Public Education in Turbulent Times

Faiza M. Jamil • Javaid E. Siddiqi

Public Education in Turbulent Times

Innovative Strategies for Leadership and Learning

Faiza M. Jamil
College of Education
Clemson University
Clemson, SC, USA

Javaid E. Siddiqi
The Hunt Institute
Cary, NC, USA

ISBN 978-3-031-43236-1   ISBN 978-3-031-43237-8   (eBook)
https://doi.org/10.1007/978-3-031-43237-8

© The Editor(s) (if applicable) and The Author(s), under exclusive licence to Springer Nature Switzerland AG 2023

This work is subject to copyright. All rights are solely and exclusively licensed by the Publisher, whether the whole or part of the material is concerned, specifically the rights of translation, reprinting, reuse of illustrations, recitation, broadcasting, reproduction on microfilms or in any other physical way, and transmission or information storage and retrieval, electronic adaptation, computer software, or by similar or dissimilar methodology now known or hereafter developed.

The use of general descriptive names, registered names, trademarks, service marks, etc. in this publication does not imply, even in the absence of a specific statement, that such names are exempt from the relevant protective laws and regulations and therefore free for general use.

The publisher, the authors, and the editors are safe to assume that the advice and information in this book are believed to be true and accurate at the date of publication. Neither the publisher nor the authors or the editors give a warranty, expressed or implied, with respect to the material contained herein or for any errors or omissions that may have been made. The publisher remains neutral with regard to jurisdictional claims in published maps and institutional affiliations.

This Palgrave Macmillan imprint is published by the registered company Springer Nature Switzerland AG.
The registered company address is: Gewerbestrasse 11, 6330 Cham, Switzerland

Paper in this product is recyclable.

*To all the incredible educators
who tirelessly supported their students and communities
through the most turbulent times.*

Foreword

From teaching to serving as U.S. Secretaries of Education, we thought we had experienced it all throughout our education careers and then the COVID-19 pandemic shook the field to its core. While education never stopped, educators across the nation suddenly had to adapt and reimagine its delivery. It would be an injustice to students and educators alike not to apply the lessons learned during this time of adaptation to better education for the future. No two individuals are better suited to articulate these lessons and help us reimagine education than the authors of this book.

During his time as Deputy Secretary and later Secretary of Education for the Commonwealth of Virginia, Dr. Javaid E. Siddiqi increased accountability of schools while leaning on his experience as a teacher and principal to ensure student-centered policymaking. Dr. Faiza Jamil, Associate Professor of Education and Human Development at Clemson University, brought together her experience as a K–12 teacher and developmental scientist to help found a Ph.D. Program in Learning Sciences that trains a new generation of education scholars and thought leaders. The juxtaposition between policy experience and research expertise offered by these co-authors makes this book and its lessons a game-changer for education.

Margaret Spellings

As U.S. Secretary of Education, and later President of the University of North Carolina System, I addressed challenges of access, affordability, quality, and accountability across our nation's K–12 and postsecondary landscape. The COVID-19 pandemic upended our normalcy, but with it our complacency and reluctance to change. Across the education continuum, there was an impetus to change, but also a genuine concern of what changes were actually effective.

COVID-19 upended how we delivered education, but we did not change the fact that we had to educate students. In this uncertain environment, assessing how and what students learned became more complex, but arguably even more important. Test scores were used to shed light on which students were most affected by the pandemic and what delivery methods were effective. But the pandemic also showed us that assessment has to be holistic, that what is happening in a student's life impacts their ability to learn and succeed. What measures we use to assess education will evolve, but so too will our understanding of achievement.

In full, this book demonstrates that in times of great threat and anxiety, communities come together to support one another. Still today, we are determining which changes to education were most beneficial to students and which ones we should keep in the future. *Public Education in Turbulent Times: Innovative Strategies for Leadership & Learning* situates the decisions and actions one takes in their culture and history and highlights best practices for educators to serve each individual student.

ARNE DUNCAN

As CEO of Chicago Public Schools and then U.S. Secretary of Education, I worked to build consensus and improve test scores for millions of students. We always knew our best innovators were those closest to students—the educators. However, they were tasked with so much that they could barely keep their heads above water, much less innovate. The COVID-19 pandemic forced us to adjust our priorities and innovate or risk an entire generation of students falling behind. As you will see in this book, teachers adapted lesson plans to deliver them remotely, principals organized lunch delivery to students, and superintendents created networks with community partnerships.

Reading these stories reminded me of my time in Chicago and the community schools that were so critical to addressing challenges to public education. Community schools provide students with an education and community members with health care, IT support, and numerous other public services, ultimately serving as a hub for the neighborhood. Neighborhoods and students benefit when communities come together and harness their resources. These stories from *Public Education in Turbulent Times: Innovative Strategies for Leadership & Learning* are a perfect example of those tangible and intangible benefits of a community united with its school.

These actions of the educators in this book to create classrooms, schools, and education systems that are more accessible, supportive, and equitable should extend beyond our faintest memories of 2020. I look forward to the conversations this book will spur and the benefits students will experience throughout their education from these lessons.

Together, we have spent our careers working to better education alongside students, parents, teachers, principals, superintendents, elected officials, and ultimately presidents. We have seen a wide range of policies, proposals, and attempts to reimagine education, some more successful than others. But what Dr. Jamil and Secretary Siddiqi bring in person, and in this book, is a desire to learn and better education. Their approach to coupling data and research with interviews results in stories that led us to think differently and imagine what is possible. In addition to addressing specific challenges related to the COVID-19 pandemic, such as hunger and internet connectivity, they also convey lessons from their discussion on issues like social protests and parental involvement that have been simmering below the surface for years.

These lessons will be important for education systems across the country as well as for the next generation of students. At a time of intense debate about the direction of the American education system, this book provides an optimism about the work dedicated educators are doing across the nation. *Public Education in Turbulent Times* cuts through the political discourse to reimagine how we approach education to ensure every student has an opportunity to achieve their dreams.

Arne Duncan
Margaret Spellings

Margaret Spellings was the 8th U.S. Secretary of Education under President George W. Bush from 2005 to 2009. She currently serves as President and CEO of Texas 2036, a nonprofit envisioning Texas' future for its bicentennial.

Arne Duncan was the 9th U.S. Secretary of Education under President Barack Obama from 2009 to 2016. He currently serves as a Senior Fellow at the University of Chicago Harris School of Public Policy.

Contents

Part I Looking Back to Look Ahead 1

1 Introduction 3
Transformation Requires Vulnerability 4
Motivating Factors for the Authors 9
Building Bridges in Our Work 15
References 17

2 Giving Voice to the Challenges 19
The Complex Challenges of 2020 20
Bringing the Stories to Light 27
The Threads that Connect Us 30
Conclusion 34
References 35

Part II Stories of Education in Trying Times 39

3 Education in a Time of Trauma: A Story of Resilience 41
The District Context of the Bronx 42
The Evolving Trauma Experience 47
Adapting to Trauma with Resilient Responses 52
Lessons Learned from the Bronx 62
References 65

4 Education in a Time of Danger: A Story of Choice 69
The District Context of Lubbock 71
The Evolving Experience of Danger 74
Addressing School Danger Through Choice 80
Lessons Learned from Lubbock 88
References 92

5 Education in a Time of Need: A Story of Community 95
The District Context of Los Angeles 96
The Evolving Experience of Need 102
Meeting Need with Community Cultural Wealth 105
Lessons Learned from the LAUSD and Cudahy 111
References 116

6 Education in a Time of Change: A Story of Justice 119
The District Context of Minneapolis 120
The Evolving Experience of Structural Inequalities 127
Challenging Inequality Through Just Policy 130
Lessons Learned from Minneapolis 136
References 140

Part III On Reimagining Education 145

7 The Circle Model 147
Adapting the Conversation to the Times 148
The Guiding Principles of Progress 155
References 159

8 Reimagine Where Schools Fit: Purpose and Context 163
Reaching Consensus on School Purpose 164
Situating Schools in Ecological Systems 170
Finding Innovative Funding Solutions 172
References 175

9 Reimagine How Schools Work: Structures and Personnel 179
Planning for Pluralistic Structures 180
Taking the Time to Thrive 184

Establishing Resilient Educator Pipelines 189
Rewarding Excellence to Retain Teachers 192
References 196

10 Conclusion: Innovation and Inclusion 201
Leadership and Learning in Communities 202
Collective Responses Beyond the Crisis 206
Future Schools: Places of Inclusion, Safety, and Purpose 207
The Rubber Band: A Final Thought 210
References 211

Index 215

About the Authors

Faiza M. Jamil is a tenured associate professor of Education and Human Development at College of Education, Clemson University, USA. She holds a Ph.D. in Educational Psychology—Applied Developmental Science from the University of Virginia. She also received an M.Ed. in Elementary Education from The College of New Jersey and an Undergraduate Degree in Psychology from Bryn Mawr College. Faiza teaches courses related to child and lifespan development in the Learning Sciences Doctoral Program and Undergraduate Teacher Education Programs. Her courses include a strong focus on how social, economic, cultural, and historical contexts influence human development, and how developing humans influence their environment. She also brings her own experiences as a K–12 teacher in three countries to her university courses.

Faiza is the founder and director of the Contexts of Learning and Development (CLAD) Lab, where she conducts interdisciplinary research in collaboration with a team of faculty members and doctoral students. Her research follows two complementary strands, with a particular focus on issues of educational equity: (1) understanding the underlying psychological processes—cognitive, social, and emotional—that influence teachers' classroom behaviors and career decisions; and (2) understanding the ways in which teacher-child interactions influence children's learning and development. Her research projects apply both strands of research in support of strengthening and diversifying the teacher pipeline in the United States to support more equitable student learning and development outcomes.

Among her many different service commitments to the field of education, Faiza has served as the Dean's Fellow for Inclusive Excellence at Clemson University's College of Education. In this position, she led the implementation of the College of Education's strategic plan to increase diversity, equity, and inclusion across its teaching, research, and service endeavors. Faiza also serves in the field of education scholarship as a member of the editorial review panel for *The Education Forum*.

Javaid E. Siddiqi is a former Virginia Secretary of Education. He is the president and CEO of The Hunt Institute. During his tenure, The Institute has more than tripled its staff and has expanded its scope of work beyond K–12 to include the entire education continuum from early childhood to postsecondary and the workforce. Javaid works with the leadership team to guide the strategic plan for The Institute and develops The Institute's relationships with partners and funders across the nation. He works with senior-level elected officials across the political aisle to help design strategy, shape policy, and drive educational improvements on the national and state levels.

Javaid's career spans more than 20 years in education, education reform, and policy. He began his professional career as a high school teacher, assistant principal, and principal in Chesterfield, Virginia, where he led the implementation of Expeditionary Learning—a nationally recognized school reform model. As secretary of education in Virginia Governor Bob McDonnell's Cabinet, Javaid assisted in the development and implementation of the Commonwealth's education policy and provided guidance to sixteen public universities, the Virginia Community College System, five higher education and research centers, the Department of Education, and state-supported museums. Prior to his appointment, he served as deputy secretary of education, where he focused his efforts on teacher quality and improving educational outcomes for all students.

In addition to an extensive history of leadership and service, Javaid actively continues to serve his community and state. He is an Aspen Institute Fellow, former Vice-Rector of the Radford University Board of Visitors, and a former member of the Chesterfield County School Board. He currently serves on the Elevate Early Education board and the National Center for Teacher Residencies board. Javaid is a graduate of Richard Bland College, Virginia State University, and Virginia Commonwealth University where he received both his undergraduate degree and his Doctorate in Educational Leadership.

PART I

Looking Back to Look Ahead

CHAPTER 1

Introduction

> *It created a space of vulnerability for all of us, where we had to step outside of our roles.*
> —Ed Graff, Superintendent, Minneapolis Public Schools

In *The Power of Vulnerability*, Brené Brown claims that "[v]ulnerability is the birthplace of innovation, creativity, and change," laying out a fundamental roadmap for growth [1]. While learning, creating, problem-solving, and growing are acts of living undertaken by all people—an evolutionary imperative for survival—the role that formalized education should play in these processes has served as fodder for intense debate through much of recorded history. Those who have challenged widely accepted beliefs in this debate have also met dramatically different responses from their contemporaries. For questioning the political and religious norms of Athenian society in his day, Socrates, considered a founder of Western philosophy, was tried for corrupting the youth of Athens and executed through the ingestion of hemlock in 399 B.C. British author Sir Ken Robinson's ideas on how the structures and goals of school must be overhauled to promote creativity and divergent thinking garnered him numerous awards, the most-watched TED Talk of all time [2], and a knighthood. For advocating for the right of girls and women to be educated, Pakistani education activist Malala Yousafzai survived an assassination attempt by the Taliban, but also became the youngest recipient of the Nobel Peace Prize at age 17 [3].

Society's tolerance for questions about what is required of the educational establishment, what it is able to provide successfully, and where it needs to evolve appear deeply grounded in time and place. Perhaps a war-ravaged Athens, emerging from the decades-long Peloponnesian War, was a place focused on restoring a bygone era of political and cultural dominance, whereas the Western economies of the early 2000s were looking forward to their new technology-oriented economies and wondering how to educate a future workforce for jobs that no one had yet imagined. At a time of intense infighting for its future direction and leadership [4], the Pakistani Taliban's militant and political forces perceived Malala's act of speaking truth to power about the educational rights of girls as defiant rebellion, a sharp contrast to the perception of so many others around the world who saw her as a heroic social activist. In times of societal vulnerability, we can fear novel ideas and look backward, or we can embrace innovation, and move forward with an eye to transformation and rebirth.

Transformation Requires Vulnerability

In this book, we contend that America is currently in a time and place of vulnerability that can be conducive to re-examination of its educational institutions, their purpose, and their practices. Other times of uncertainty and vulnerability in history—World Wars, the Spanish flu, the Great Depression—touched large parts of the global population, and were followed by historic shifts in geopolitical processes, world economies, and cultural norms. Our darkest times hold within them an opportunity for the most honest examination of what is, and reimagining what it could be. As Desmond Tutu once said, "It is a risky undertaking but in the end, it is worthwhile, because in the end only an honest confrontation with reality can bring real healing."

At very few other points in history has American society been simultaneously faced with the breadth and depth of challenges to health, wealth, and culture such as those that began in the year 2020. While the global pandemic moved out of most people's daily concerns, and the global economy broadly escaped the long-lasting global recession that was feared, the vulnerabilities that were exposed in 2020 must still be addressed to ensure future thriving. Unprecedented global school closures to combat the spread of COVID-19 meant that a broad swath of learners around the globe experienced educational disruptions, distance learning, and even complete economic lockdown in March and April of 2020. Reports by UNESCO suggested that in the ten days preceding March 24, 2020, approximately 1.37 billion students, representing more than 80% of school and university students across the globe, were home from school [5]. While in places short-lived, these disruptions left lasting impressions on our ideas about education that should be reflected in our educational experiences moving forward.

Over the next two years of the global pandemic, children and youth experienced the trauma of hundreds of millions sickened by COVID-19 globally, with American students facing life in the nation with the largest number of pandemic deaths. The magnitude of this shared trauma was coupled with a chaotic, if short-lived, economic recession, and growing inflation, adding to the stress, as families struggled to keep food on the dinner table. Even as the pandemic wound down and official government declarations of health emergencies and financial assistance programs were brought to an end across the globe through the spring of 2023 [6], the protections offered through these programs were also rolled back, creating new financial pressures on families and communities struggling with the rising cost of living across the country.

While the economic and pandemic challenges were global, they also starkly highlighted aspects of systemic racism and structural inequality that seem uniquely American—the disproportionate police brutality and shooting deaths of individuals of color. The murder of George Floyd, while sadly not unique, resulted in a global outcry in its particularly palpable dehumanization. The racial reckoning around the world triggered by the cell phone camera footage captured by teenager Darnella Frazier in a brave act of citizen journalism, earned her a special citation by the Pulitzer Prize committee [7]. This instance of youth activism emphasized the importance of individual voices and stories to make sense of the chaos—it served as a reminder that the vulnerability the world bore witness to in that video, while new and horrifying to many, was familiar to too many Americans.

The challenges that American society and the children in its schools faced during the pandemic years were not new for many. Economic inequality and racial injustice are the drivers of the systemic oppression that has always been experienced by the less privileged and less powerful in America. In recent years, this inequality showed itself in the disproportionately negative developmental outcomes of minoritized children across the country [8]. Their communities experienced more learning loss due to poorer internet access and school quality during virtual schooling, more sickness and death due to unequal access to medical care, and more economic hardship due to higher rates of job loss during lockdowns [9]. What made this upheaval different from other national tragedies was that the learning loss, trauma, and economic hardship that had traditionally been experienced by the most vulnerable in our society were experienced by many more.

As our system noticeably stops meeting the needs of more and more people, perhaps we find ourselves in a place of enough vulnerability that we can no longer avoid looking more deeply and more honestly at the purpose of our schools and how well it is met through current policies and practices. Education scholar Joel Spring posits that throughout the nation's history, the purpose of American schools has traditionally fallen into three broad areas: political, social, and economic, with different goals taking on varying levels of importance at different times [10].

Political Purpose

The political goal of schools has focused on developing the next generation of citizens and patriots, furthering conformity toward the nation's founding democratic ideals. Who has been considered a citizen has changed over time, through battles waged in courthouses and on city streets. Debates have been won through the power of the pen, and the funding of political action committees. Yet through it all, the cultivation of civic-mindedness and the concept of citizenship has been imbued in future generations in classrooms.

In the polarized climate of recent years, educators have played a pivotal role in preparing the most diverse generation of public school students [11] to use the power of their vote and their voice to shape the direction the nation will take. However, they face increasing pressure from state legislatures and school boards to restrict the diversity of perspectives and experiences represented in their teaching. In fact, since the beginning of 2021, at least 36 states have introduced legislation or used other measures to curtail the teaching in schools of Critical Race Theory (CRT), a perspective that seeks to explain the structural mechanisms of racism [12]. Although CRT is not a formal subject taught in schools, it serves as a conceptual framework employed in higher education and legal studies to comprehend the role of race in public policy and history, and it can inform the development of curricular materials and instructional approaches. In effect, this legislation targets the removal of topics, books, and historical perspectives from the curriculum that are associated with people's differences, and it is also being used to cut administrative positions such as diversity and equity officers from district leadership, by connecting them to the CRT conversation.

And while this is just the latest debate, those with political power have always used their influence to shape the narrative of the nation's history taught in schools. Even as it takes on an outsized importance in American life, the political goal of education has become a chimera—elusive and unattainable in a divided nation.

Social Purpose

The social goal of education represents morality and character development among youth and prepares them to be positive members of the community. As the American population has grown increasingly diverse, determining whose morals and values schools will disseminate to their students has become an increasingly complex endeavor, in a large part because diversity makes it harder to see *only* the belief systems and ideologies that conform with our own. Like so many recent efforts at legislating away diverse concepts, on February 24, 2021, the Florida House of Representatives passed HB7, or the Individual Freedom Act [13]. Commonly referred to the *Stop Wrongs Against our Kids and Employees Act* (Stop WOKE Act), one part of this bill limits the teaching of any ideas that lead a student to "feel guilt, anguish, or other forms of psychological distress because of actions in which the person played no part" if they were committed by someone of the same race or sex.

As bills with similar intent are introduced in other state legislatures, they have the potential to discourage intellectual debate or even limit the content of history lessons. The use of legislation in this context is undoubtedly political as well as social, as it shapes education policy and practices. It is essential to recognize the interconnection between social, political, and economic purposes of schooling. By understanding how social goals influence education policies and decisions, we can better appreciate the broader implications and complexities surrounding issues in the education system.

Incorporating divergent experiences and perspectives into school curricula is a mark of progress for those seeking to build a more inclusive future, but it represents an existential threat to those who benefit from long-existing systems of societal oppression. Privilege and power, once enjoyed, are unsurprisingly difficult to part from, but surprisingly difficult to acknowledge, as equity can feel like oppression when one has been privileged for so long. At a time when we have access to information from numerous perspectives, remaining in a polarized bubble of our choosing can lead us to perceive even scientific facts, such as how viruses spread, as matters of opinion. In a nation with the highest number of COVID-19 infections and deaths in the world, even while enjoying access to the largest stockpiles of vaccines, information is power, and both disseminating it and consuming it come with a moral responsibility.

How can our nation balance economic power with the loss of human life? When does public health outweigh profits? How can we become critical thinkers open to differing opinions? How do we balance individual needs and desires with the greater good [14]? It falls to educators to pose these challenging questions and teach the next generation of Americans to evaluate information and make sure the choices they make live up to their professed ideals. In a time of such immense loss of life and so much shared trauma, schools can and must be places to learn compassion for others, their experiences, and their ideas. Perhaps the shared pandemic experience, as unimaginably painful as it has been, opens a door for a shared vision of how society can be rebuilt for the future.

Economic Purpose

Finally, the economic goal of schools is workforce development, simultaneously touting education as the great equalizer and serving as a mechanism of social reproduction that both creates and inhibits opportunity. The promise of public education has long been held as an essential component of the American Dream. Guaranteed access to a free education was supposed to mean that all Americans, regardless of the circumstances of their birth, could chart a course for the future they chose.

American exceptionalism has been grounded in the belief that through hard work and learning, anyone could make their way to their best life. Perhaps, the hubris of human nature leads many who enjoy privilege to overlook that their exceptionalism may not solely result from their own good choices, but rather from the advantages and opportunities they had—advantages that were not equally available to many of their marginalized peers. The ideals of the American Dream have also been the engine on which the largest economy in the world has run for generations—through strong public education, the country could continue to produce an innovative workforce that would both create and consume its way to global power. While this version of the American Dream has attracted an immense pool of fresh talent to American universities and corporations for decades through immigration, the cultural and political environment, marked by division, and ongoing decreases in the nation's global competitiveness in education [15], leave American public schools and the economy vulnerable in the post-pandemic world.

At a time when the workforce purpose of education is clearly relevant, we must evaluate the current models of education we employ, many of which were developed for a very different time and place. As we prepare students for a future in an evolving workforce that increasingly requires education after high school, especially in the face of unstable economic conditions, we have an opportunity to reimagine the endeavor of education more broadly. Perhaps, schools might finally approach the understanding of the American Dream with more nuance, accounting for the vast divide in educational experiences and economic opportunities currently available to different segments of the population. The brief and intense economic recession that followed the start of the COVID-19 pandemic resulted in disproportionate job losses among Black and Latinx workers [16], and the subsequent recovery has been less favorable for them when compared to their white counterparts [17], especially among Black women and teens [18]. While the structural biases that contribute to this phenomenon can be addressed under the political and social purposes of school, our experiences since the start of the pandemic leave no doubt that leveraging emerging communication technologies and innovative, flexible approaches to education have to be part of an effective, equitable approach to preparing the future workforce for success.

Motivating Factors for the Authors

Like individuals across the globe, as the authors of this book, we have spent the pandemic and post-pandemic years watching, and living, the incredible vulnerability of human experience unfolding. We have filtered our observations through our own lenses as educators, parents, and people, with each anecdote shaping us as we have watched deep devastation and incredible resilience unfolding in schools and communities around us. In our own experiences of vulnerability, we have seen an opportunity for honest examination and innovative thinking about schools and the important role they play in the lives of young people. We hope to share these reflections grounded in the stories of committed, passionate education professionals who have navigated some of the most challenging times in their careers with an abundance of selflessness and grace. For each of us, the path that brought us to this work is different, both in our broader experiences and expertise in the field of education and in the particular experiences through this unique time that motivated us to reach out to educators in different parts of the country and bring their stories to light.

Dr. Faiza Jamil: Tales of Transformative Teachers

Education has always played a central role in my life, but I am not sure I ever set out to be a teacher. In my case, my career in education was something that found me after a few years in the business world. But it seems somewhat inevitable in retrospect. My maternal grandfather was an engineering professor in Pakistan, and my father was his favorite student. His mentorship played such a huge role in my father's life, that not only did he help my father navigate his education, and find his first job after graduation, but he was also responsible for helping my father find his life partner of over 50 years. In some ways, I exist because my grandfather was such an influential teacher. Although my grandfather passed away before I was born, his story has loomed large in my life and silently influenced many of my choices. My mother carried her father's love for learning in her and passed it on to her children. In her eyes, doing well in school was the path to achieving our dreams. My father showed us the culmination of his mentor's teachings in his own hard work.

As I grew up, numerous teachers touched my life. From my fourth grade teacher in Kuwait, who noticed that I was ready for more challenging work, to my seventh grade English teacher in Pakistan, who saw that as a Gulf War refugee, I was struggling to fit in, they all recognized individual needs and reached out with care. In high school, my journalism teacher let me borrow his guitar over winter break so I could practice the few chords he had taught me and decide if I wanted to take up playing the instrument more seriously. In the end, I did not, but his ability to connect with every student in the class and tap into what made them unique helped us all see ourselves and each other as so much more. I had the privilege of working on the faculty with my former journalism teacher in my first teaching position, and the best part of my first day on the job was telling him how his small acts of inspiration had changed my life and made me want to teach.

While I loved the daily interactions with young people as a teacher, the constant problem-solving required to understand my students' individual needs was what always kept me motivated to innovate and improve my craft. I had the good fortune of working with experienced teachers who offered mentorship and collaboration, all of us striving to support our students' learning and growth.

Perhaps this drive to better understand my students as developing humans was what first made me consider a life in academia, but the true motivator was observing the burnout and exhaustion of my colleagues over the years. I witnessed the immense impact they had on the lives of the students in their care, and wondered how the stress they carried was impacting their ability to stay in the field. How could we take care of our students and still take care of ourselves? What reasonable supports could we expect from our schools to aid us in this goal? What impact was the constant churn of teachers in and out of school having on our students over time?

These were the questions that led me to doctoral study in Educational Psychology and Applied Developmental Science at the University of Virginia, and my position as a faculty member in the Learning Sciences at Clemson University. As teacher shortages have continued to grow in the years leading up to the global pandemic, the true impact of what we have asked of teachers in recent years, and the consequences it will have for the profession in the future are still unfolding. Even through these challenging times, countless teachers in the field have continued to adapt and support their students, and colleges of education have continued to enroll and prepare future teachers for an evolving educational landscape. Every day, educators at all levels of the system ask: *What comes next and how do we prepare for it?*

Looking back on my time as a student, an elementary school teacher, and a college professor, I see a common thread: teachers transform lives. All too often, they engage in small acts of kindness and courage and never see the true impact they have. During the first year of the COVID-19 pandemic, I heard countless stories about teachers going above and beyond the expectations of employment to support students and families that reminded me of the transformative power of teachers. As schools began reopening and the winter COVID surge of 2020 occurred, the narratives about teachers began to change from the heroes of the early pandemic to individuals who did not want to work and did not care about the harm that distance learning was doing to children. None of the teachers I spoke with expressed this feeling. They all expressed deep concern for the impact that virtual learning was having on their students, but many feared for their own safety, as well as the safety of their students as school reopened. In the absence of a vaccine, many craved the protection of masks, better ventilation, and social distancing. *I also saw one critical incident that reminded me how the essential contribution of educators is all too often overlooked. That was the day I decided to write this book.*

On January 21, 2021, I read several news reports and watched television coverage of a school board meeting that had taken place that day in Cobb County, Georgia, one of the state's more populous districts [19]. Three teachers in the district had died from COVID-19 in the preceding month, and over 100 teachers attended the school board meeting that day to protest the lack of care that they perceived the district was showing for their safety during the return to in-person instruction. While speaking to the board, district employee Jennifer Susko asked the board members who were not masked to put on a mask in honor of beloved kindergarten teacher Patrick Key, an avid mask advocate, who had passed away from COVID-19 on Christmas Day. While many board members were already masked, the refusal of district superintendent, Chris Ragsdale, to don a mask in solidarity with the teachers in his district made national headlines.

As I reflected on this incident, I wondered, what was the superintendent's refusal to wear a mask meant to communicate? A political stance? A refusal of liability? For that matter, why were the teachers asking for the masking to begin with? To shame the school board? Or were they drawing attention to the plight of so many educators around the country—trying to reconcile their desire to serve their students with their fear of a dangerous virus that was claiming thousands of lives each week?

When the world shut down, educators moved their classrooms online, and kept teaching our children. District personnel packed lunches for delivery, built partnerships to increase technology access, supported parents on their journey as reluctant co-teachers, and drove in neighborhood parades to cheer up their isolated students. Overnight, they became a virtual lifeline to millions of students to help them navigate trauma, make academic progress, and stay connected, all while trying to manage the upheaval in their own personal lives. When schools reopened, teachers put their lives in danger to continue their service, asking that we protect and care for them in the same way they had spent their careers caring for so many.

Watching the incident in Cobb County unfold made me realize that even as teacher shortages have grown over the last decade—with declining enrollments in teacher education programs and perpetual retention challenges due to difficult working conditions—the world needs its educators more today than ever before. Stable schools and classrooms will be an asset in recovering from trauma and lost learning opportunities, and the teachers who have shown resilience in the most challenging contexts during the pandemic have much to tell us about how to rise to educational challenges in the coming years. As we reimagine what comes next in education, we must start by honoring the stories of those who have helped us survive these challenging times. One of the greatest privileges of writing this book for me has been the opportunity to give voice to the narratives of everyday heroes who have gone largely unrecognized for the immense contribution they have made to the lives of the children in their communities over the course of the pandemic.

Dr. Javaid Siddiqi: Lessons in Leadership

Beginning early in my childhood, my father instilled in me the importance of education. Immigrating to the U.S. from Pakistan in 1965 to pursue his Ph.D. at the University of South Carolina, my father demonstrated he was willing to sacrifice all he had for a better education. Throughout life, he always reminded me that education was the great equalizer and that everyone deserved an opportunity to receive that education. I did not know it at the time, but it was his passion for education and his commitment to giving each and every student their opportunity that led me to pursue teaching, and ultimately, educational leadership.

During his time at the University of South Carolina, my father met and married a woman from New York, and soon after, I and my three brothers were born. Shortly after my birth, my father was offered a position at Virginia State University (VSU), a historically Black land-grant university, and the first state-funded four-year university established for the higher learning of Black Americans. We packed up the house and headed north to Chesterfield County, Virginia, where unbeknownst to me, I would make my home, and where my own children would also spend their entire K-12 experiences.

Having a father who was a professor had its perks: I was able to roam the campus and soak in the environment, something I would later learn was uncommon, especially for students of color. We had conversations about everything: why do some students succeed, when others do not? What does it take to be successful in education and in life? How is education different for me, as a person of color, compared to my white classmates? Throughout these conversations, a common theme was always present: there was so much potential and opportunity that could be realized through a quality education, but it would take bold leaders to provide that opportunity to all students.

After high school graduation, I stayed close to home in Virginia, completing my undergraduate (and later my Doctorate) degree in education at Virginia Commonwealth University. I then returned home to Chesterfield County in 2000 to teach biology at a local high school. I was less than two years into my teaching career when 9/11 terrorist attacks occurred in 2001. As the son of a Pakistani immigrant, I experienced blatant racism and xenophobia. What hurt more was seeing my students exposed to similar adversity. At the same time, many students from military families experienced their parent(s) being deployed. It was during this time of intense national trauma and emotional upheaval that I realized what my students needed the most was a place to belong. Along with a colleague, I started a student group that met on a weekly basis and provided a space for students to connect, share, and ultimately, belong. Through these meetings, I truly realized what it would take to make education the great equalizer, and I was even more inspired to do the work.

My career in education has now spanned over 20 years, from being a teacher to an assistant principal to a principal; I then left my role as principal to serve Virginia Governor Bob McDonnell as Deputy Secretary of Education, and later, Secretary of Education. Currently, I serve as the President and CEO of The Hunt Institute, an education nonprofit founded by four-term North Carolina Governor Jim Hunt, that provides unbiased research, technical expertise, and learning opportunities to equip and empower educators and policymakers to drive equitable reforms and become audacious champions for education. Governor Hunt, known as the "education governor," had a vision for The Hunt Institute, which was to create "an equitable American education system through which all learners achieve their highest potential in school and life," and this work continues the ideals that my father instilled in me so long ago.

At the end of 2019, no one could predict what 2020 had in store for the world, much less the impact it would have on education. In March

2020, I vividly remember the fears I had, as I shared with our Vice President my plans to keep The Hunt Institute running with a pivot to virtual operations. Once the dust settled, and we had time to reflect, I realized that if our transition to virtual work was difficult, it had to be challenging for schools and families as well. These concerns were quickly verified, as we started to hear from education leaders across the country about the issues educators were facing. As you will hear later in this book, educators did not just have to pivot to emergency virtual learning, they had to become so much more.

These challenging times for education also arrived at my dining room table. As a father of a daughter who was then in high school and a son in middle school, not only did I see the pandemic from the perspective of an educator, I saw it as a parent. Luckily, my children have two loving parents who were able to provide the support they needed to succeed, despite the obstacles, but that was not the reality for all students.

My personal and professional experiences leading up to and through the pandemic are what led me to co-author this book. Throughout my life I have strived to live out the ideal instilled in me by my father, that education is the great equalizer. I also know that this pandemic has had outsized effects on students of color and students from low-income communities. Every student should have access to a quality education and an opportunity to achieve the American dream. It is my hope that this book tells the stories of teachers, principals, and education leaders across the nation who believe in that same ideal, and who reimagined education during this time of crisis to keep that opportunity alive for all students.

Building Bridges in Our Work

No doubt, our individual stories represent some shared aspects of cultural heritage, as well as vast differences in our experiences and expertise within the field of education. Perhaps, it was seeing a Pakistani name in the context of American education scholarship that, in some small way, first led us to connect to discuss this book project. For those who believe that representation matters, this should come as no surprise. Ultimately, the value we have found in combining our different perspectives, in the interest of meaning-making, has brought this book to fruition.

The challenges of education, especially in the midst of a global pandemic, are large and complex, and require complex thinking that leverages diverse experiences. These challenges also require bridging what often seem like insurmountable distances in how we understand and address problems. In schools, these distances tend to appear between the thinking of teachers and principals, schools and school districts, and sometimes even school districts and the state. As we have conceptualized this book, conducted interviews, and put pen to paper (or really fingers to keys), we have made deliberate decisions to harness the perspectives of educators in different levels of the education system. We have also challenged each other to bridge the distances between our own perspectives as former teacher and former principal, developmental scientist and policymaker, education scholar and nonprofit leader.

The structure of this book and our collaboration represent an act of bridge building. Albert Einstein theorized that vast distances in space could be traversed through an Einstein-Rosen bridge, more commonly known as a wormhole, achieved by bending the very fabric of space-time. A demonstration used in many classrooms illustrates the concept of a wormhole using a sheet of paper. The two edges at the top and bottom of the paper are furthest away from each other, but if you bend the paper to form a tube, these same edges can be placed right next to each other. Similarly, the distance between different perspectives—teacher, principal, superintendent—can also be traversed by layering them on top of each other within an educational context and examining the same meaningful events to find points of overlap and variation.

Bridging the differences in our perspectives, we have discovered that we asked different questions and reached different conclusions in this work compared to what we would have done individually. Bridging the perspectives within school districts showed us that even in the most challenging times, educators were able to combine their efforts to produce innovative responses to the needs of their students. It is the numerous acts of resilience—the *positive* adaptations made in response to *extreme adversity*—that we set out to share in this book. Too often, we think of resilience as a quality or trait of individuals. It is something they possess or do not possess. Developmental science research suggests that resilience occurs in response to adversity [20]. The interviews captured for this book during the pandemic have demonstrated that resilience occurred even in the most challenged school contexts, a result of adaptive decision-making. As the world emerges from the pandemic, we turn to the stories of these resilient educators to imagine what might come next for American education.

REFERENCES

1. Brown, B. (2010). *The power of vulnerability* [Video]. TED Conferences https://www.ted.com/talks/brene_brown_the_power_of_vulnerability
2. TED Conferences. (2023). *Do schools kill creativity?* TED Conferences. Retrieved August 1, 2023, from https://www.ted.com/playlists/171/the_most_popular_ted_talks_of_all_time
3. Nobel Prize Outreach AB. (2014). *Malala Yousafzai facts.* Nobel Prize Outreach AB. Retrieved August 1, 2023, from https://www.nobelprize.org/prizes/peace/2014/yousafzai/facts/
4. Zahra-Malik, M. (2012, December 6). Exclusive: Emerging Pakistan Taliban chief to focus on Afghan war. *Reuters.* https://www.reuters.com/article/us-pakistan-taliban-idUSBRE8B50G920121206
5. UNESCO. (2020, March 24). *1.37 billion students now home as COVID-19 school closures expand, ministers scale up multimedia approaches to ensure learning continuity.* UNESCO. Retrieved April 2, 2023, from https://www.unesco.org/en/articles/137-billion-students-now-home-covid-19-school-closures-expand-ministers-scale-multimedia-approaches
6. Lafraniere, S., & Weiland, N. (2023, January 31). Biden says U.S. will allow public health emergency for covid to expire in May. *New York Times.* http://libproxy.clemson.edu/login?url=https://www.proquest.com/newspapers/biden-says-u-s-will-allow-public-health-emergency/docview/2770841680/se-2
7. The Pulitzer Prizes. (2021). *The 2021 Pulitzer Prize winner in special citations and awards.* The Pulitzer Prizes. Retrieved April 6, 2023, from https://www.pulitzer.org/winners/darnella-frazier
8. Hanks, A., Solomon, D., & Christian W. (2023) *Systematic inequality: How America's structural racism helped create the black-white wealth gap.* Center for American Progress. Retrieved August 1, 2023, from https://www.americanprogress.org/article/systematic-inequality/
9. Edwards, K., & Lopez, M. H. (2021, May 12). *Black Americans say coronavirus has hit hard financially, but impact varies by education level, age.* Pew Research Center. https://www.pewresearch.org/fact-tank/2021/05/12/black-americans-say-coronavirus-has-hit-hard-financially-but-impact-varies-by-education-level-age/ft_2021-05-12_blackamericanscovid_01/
10. Spring, J. (2018). *American education* (18th ed.). Routledge.
11. Wang, H. L. (2018). *Generation Z is the most racially and ethnically diverse yet.* National Public Radio. Retrieved August 1, 2023, from https://www.npr.org/2018/11/15/668106376/generation-z-is-the-most-racially-and-ethnically-diverse-yet

12. Schwartz, S. (2021, June 11). Map: Where Critical Race Theory is under attack. *Education Week*. Retrieved April 6, 2023, from http://www.edweek.org/leadership/map-where-critical-race-theory-is-under-attack/2021/06
13. Geggis, A. (2023, March 22). Judge rules against DeSantis-backed 'Stop WOKE Act'. *The Miami Times*. https://www.miamitimesonline.com/news/florida/stop-woke-act-passes-in-the-fl-house/article_38b2f584-95c6-11ec-b83f-f39a5e94dc7e.html
14. Lakoff, G. (2006). *Whose freedom?: The battle over America's most important idea*. Farrar.
15. DeSilver, D. (2017, February 15). *U.S. students' academic achievement still lags that of their peers in many other countries*. The Pew Research. https://www.pewresearch.org/fact-tank/2017/02/15/u-s-students-internationally-math-science/
16. Kochhar, R. (2020). *Hispanic women, immigrants, young adults, those with less education hit hardest by COVID-19 job losses*. Pew Research Center. Retrieved August 1, 2023, from https://www.pewresearch.org/short-reads/2020/06/09/hispanic-women-immigrants-young-adults-those-with-less-education-hit-hardest-by-covid-19-job-losses/
17. Rogelio, S., & Sparks, C. (2020). *The inequities of job loss and recovery amid the COVID-19 pandemic*. Carson School of Public Policy. Retrieved August 1, 2023, from https://carsey.unh.edu/publication/inequities-job-loss-recovery-amid-COVID-pandemic
18. Broady, K., & Barr, A. (2022, January 11). *December's jobs report reveals a growing racial employment gap, especially for black women*. Brookings Institution. Retrieved April 11, 2023, from https://www.brookings.edu/blog/the-avenue/2022/01/11/decembers-jobs-report-reveals-a-growing-racial-employment-gap-especially-for-black-women/
19. Kornfield, M. (2021, March 25). Raw feelings in Georgia after mask request to honor teacher is met with silence. *The Washington Post*. https://www.washingtonpost.com/education/2021/01/24/georgia-teachers-deaths/
20. Masten, A. S., Best, K. M., & Garmezy, N. (1990). Resilience and development: Contributions from the study of children who overcome adversity. *Development and Psychopathology, 2*(4), 425–444.

CHAPTER 2

Giving Voice to the Challenges

> *I was trying to find ways to share this journey of where we went and the direction we went. It allowed for a lot more voice to happen in our community. And as the voices started to speak, we started to put things into action.*
> —Rafael Alvarez, Superintendent, Bronx CSD 7

At no other time in American education was resilience needed more than during the events that started unfolding in February of 2020. Between March and June of that year, a series of events touched the lives of people across the country and around the world. While it is easy to forget that the major challenges of 2020 did not occur simultaneously in all places, it is crucial to remember the evolving nature of the tragedy over months as we analyze the experiences of educators in different communities.

Yet even as the tragedies of that year emerged over many months, their impact on education was swift. No longer could education continue its slow roll toward progress and change, but rather schools, administrators, teachers, parents, students, and so many others were thrust into an environment unlike anything experienced previously. The status quo was no longer sufficient for this generation of students. Quickly and drastically, schools across the nation had to reimagine how they would educate their students. In the context of a lengthy and unpredictable global pandemic, an economy that remains unstable, and unfolding discussions of racial equity that will likely continue for generations to come, this reimaging of education, at times, seemed like a moving target. While necessity guided educators to flexibly address challenges as they emerged, these were just steps toward the deeper reconsideration of educational philosophy, policy, and practice we propose must continue to occur as a post-pandemic sense of normalcy is fully realized [1]. We cannot be sure what this new normal will look like over time, but we can be sure that learning from what has been occurring since the start of the pandemic will surely leave us better prepared to collectively shape this new reality.

THE COMPLEX CHALLENGES OF 2020

The tripartite challenges that defined the spring and summer of 2020 developed gradually. First, a dangerous virus spread trauma and fear along the coasts, and then permeated further inland to cities, towns, and eventually rural areas in every state. As stay-at-home orders began in an effort to reduce the spread of the virus, the hardships of an economic recession spread more quickly than the virus, starting with industries that required face-to-face interactions, and trickling through the economy. In June, the public reckoning of racial inequities rocked the world as video of the murder of George Floyd flooded the airways. Each additional challenge that came seemed to emerge faster and with greater impact as an already-stressed nation and world flexed further and was forced to adapt to more difficulty. Indeed, there were days in 2020 when the world seemed to be riding a runaway train that was about to jump the tracks, and the many challenges aligned to create an inflection point in education.

The COVID-19 Pandemic

Entering 2020, no one could have expected our lives and routines to be upended the way that they were. While the U.S. did not officially declare a National Emergency until March 13, 2020, as we know from our interviews, discussions regarding preparations for the pandemic and possible school closures started much earlier. As early as mid-February, schools shut down and moved their students to virtual learning. These early school closures were mainly isolated to New York and Washington state, as residents experienced the first waves of COVID-19, but by March 11, over one million students had been impacted by school closures, and that number only continued to grow. By March 25, all U.S. public school buildings had closed [2]. For the first days of the pandemic, the transition to emergency online learning was a blur. Administration, faculty, and staff were learning as they went, trying to provide some semblance of a *normal* classroom experience while students learned virtually from home. It was not long before educators were also supporting students and community members as they faced personal trauma and navigated the dangers of the virus both at home and eventually in school.

Trauma. As COVID-19 spread across the nation, the evolving virus strains, increasing scientific understanding of the disease, and the variations in state and local policy created diverging experiences for school children based on geography. Once the immediateness of the transition to emergency virtual learning wore off, communities that experienced infection surges and high death rates from the earliest strains of the coronavirus found themselves suddenly contending with another foe: trauma. The high death rates in the early stages of the pandemic led to extreme lockdowns and numerous unknowns that left many scared and confused. The CDC found that students reported experiencing greater symptoms of depression and anxiety. Needs for mental health services increased. Drug overdoses showed their largest single-year increase in over 20 years [3]. Some educators suddenly found themselves serving as grief counselors in areas that were hit hard by the pandemic [4]. Many of these same educators were also simultaneously coping with the loss of loved ones to the virus, facing financial challenges in their personal lives, and supporting their own children in virtual learning. Like so many frontline workers, educators supported their communities through trauma and loss, while putting their own safety and well-being on hold.

While the acute trauma experienced in urban centers like New York City during the early days of the pandemic was expected, the subsequent forms of trauma being experienced by school-aged children was, perhaps, more difficult to address. For example, the number of emergency room visits for suspected suicide attempts by girls between 12 and 17 years of age between February 21, 2021, and March 20, 2021, was more than 50% higher than the same span in 2019 [5]. Even as schools and communities rose to the challenge of providing additional mental health support during the times of acute hardship, when morgues overflowed and refrigerated trucks were parked outside hospitals to store the dead, the ongoing impacts of the trauma will likely continue to unfold over many years to come.

As educators, students, and their families navigated a return to school amid the pandemic, and the virus continued to claim lives, the experiences of trauma in schools became more chronic and complex. Masks helped slow the spread of disease, but they also hid the smiling faces of those who would comfort students in times of hardship. Trauma of lost loved ones also evolved into a more complex trauma of emotional deprivation as young people developed with fewer social interactions and in conditions of more uncertainty. Teachers and school leaders continued to cope with their own losses and fears, but also experienced growing vicarious trauma as they supported their students and parents back toward a semblance of normalcy. An important step in more comprehensively addressing the mental health needs of the school-aged population in the post-pandemic years may need to include new ideas on the role of schools in healthy development. Once trauma becomes an expected part of life in schools, it can no longer be an afterthought or add-on to the business of educating—we must turn to the successful examples from the front lines to plan for the future.

Danger. While high death rates in the early stages of the pandemic were isolated to certain geographical areas, everyone was affected by this new great unknown that was COVID-19. We all remember the stories of people attempting to stay safe by leaving their mail outside for 48 hours or wiping down groceries as they were brought in the house. There was so much uncertainty coupled with the certainty that a deadly, contagious virus was making its way across the globe. This unknown highlighted another challenge that schools had to overcome: *danger*.

Unfortunately, danger is not a new characteristic of education in America. Since the Columbine Massacre of 1999, schools have constantly been under the danger of school shootings. By some estimates, almost 300,000 children have experienced gun violence in school since Columbine [6]. The generation of Americans that has come of age over the last twenty years has not had the luxury of viewing schools as safe places, and little has been accomplished in the policy arena to address this reality. Increases in bomb threats, intruder scares, bullying, cyberbullying, and so many other dangers have become commonplace in our schools. Increases in extreme weather events have also led to dangers such as tornadoes, flooding, and even excessive temperatures that the school buildings were not designed to accommodate. These dangers continue to dismantle the idea of a school building as a safe space and force educators to prepare for the worst.

And yet, even with all these present dangers, no one could have been prepared for the unique dangers that the COVID-19 pandemic presented. All the previous dangers were quick-passing, and geographically isolated. If administrators and/or local law enforcement could locate the source of a threat, such as a school shooter or bully, it could usually be neutralized. Even weather events, which might impact the entire Eastern Seaboard over the course of a week and circulate heavily through the media, remain passing events in much of the nation's consciousness. However, with COVID-19, especially in the early stages, no one could predict what the end of the pandemic would look like. Once the realization set in that this pandemic would not pass quickly, educators across the nation had to determine which risks were worth taking to ensure that a student received a proper education. Schools had to decide what calculated risks to take, and whether it was worth it to reopen schools during the pandemic, even before a vaccine became available. These risk calculations resulted in different strategies emerging across different districts, and as a result, the U.S. saw a hodgepodge of school reopening decisions across the nation. While this variation proved a source of great contention, it also affords an opportunity for meaningful learning for the future.

Ultimately, what remains a fact is that the pandemic evolved, and we evolved to keep up with its impacts. Educators debated through three years of national emergency how to provide safety in schools and recover from the harm that had already occurred to the psyche of a generation of students. Each day offered a new risk assessment that involved weighing disease prevention against psychological harm from isolation. Each set of results from school assessments raised, and continues to raise, questions about how to recover lost learning and build back lost trust between America's schools and their stakeholders. How do we help children re-establish the safety required for learning in a polarized environment when what makes some people feel safe—physically and psychologically—actively raises the anxiety of others? How do we keep our classrooms staffed by qualified teachers when so many are disillusioned by the profession and what it requires of them? These are just some of the questions that a dangerous, ever-mutating virus challenged us to keep grappling with, even as it sometimes undermined our best efforts.

The Economic Recession

While the pandemic brought along health-related challenges that varied based on local infection rates, mitigation strategies, and a multitude of other factors, the *economic recession* that resulted from the pandemic was much more widespread and was faced fairly simultaneously across the nation. Numerous news channels reported on the food bank lines that stretched for miles [7, 8]. Over 22 million people became unemployed when businesses were forced to shut down in March of 2020 [9]. An economy that was thriving and growing suddenly came to a halt, and numerous economic repercussions reverberated through every facet of life. Education was no exception.

Education funding has always been a contentious issue [10]. Funding for education fluctuates. During times of economic growth, more money is invested in schools; however, when an economic recession arises, education is often one of the first areas to see budget cuts. This was the case with the 2007 Great Recession, as states dramatically reduced their investment in public education as a budgetary response [11]. Even when state economies recovered, states failed to restore their investments in education. As a result, schools across the nation were already operating at reduced capacity and with strained budgets prior to the onset of COVID-19.

The massive unemployment and widespread economic hardships that employees faced across the nation manifested themselves in schools. Educators began preparing deliverable lunches so that students whose parents had lost their jobs could have food. They created funding campaigns to help cover utility costs for families in need. They scheduled regular check-ins with students and families to provide mental health and social support [12]. Suddenly, teachers and administrators found themselves not just educating, but serving as the last line of defense for their students' well-being. At the same time, educators were also impacted by the economic recession in their own personal lives. As family members in other industries lost jobs, household incomes shrank. Over the course of the pandemic, already underpaid teachers were asked to give more of themselves, leaving states with brewing teacher shortages in dire straits post-pandemic, as thousands of teaching positions went unfilled [13].

The true impact of the economic recession that occurred during COVID lockdowns is yet to be fully understood, but several key findings continue pointing to potential looming challenges. First, one of the most surprising aspects of the recession was its short duration, lasting only two months, despite being one of the worst in U.S. history, as cited by most economists [14]. Thanks to an enormous government bailout of the economy, a large number of Americans were able to continue paying their bills, and living in their homes, and as mitigation strategies slowed the spread of the coronavirus, many business operations were able to return to levels approaching normal [15]. As with so many aspects of economic life in America, this quick recovery was not an experience shared by all Americans everywhere, and the long-term impact of COVID on financial stability for some has been quite hard. Some economists believe that the learning loss incurred during lockdown by students in grades 1–12 might result in a 3% reduction in their lifetime earnings. At the national level, this could translate to a 1.5% reduction in annual GDP for the rest of the century [16]. This means that while the recession that occurred during COVID was short and spared many, the ongoing economic impacts of stay-at-home orders and emergency virtual learning, and what they mean for the future of schools and communities, may be much larger and will require the best efforts of the field of education to overcome.

As part of these government efforts to navigate the virus, schools received massive amounts of money from the Elementary and Secondary School Emergency Relief (ESSER) Fund, to support the safe return to school and the recovery of lost learning [17]. This funding had several positive outcomes—allowing school districts to obtain technology to support emergency virtual education, to address expected and unexpected food insecurity experienced by families in their districts, and to invest in much-needed mental health support for students and district personnel. Some schools used funding to update ventilation systems in old buildings and purchase additional cleaning supplies to prepare for a safe return to in-person schooling. Most importantly, schools used ESSER funds to address the learning loss experienced by their students through extended calendars and additional programming, including extending learning programs, diagnostic assessment, and professional development for teachers to understand how to use assessment data to provide targeted learning support [18]. However, while these ESSER funds were essential to keep schools running, as the pandemic continued to alter traditional school operations, additional funds were not available.

While some schools started allocating COVID recovery funds to improve teacher recruitment and retention, economic realities outside of school systems provided additional, unexpected challenges in this area as the pandemic-related economic recovery continued. Teacher shortages were already occurring before the start of the pandemic, and studies showed that the low pay of teaching jobs required about 20% of the teacher workforce to hold a second job to make ends meet [19]. The broader labor shortage has emerged in the U.S. economy, a portion of which has been attributed to increasing disability in the workforce resulting from long-haul COVID symptoms, has created opportunities for teachers to leave the profession that might not have existed before [20]. As business operations moved online during lockdowns, the demand for instructional design professionals exploded. Simultaneously, teachers switched physical classroom teaching to emergency online instruction and received intensive real-world experience, retooling their existing skills for a new classroom environment. The convergence of new, high-paying job opportunities and a teaching force that had endured dangerous working conditions, low morale, and acquired new skills to meet the demands of the emerging workforce has left schools in a tenuous staffing position for the near future. While the immediate recession subsided, the rising cost of living and inflation have continued to stress an already-stressed education system as teachers leave for higher-paying jobs. Additionally, America's minoritized youth, already suffering from ongoing economic insecurity in society's most under-resourced segments, are likely to feel disproportionately impacted by the exodus of qualified teachers in the months and years to come.

The Racial Reckoning

Given the racial inequalities apparent in both the experience of the coronavirus and the pandemic recession, it makes sense in hindsight that a racial reckoning that had been brewing under the surface for years burst forward during the summer of 2020. The third major challenge of that year, while not directly related to the COVID-19 pandemic, nonetheless emerged during this critical time for the education system and might perhaps have had the broadest societal impact. On May 25, 2020, George Floyd, a 46-year-old Black man, was murdered in front of numerous witnesses, as Minneapolis police officer Derek Chauvin kneeled on his neck for over eight minutes, despite pleas by onlookers and Floyd, alike, that he could not breathe. Cell phone video of the Floyd murder, which spread quickly across the globe, sparked protests against the systemic racism toward African Americans in the United States [21]. As the world watched the agonized last breaths of a helpless man, the U.S. was plunged into a ***racial reckoning***.

The racial reckoning that began in 2020 is, by no means, an indication that some new form of racism was emerging, rather that something which had existed for hundreds of years was being recognized or seen in a new way. The U.S. has an enduring legacy of a society built on racial hierarchy and repression. While there have been attempts to rectify these racial injustices, the lack of social progress toward the equitable treatment of minoritized individuals in America demonstrates the difficulty that the United States has with reconciling the parts of its history that are at odds with its ideals of liberty. The murder of George Floyd was a catalyst for the current discussions on racial justice and police brutality around the world. Further, the efficacy of resource officers in schools and law enforcement's role in society soon permeated every discussion, including those occurring in educational contexts.

The racial reckoning of 2020 was unique in specific ways, though. First, it was happening at a time of great political and cultural division in our country. A heated presidential campaign was in full swing, and candidates were not shy to use racially charged rhetoric. Further, since schooling was virtual, classrooms for the first time were open to parents and guardians, who were previously unaware of how discussions on race and equity were handled in schools. Witnessing unadulterated classroom discussions on race, equity, and oppression resulted in a vocal opposition to these topics. Soon, protests about the dangers of Critical Race Theory (CRT) began occurring in school board meetings and state legislatures, and some states even sought to implement anti-CRT laws. As the horror of the very public and brutal murder of a Black man raised the critical consciousness of people around the world, it also threatened the long-standing structures of power that too many Americans had relied on to maintain their privilege. At the same time, individual schools, districts, towns, and cities took on the challenges of racial equity and faced the country's history of racial injustice bravely. These contexts hold within them examples of how the willingness to be uncomfortable can unleash our potential to educate a future generation to build a more just society.

Bringing the Stories to Light

In the following chapters, we aim to give voice to the experiences of teachers and leaders in school districts that were heavily impacted by the COVID-19 pandemic in the United States through the end of 2020, and how they have continued to approach education through the duration of the pandemic. News reports of the pandemic, especially early on, tended to report infection rates and death rates related to the pandemic, as well as school closure and reopening experiences in different states. While the policies guiding the return to in-person instruction at different points in the pandemic have been debated and written at the state level, the impact of the virus or of school policies was not experienced in the same way across various communities in most states [22, 23]. In the following chapters, we examine the impact of these phenomena through the stories of teachers and leaders in diverse communities across the country, considering the existing inequalities in wealth, healthcare access, and school quality at the start of the pandemic to better understand how teachers and leaders navigated this challenging time to best serve their students. As we have spoken to educators and collected these stories, we have not only found the myriad challenges faced in the most disadvantaged school settings around the country, but also seen how they fit in the broader national conversation on racial and economic equity and the historical roots of structural racism in America's schools. While this is a narrative of trauma and loss on the surface, it is also an illustration of extreme resilience: even through the tears, teachers and school leaders have selflessly answered the call to support students.

While the inspiring stories of pandemic education experiences are too numerous to count, these stories are drawn from four school districts that illustrate some of the greatest challenges (i.e., trauma, danger, economic recession, and racial reckoning), but have also banded together within their communities to develop innovative approaches to addressing challenges that can benefit the field at large.

When considering the trauma of death and despair experienced in the early days of the pandemic in the United States, few places come to mind in the same way as New York City. While the rest of the nation waited with bated breath, locked down in homes, watching the news, and wondering when the silent killer would walk among its loved ones, the residents of New York lived through the first coronavirus surge. The Bronx, one of the five boroughs of New York City, is the third most densely populated county in the U.S., and unfortunately, was one of the hardest hit areas in the first stage of the pandemic. The Bronx had the highest COVID-19 death rate per capita for any county with over 100,000 residents in December 2020 [24]. Concourse Village Public School 359, a preK-5 school in New York City Community School District (CSD) #7, in the Bronx, faced first-hand the trauma that the COVID-19 pandemic created for students. Even though PS 359 has the distinction of being in what at the time was the poorest congressional district in the country, the richness of community connections that guided the district through the darkest days of the pandemic was evident in every conversation we had with educators there. The story of their district emphasizes the deep pain and suffering that so many, including young children, experienced during the pandemic, the way leaders and teachers stepped in to support students through such trying times, and the innovative solutions that emerged from their work.

The greatest danger that educators and schools faced during the pandemic was the risk of COVID infection. In the early months of the pandemic, there was limited availability of testing, and even though the virus spread quickly in America, proportionately very few people had acquired immunity through infection. In the absence of a vaccine, the virus had a high mortality rate [25]. While many schools around the country did not return to in-person schooling until well into 2021, Monterey High School in the Lubbock Independent School District is one of the districts that was forced to contend with the dangers of in-person schooling prior to the wide distribution of vaccines. Lubbock, Texas, home to Texas Tech University, had the highest COVID-19 infection rate of any county over 100,000 residents as of December 2020 [26]. Many of these infections occurred later in the year, by which time mortality rates from the virus were lower than those that devastated the Bronx in the first pandemic wave during the spring of 2020, even as the virus evolved to become more transmissible [27]. However, due to issues with access to wireless internet and high absentee and failure rates in the virtual academy, schools in Lubbock ISD returned to in-person learning early in the pandemic. Their story speaks to the inherent dangers that came with opening their schools during a period of high infection rates, the ways they safely supported their students through the process, and best practices they hope to continue into future school years.

The economic challenges of the COVID-19 pandemic were even more pronounced in school districts where communities had pre-existing income inequities and contended with ongoing economic challenges. Los Angeles Unified School District (LAUSD) is one of the largest districts in the country and illustrates these inequities. While it includes the wealth and privileged lifestyles of communities like Hollywood, parts of the district also suffered some of the highest pandemic-related unemployment rates. Nowhere were the vast economic inequities in the district more noticeable than in Cudahy, California. Part of the Los Angeles Unified School District, Ellen Ochoa Learning Center sits in one of the most densely populated cities in the country [28]. As a result of this density, high housing costs and extreme poverty for some residents create unique challenges for the education system. The economic recession resulted in high levels of housing and food insecurity, which affected students. Their district's story speaks to the resilience, innovation, and community support needed to sustain learning through difficult times.

The racial reckoning of 2020 began in the streets of Minneapolis, and there was no more fitting place to understand its true implications for schools than in Minneapolis itself. While the murder of George Floyd changed the conversation on racial justice for so many schools, one school, Patrick Henry High School of the Minneapolis Public Schools (MPS), was able to continue its work. For Patrick Henry High School, and MPS, the murder of George Floyd did not bring to light new injustices, rather it affirmed the need for the racial equity work they were already doing. As we heard in their interviews, educators in MPS are committed to embracing the diversity of their students, faculty, and staff. Minneapolis is all too aware of racial violence and unrest. Before George Floyd, there were Philando Castile, Jamar Clark, Christopher Burns, David Smith, and still others, all Black people killed by police officers in or near Minneapolis. The murder of George Floyd did not change the work educators were doing in Minneapolis, but it did change the eyes that were watching what they did. The story of this district speaks to their community's tenacity and mission to eliminate racial injustices and ensure that all students have access to a safe, quality education.

The Threads that Connect Us

Each and every school district was affected by the challenges of 2020 in unique ways, but it was our goal to bring these stories to light so that we can formulate best practices and ensure that students have equitable opportunities in the future. As we conducted interviews with superintendents, principals, and teachers in multiple districts, seven main themes emerged in our conversations with educators. While the exact nature of what was discussed in these areas varied considerably from one school to the next, the consistent focus by school personnel on these topics highlighted their importance in our discussions of education and learning during the pandemic. These themes give us the opportunity to see new potential in these spaces and ultimately reimagine what education can look like in the post-pandemic era.

Broader Purpose of School

Throughout the pandemic, schools have been forced to expand their purpose beyond education to so many other supports. While schools and educators were trying to adjust to virtual learning, they were also serving as technology troubleshooters, food delivery workers, mental health advocates, and so much more. Educators had provided similar services before, but never at this scale. Usually managed on an individual basis, leaders suddenly saw a whole community in need of support and stability. Throughout each of the next chapters you will hear stories of educators who went beyond their job description, ensuring that students and their families could survive and persist through the pandemic, and reimagined education to create a community around their schools. As we look ahead, we are left to consider if, perhaps, schools have always done more for some than teaching reading, writing, and arithmetic. Maybe in this new era of education, in a post-pandemic world, an expanded purpose of school is needed for all students to thrive?

Equity and Access

The pandemic and economic recession also highlighted the inequities that still exist so prevalently in our society. The transition to virtual learning highlighted the economic and technological inequities, as some students were without devices or internet to attend school online. A Pew Research Center poll conducted in April 2020 showed that roughly one in five parents said their children would not be able to complete their schoolwork because they do not have access to a computer at home, and about three in ten parents reported that their children had to do their schoolwork on a cell phone [29]. Even when internet connections were available, social and economic inequities made the cost unaffordable for some. All the schools featured in the subsequent chapters will highlight the ways they went beyond the classroom to ensure all students had access to the technology and resources they needed to continue education. But these efforts call into question our larger education policies—how do we close these access gaps moving forward?

Teacher Pipeline

The snowball effect of a teacher shortage has been slow rolling through the U.S. for years, but no one anticipated the rate at which the pandemic would hasten its course [30]. Schools across the nation have been scrambling to fill teacher vacancies, as experienced teachers retire at higher rates and the number of new teachers entering the field continues to dwindle [31]. In a survey of teachers by the National Education Association and American Federation of Teachers, 75% of teachers reported frequent job-related stress, compared to only 40% of other working adults [32]. Teachers said this stress came from a multitude of factors including maintaining contact with students and their families, supporting students' social-emotional health, and keeping students engaged virtually. As you will see in the stories of the education leaders interviewed, they were forced to take new approaches to retain and support teachers. The question we are left with as a field is: how can the innovative approaches that emerged in a time of crisis help us reimagine our teacher pipeline and ensure a sustainable educator workforce?

Leadership Philosophy

Throughout our interviews and discussions with education leaders, the impact of leadership philosophy emerged. Each leader's style was seen across his or her school district, rooted in values and principles that defined that educator, and it was these values that kept them motivated, even through the most challenging times of the pandemic. In speaking to district and school leaders, it was clear that leaders were the creators and disseminators of professional culture, and they played an essential role in how those in their charge fared through the darkest days. Regardless of the leadership style, the idea of trust was pervasive. However they chose to enact this idea, the pandemic taught the leaders we interviewed that education is a business of developing humans and could only be successfully approached from a place of humanity. As we recalibrate through our field's exit from this global pandemic, how can we retain this important learning and instill it in current and future education leaders?

Community Resources

While the way the schools embraced their communities was clearly important in our conversations across districts, communities also contributed a tremendous wealth of resources to the schools. Community organizations, familiar with how embedded education is within society, recognized the need to serve the whole child. Students are more successful when they are safe, healthy, and well-fed. Community organizations, such as the YMCA, stepped up and provided a place for children of first responders to attend virtual school in a safe, supervised environment. This is just a tiny example of the ways faith-based institutions, nonprofits, and other local organizations united to provide social support services to schools and their community. No matter where the communities were located, what their level of affluence was, or what their needs were, local communities met their schools with creativity and responsiveness. Every community had care and cultural wealth to offer, and leaders leveraged their community relationships to ask for innovative supports from their communities. The stories you will hear from education leaders speak to their efforts to secure these resources for their students and to ensure that all students in their district were served. Considering the unique attributes of different communities, we must consider—what sources of cultural wealth have gone unacknowledged in our approaches to education? Does the evolving landscape of education in a post-pandemic world afford a space for more robust and authentic school-community partnerships?

Communication

Communication was key to successfully navigating most pandemic challenges in schools, even as it took different forms in different situations. For one, every person interviewed conveyed the importance of communication within the school building. This included weekly virtual meetups of teachers from the same grade, daily addresses by principals to their teachers, and even individual check-ins between supervisors and supervisees to discuss the stress and weight of the pandemic. Communication was also key outside of the school building, as teachers emphasized the importance of disseminating information to families. In a time where conditions, knowledge, and best practices were changing constantly, communicating clearly and frequently with students and families was important. Most of all, you will see from our interviews that transparency in communication was of utmost importance. Even if someone did not agree with the decision being made, communicating *why* helped alleviate fears and frustrations. In an era of great polarization of perspectives, how can schools and society cultivate clearer communication practices that aim to understand as much as they aim to convince?

District Readiness

The final theme of district readiness speaks specifically to how prepared schools were to deal with the tripartite challenges of 2020—coronavirus pandemic, economic recession, and racial reckoning—that were before them. It should come as no surprise that having leaders, systems, and policies in place before a challenge can greatly ease the burden of navigating it. For one, many of the programs and services that schools provided were happening already, just on a much smaller scale. The challenge was quickly scaling up these services in a way that made them sustainable. Whether it was ordering thousands of masks for their school to reopen, raising money to pay internet bills, or providing lessons on race made for students and their parents, school leaders were consistently preparing for the next challenge. No district could have been truly "ready" for what was to come, but as you will see from our discussions, educators demonstrated ingenuity and were ready to do what it took to make sure their students and their schools succeeded. As we imagine what comes next for education in America, perhaps the idea of readiness is more important than ever. How can the lessons learned over the course of the COVID pandemic help us prepare for the next upheaval? How can we develop forward-thinking policies and procedures in our schools that are not responding to challenges of bygone eras, rather anticipating future challenges, and building the capacity of the next generation to meet them?

CONCLUSION

In closing, the seven themes highlighted in this chapter: (1) the broader purpose of school, (2) equity and access, (3) the teacher pipeline, (4) leadership philosophy, (5) community resources, (6) communication, and (7) district readiness were used to inform the way we analyzed interviews and compiled our thoughts for writing. Each of these themes highlights the significant time, energy, and thought educators put into all aspects of their profession. The following four chapters tell the comprehensive account of the four school districts of Bronx Community District #7, Lubbock Independent Schools, Los Angeles Unified School District, and Minneapolis Public Schools. These seven themes permeate our discussions of the trauma and fears of the pandemic, the economic recession, and racial reckoning, as evident from interviews with superintendents, principals, and teachers. While each school district was chosen for a specific reason, every one of the large challenges that defined 2020 and carried through the subsequent years influenced decision-making in each district. It is our hope that the following four chapters tell the stories of triumph and ingenuity of four school districts that charted a course for reimagining education for years to come.

REFERENCES

1. Johnson, C., & Sdunzik, J. (2023). Introduction to special issue: Re-imagining teaching and learning in the context of current crises. *Research in Educational Policy and Management, 5*(1), i–iii. https://doi.org/10.46303/repam.2023.1
2. Decker, S., Peele, H., & Riser-Kositsky, M. (2020, July 1). *Education Week.* https://www.edweek.org/leadership/the-coronavirus-spring-the-historic-closing-of-u-s-schools-a-timeline/2020/07
3. Centers for Disease Control and Prevention. (2021, November 17). *Drug overdose deaths in the U.S. top 100,000 annually.* Centers for Disease and Prevention. Retrieved August 1, 2023, from https://www.cdc.gov/nchs/pressroom/nchs_press_releases/2021/20211117.htm
4. American Federation of Teachers. (2020, October 21). *Educators say COVID-19 has greatly exacerbated the grief support crisis in schools, according to new survey.* American Federation of Teachers. Retrieved August 1, 2023, from https://www.aft.org/press-release/educators-say-covid-19-has-greatly-exacerbated-grief-support-crisis-schools
5. Yard, E., Radhakrishnan, L., & Ballesteros, M. F., Sheppard, M., Gates, A., Stein, Z., Hartnett, K., Kite-Powell, A., Rodgers, L., Adjemian, J., & Ehlman, D. C. (2021). Emergency department visits for suspected suicide attempts among persons aged 12–25 years before and during the COVID-19 pandemic. *Morbidity and Mortality Weekly Report, 70*(24), 888–894. https://doi.org/10.15585/mmwr.mm7024el
6. Cox, J. W., Rich, S., Chong, L., Muyskens, J., & Ulmanu, M. (2018, April 20). More than 348,000 students have experienced gun violence at school since Columbine. *The Washington Post.* https://www.washingtonpost.com/graphics/2018/local/school-shootings-database/
7. Alonso, M, & Cullinane, S. (2020, November 16). Thousands of cars form lines to collect food in Texas. *CNN.* https://www.cnn.com/2020/11/15/us/dallas-texas-food-bank-coronavirus/index.html
8. Abou-Sabe, K., Romo, C., McFadden, C., & Longoria, J. (2020, April 8). COVID-19 crisis heaps pressure on nation's food banks. *NBC Universal.* https://www.nbcnews.com/news/us-news/covid-19-crisis-heaps-pressure-nation-s-food-banks-n1178731
9. Mutikani, L. (2021, July 29). U.S. economy contracted 19.2% during COVID-19 pandemic recession. *Reuters.* https://www.reuters.com/business/us-economy-contracted-192-during-covid-19-pandemic-recession-2021-07-29/

10. Ravitch, D. (2020). *Slaying goliath: The passionate resistance to privatization and the fight to save America's public schools.* Vintage.
11. Farrie, D., & Sciarra, D. G. (2020). *$600 Billion Lost: State Disinvestment in Education Following the Great Recession.* Education Law Center. Retrieved April 1, 2023, from https://edlawcenter.org/research/$600-billion-lost.html
12. Truong, D. (2020, September 17). In D.C. neighborhoods devastated by COVID-19, school workers become 'emergency responders.' *WAMU 88.5 American University Radio.* https://dcist.com/story/20/09/17/dc-school-workers-pandemic-emergency-responders-covid19/
13. Walker, T. (2022, February 1). Survey: Alarming number of educators may soon leave the profession. *NEA News.* https://www.nea.org/advocating-for-change/new-from-nea/survey-alarming-number-educators-may-soon-leave-profession
14. NBER. (2021, July 19). Business cycle dating committee announcement. *NBER News.* https://www.nber.org/news/business-cycle-dating-committee-announcement-july-19-2021
15. Parlapiano, A., Solomon, D., Ngo, M., & Cowley, S. (2022, March 11). Where $5 trillion in pandemic stimulus money went. *The New York Times.* https://www.nytimes.com/interactive/2022/03/11/us/how-covid-stimulus-money-was-spent.html
16. Hanushek, E. A., & Woessmann, L. (2020, September). *The economic impacts of learning losses.* OECD. Retrieved April 15, 2023, from https://www.oecd.org/education/The-economic-impacts-of-coronavirus-covid-19-learning-losses.pdf
17. Office of Elementary & Secondary Education. (2023, May 17). *Elementary and secondary school emergency relief fund.* U.S. Department of Education. Retrieved August 1, 2023, from https://oese.ed.gov/offices/education-stabilization-fund/elementary-secondary-school-emergency-relief-fund/
18. The Hunt Institute. (2020, December 27). *Elementary and secondary school emergency relief fund ii: Menu of options.* The Hunt Institute. Retrieved August 1, 2023, from https://hunt-institute.org/resources/elementary-and-secondary-school-emergency-relief-esser-funds/
19. Will, M. (2018, June 19). To make ends meet, 1 in 5 teachers have second jobs. *Education Week.* https://www.edweek.org/leadership/to-make-ends-meet-1-in-5-teachers-have-second-jobs/2018/06
20. Bach, K. (2022, January 11). Is 'long Covid' worsening the labor shortage? *Brookings.* https://www.brookings.edu/research/is-long-covid-worsening-the-labor-shortage/
21. Silverstein, J. (2021, June 4). The global impact of George Floyd: How Black Lives Matter protests shaped movements around the world. *CBS Interactive Inc.* https://www.cbsnews.com/news/george-floyd-black-lives-matter-impact/

22. Ferren, M. (2021, July 6). *Remote learning and school reopening: What worked and what didn't*. The Center for American Progress. Retrieved August 1, 2023, from https://www.americanprogress.org/article/remote-learning-school-reopenings-worked-didnt/
23. Office of Civil rights. (2021, June 9). *Education in a pandemic: The disparate impacts of America's students*. U.S. Department of Education. Retrieved August 1, 2023, from https://www2.ed.gov/about/offices/list/ocr/docs/20210608-impacts-of-covid19.pdf
24. Johns Hopkins University. (2023, March 10) *Coronavirus resource center*. Johns Hopkins University. Retrieved August 1, 2023, from https://coronavirus.jhu.edu/map.html
25. Mervosh, S., & Fernandez, M. (2020, July 6). Months into virus crisis, US cities still lack testing capacity. *New York Times*. https://www.nytimes.com/2020/07/06/us/coronavirus-test-shortage.html
26. Johns Hopkins University. (2023, March 10). *Coronavirus resource center*. Johns Hopkins University. Retrieved August 1, 2023, from https://coronavirus.jhu.edu/map.html
27. Oladunjoye, O., Gallagher, M., Wasser, T., Oladunjoye, A., Paladugu, S., & Donato, A. (2021). Mortality due to COVID-19 infection: A comparison of first and second waves. *Journal of Community Hospital Internal Medicine Perspectives, 11*(6), 747–752. https://doi.org/10.1080/20009666.2021.1978154
28. Business View. (2017, February). Cudahy California: Small city, big plans. *Business View Publishing*. https://businessviewmagazine.com/cudahy-california-small-city-big-plans/
29. Vogels, E. A., Perrin, A., Rainie, L., & Anderson, M. (2020, April 30). 53% of Americans say the internet has been essential during the COVID-19 outbreak. *Pew Research Center*. https://www.pewresearch.org/internet/2020/04/30/53-of-americans-say-the-internet-has-been-essential-during-the-covid-19-outbreak/
30. Schmitt, J., & deCourcy, K. (2022, December 6). *The pandemic has exacerbated a long-standing national shortage of teachers*. Economic Policy Institute. Retrieved August 1, 2023, from https://www.epi.org/publication/shortage-of-teachers/
31. National Center for Education Statistics NCES. (2022, March 3). *U.S. schools report increased teacher vacancies due to covid-19 pandemic, new NCES data show*. U.S. Department of Education. Retrieved August 1, 2023, from https://nces.ed.gov/whatsnew/press_releases/3_3_2022.asp
32. Steiner, E. D., & Woo, A. (2021). *Job-related stress threatens the teacher supply*. RAND. Retrieved March 1, 2022, from https://www.rand.org/pubs/research_reports/RRA1108-1.html

PART II

Stories of Education in Trying Times

CHAPTER 3

Education in a Time of Trauma: A Story of Resilience

> *The lesson that our community learned is that we're definitely stronger together. We are each other's assets, able to lean on one another, and have one another at all times.*
> —Alexa Sorden, Principal, Concourse Village Elementary School

The earliest days of the COVID-19 pandemic were full of fear and uncertainty. While none of us knew exactly how bad things would be, by the time infection rates started to climb rapidly in New York City, one thing was clear: we were in the midst of a shared global trauma that was being experienced in real terms by some, and vicariously by everyone else through the news coverage of events. This was a disruption event unlike any other, and one that immediately exacerbated existing structural inequalities in our education system and in our society.

In a book on the life and work of renowned psychotherapist and Holocaust survivor, Victor Frankl [1], author Stephen Covey states, "Between stimulus and response there is a space. In that space is our power to choose our response. In our response lies our growth and our freedom." Covey saw that sometimes, our moments of greatest hardship can be transformed into our greatest achievements through the power of choice, self-awareness, and ultimately, meaningful impact. Amid the chaos and upheaval of the early days of the COVID-19, every person had to choose a response, and educators, in particular, impacted a great many people through the responses they chose.

The unknown, deadly coronavirus was the stimulus causing pain and trauma. There was no silver lining. No looking on the bright side. People were dying in the thousands and no end was in sight; but in this trauma emerged a small space where the broader community, and a remarkable group of educators at Concourse Village Public School 359, in Bronx District 7, chose to reimagine their role in the lives of their students and families. Their resilient response and personal sacrifices not only supported their community through the darkest of days, but now provides guidance for the rest of us on the potential of schools to address trauma in its many forms in the years to come.

The District Context of the Bronx

Nestled between the Hudson River to its west and the Long Island Sound to its east, Bronx County, commonly referred to as "the Bronx" is a borough of New York City with a population of over 1.4 million residents. This 42-square-mile plot of land was originally part of the Lenape Lenapehoking territory before European colonists converted it to farmland [2]. Beginning in the late 1800s, new technology such as railways and subway systems enabled rapid population growth that only accelerated after World War I. Today, if it were its own city, the Bronx would be the ninth most populous city in the U.S. and the third most densely populated [3]. The Bronx boasts a vibrant and diverse population: 22% of residents identify as white, 35% as Black, 4% as Asian, and 2% as multiracial. Additionally, 56% of residents identify as Hispanic, making it the only Hispanic-majority county in the Northeast and the fourth most populous nationwide [3].

The Bronx has an estimated per capita income of $22,600, which is below the U.S. average of $35,600. As a result, it is considered one of the poorest counties in the nation. Additionally, the South Bronx, specifically the NY-15 congressional district, was the poorest congressional district in the country prior to redistricting after the 2020 census. Further, roughly 26% of Bronx residents live below the poverty line, more than double the average rate in the United States. This number is even higher for children, as over 37% of Bronx children live in poverty [3]. As Bronx District 7 Superintendent Rafael Alvarez stated:

> [A] school district like mine, that is in the poorest congressional district in the United States, that faces the largest opioid crisis in the New York City area, that has the income of no more than twenty something thousand dollars—that's the average income in this community—with largest number of temporary housing students within the district, we were already facing trauma and mental health pre-pandemic. Post-pandemic just exacerbated the desire and need for the collective city to say we need to do something about it.

The pandemic had an outsized effect on those from low-income and minoritized communities, and this was no doubt the case in the Bronx. For education leaders already providing extensive support to students to overcome the racial and social barriers to education equity, the pandemic only emphasized a drastic need to recalibrate and reimagine education.

Understanding the District Structure

The New York City Department of Education is divided into 32 community school districts, each with their own superintendent and school board [4]. Bronx Community School District 7 (CSD #7) is located in the South Bronx and is situated within the greater New York City Department of Education. CSD #7 comprises nearly 50 schools, including 17 elementary schools, 12 middle schools, and 18 high schools, and enrolling nearly 16,000 students yearly. Roughly 26% of students identify as Black, 70% as Latino/Hispanic, 2% white, 1% as Asian, and 1% as multiracial. Roughly 17% of students are identified as English language learners. Additionally, given the economic status of the area, 93% of students are classified as economically disadvantaged, and 16% are experiencing homelessness [5].

There were challenges aplenty for CSD #7 that any leader would have to address, and when Superintendent Rafael Alvarez stepped to the helm in 2018, he was prepared to do just that. While he had no idea what lay ahead in 2020, his military background and previous experience managing complex situations would prove that he was the right person to lead CSD #7 through the pandemic and subsequent trauma experienced by a community with the highest COVID-19 death toll in 2020. Superintendent Alvarez previously spent 13 years in the U.S. Navy, and it was this experience that prepared him to triage, strategize, and execute plans that supported his faculty, students, and community through immense trauma and grief. Part of what made his school district so successful during this time was the team of leaders he had built around him.

Just as the military strives to develop new leaders that bring fresh and innovative perspectives, Alvarez noted the importance of developing the next generation of teachers, principals, and administrators. Prior to the pandemic, his district created a Paraprofessional Institute, aimed at training paraprofessionals internally to become licensed teachers. They also developed a Coach's Leadership Institute to train those in "out-of-classroom" positions to provide useful feedback for teachers and encourage that feedback mindset. He believed new leadership was critical to bring new ideas to the forefront through collaboration, and this served the district well when the upheaval of 2020 began:

> *There has to be learning at the district level, otherwise it stays stagnant because the tendency at the district level is that everybody thinks they have all the answers. I don't have all that. … It was through collaboration [and] communication with my team, and the pushing of thoughts between principals, assistant principals, parents, and students. They came up with the answers. I just made the final decisions based on those answers.*

Ultimately, Alvarez knew that the success of his district hinged on the desire, and ability, to continue to learn and to develop education leaders.

One of the schools within CSD #7, Concourse Village Elementary School (CVES) 359, was led by someone who knew the importance of developing future principals. A former classroom teacher, Alexa Sorden was founding principal of CVES, a Pre-K through fifth grade school in the South Bronx whose goal was to end a cycle of academic underachievement that led to the closure of two previous schools in the same location. Principal Sorden previously served as a teacher, then literacy coach, then Director of Student Achievement, before being tapped to serve as principal of CVES in September 2013. A graduate of the 2018 Cahn Fellows Program for Distinguished Principals at Teachers College, Columbia University, she led CVES to achievements such as being named a 2018 Blue Ribbon School and a 2020 Best Urban School in the Nation. Through Principal Sorden's leadership, CVES developed a reputation for academic excellence through hard work, innovation, and intentional learning experiences to support all students and their journeys.

CVES is a diverse community of almost 300 students, teachers, and staff members who come from a wide range of cultures and identities. When designing the school, Sorden thought about what she wanted as a student. The daughter of a Dominican mother and African American father from Georgia, she knew firsthand the importance of centering culture and intentional design in the curriculum. Approximately 33% of students identify as Black, and 63% as Hispanic or Latinx. Further, CVES serves many families who have recently immigrated to the U.S., which creates an environment rich with linguistic and cultural diversity. Roughly 10% of students are identified as English Language Learners and 20% have disabilities. As a result, CVES has embedded inclusive instructional environments at all grade levels to ensure students have the support systems needed to be successful.

Throughout our discussions about CVES, it was clear that the core values of integrity, perseverance, optimism, willingness, empathy, and respect guided the work done at CVES. Leaders at CVES promoted and highlighted positive behaviors and strived to find opportunities to celebrate accomplishments big and small. These positive reinforcements created relationships, sense of community, and a space for growth and success.

> *I believe that every student can learn and be successful when provided with the right supports and opportunities. Our educators and staff are committed to providing all scholars with an appropriate and challenging educational experience in a respectful environment that fosters learning and growth.* (Alexa Sorden [6])

Within Concourse Village Elementary School 359, over 30 teachers dedicated their time and efforts to providing the best education possible to their students. Ms. Cynthia Cruz was one of those teachers, identified by Principal Sorden as going above and beyond during the pandemic and using innovative strategies to provide an equitable classroom experience to all students at a time of trauma and fear.

Ms. Cruz was a third-grade teacher at the start of the pandemic and had a close-knit relationship with her students. At CVES, most teachers co-teach classes and loop with their students, meaning that rather than getting a new set of students each year, teachers progress with their class. Ms. Cruz, for example, taught her class in second grade, and then moved up to teach them in third and fourth grade in subsequent years. Progressing with the students allowed Ms. Cruz to form deep relationships with both the students and their families; and these relationships were essential to the success of her classroom when the pandemic hit halfway through third grade. Students had known Ms. Cruz for over a year when the pandemic started, so in this time of uncertainty, she served as a trusted source and guide for students and their parents. Open lines of communication were already established, and this was essential for keeping learning opportunities at the forefront. As you will see throughout this book, communication was a critical part of a successful response to pandemic school closures and the switch to emergency online learning. Teachers found themselves central to important communication between schools and families, and Ms. Cruz was exemplary among her peers in her responsive support of families.

No previous experiences could prepare teachers for what the pandemic had in store, but as Ms. Cruz told us, not even a pandemic could persuade her to choose a different profession. For her, teaching was her passion and her path. Even when the pandemic forced her to find a new way to connect with her students (like playing the video game *Among Us* with her students during lunch), rather than becoming frustrated, she embraced it and found joy in the work. When asked about how the pandemic had affected teacher retention and future decisions around the profession, including her own, she said:

> *[Other teachers] found a different art and they became entrepreneurs and went on a different path. I guess everyone had their own path in all this. Me? No. I'm staying here.*

It was clear from our conversation that the deep relationships she had developed with her students and their families over their years together played an important part in her commitment to the profession and the community she served.

Together, the perspectives of these three educators in Bronx CSD #7 tell the story of a district and school whose commitment to the success and well-being of every student extends well beyond the walls of the school. The success of Bronx CSD #7 and CVES were not the results of any individual's actions, but rather a group effort where everyone's skills were uplifted for the greater good. Superintendent Alvarez explained:

> *There's a tendency in communities like [CSD #7] to think about the deficits, but we started thinking about rewriting the narrative for the South Bronx. And as we thought about the rewriting of the narrative of the South Bronx, being able to be inclusive of the community and their thoughts, and decisions, and minds collectively, helped us get through this pandemic ... without the help of [community organizations] I'm not necessarily sure we would have been able to get through ... so the greatest success was tapping into the local resources [and people] and utilizing them to their fullest potential.*

As you will see in the next section, overcoming the intense trauma and fear that resulted from the COVID-19 pandemic was a community-wide effort, and one that would unite a community, even if they couldn't physically be together.

THE EVOLVING TRAUMA EXPERIENCE

As the educators from Bronx CSD #7 reminded us during our interactions with them, their community members are no strangers to trauma. In fact, along with strong relationships and sound policies and practices, the history of resilient response to trauma in the community played an important role in how prepared district personnel and the families they serve were to respond to rapidly evolving experiences of the COVID-19 pandemic as they unfolded. As one of the first pandemic hotspots in the country in March 2020, New York City had few models from within the United States on which to rely for guidance on managing stay-at-home orders and virtual schooling for its children. In addition, because the large infection surge at this time was a result of the *alpha* strain of the coronavirus (which was considerably more lethal than the *delta* and *omicron* strains that led to later surges [7]) and occurred prior to the development of a COVID vaccine, the trauma experienced by community members in the Bronx during the early days of the pandemic was somewhat different than experiences of later surges.

While it seems a lifetime ago, and very different from the understanding of COVID-19 that we have today, in March of 2020, healthcare officials still believed that children were relatively safe from the novel coronavirus circulating in a growing number of countries, and decisions to shut down school and switch to virtual learning were still being debated. On March 13, 2020, New York City still had under 100 confirmed cases of the virus, and only one of them was related to the school system [8]. By March 15, 2020, New York City Mayor, Bill DeBlasio, had announced that New York City's public school system—the largest in the nation with over one million students and 75,000 teachers—would be shutting down from at least March 23, 2020, to April 20, 2020. At the time, the hope was that by closing through the district's spring break, the city would be able to employ the virus mitigation strategies being recommended by public health experts, and the rapidly spreading SARS-CoV-2 virus responsible for the pandemic would burn itself out due to a lack of hosts. While we now know that the pandemic took a very different course and some students did not return to in-person learning for more than a year after the initial school closures, during the first, most severe societal lockdown, administrators and teachers in Bronx CSD #7 had little notice to prepare themselves and their students for an unprecedented learning experience.

Immediately after learning that school closures might be possible, Superintendent Alvarez began daily meetings with his principals in Bronx CSD #7, warning them of the possibility of closing schools and forming digital curricula. As Alvarez reminded us, they were ready when the time came:

> *So, we had about a week's notice that this was gonna start hitting our city and there was a possibility of the potential of closing for the remainder of the school year. But I have to be honest with you. We have been preparing for this type of challenge now for the past, since I've been superintendent here, for the past three years. It's always been my belief that in District 7, we faced so many adversities that have impacted trauma and mental health in our district just from the sheer nature of the district that we have already been doing all the preparation for something like a pandemic.*

Rather than waiting for the schools to close, they prepared two curricular units in anticipation of closure, buying teachers' and leaders' time and ensuring that students did not miss learning opportunities during the pandemic.

As the district personnel navigated each new hurdle, they leaned heavily on personal experiences of trauma to guide their students and pulled together a community well-versed in supporting each other through adversity. Understanding the history of adversity that is deeply embedded in the Bronx can shine a light on the importance of Alvarez's drive to change the narrative about the South Bronx. Too often in the past, socioeconomic inequalities had led policymakers to tell a tale of deficit to describe his community. Alvarez clearly recognized that the perseverance and resilience developed through generations of struggle in the Bronx was a part of the community's identity, and a cultural asset that could empower educators, students, and parents in a time of crisis.

Generations of Trauma and Resilience

While the Bronx was a thriving borough of New York City in the first half of the twentieth century, with rapid population growth and a robust economy, socio-demographic changes that occurred between the 1950s and 1980s fed into the narrative of despair and trauma that Superintendent Alvarez had been attempting to rewrite in his time leading Bronx CSD #7. As with so many urban centers in the United States during this period, the Bronx experienced "white flight," with working-class families of European descent that had made up a majority of the borough's population leaving the city for the suburbs in large numbers in the 1950s and 1960s [9]. With this departure came new population growth, with the influx of Puerto Rican immigrants and Black families being displaced from Manhattan due to rising housing costs [10].

The development of large urban housing projects also increased the number of families living in poverty in the Bronx over the next decade, and the closure of over 300 companies that employed over 10,000 workers in the Bronx during the 1970s led to unemployment rates between 25% and 30% [11]. Increasing poverty in the borough was accompanied by what so often follows: higher crime rates and a decline in property values. Along with de-industrialization of the borough, the 1970s brought another blow to life in the Bronx—city services such as sanitation, street repairs, and fire departments were cut in response to the financial crisis that plagued the New York City government during this time. In a tragic alignment of events, the reduction in fire departments coincided with a decade of systematic arson in the Bronx, as landlords attempted to limit financial losses from the collapsing Bronx real estate market by burning buildings to collect insurance payouts. The scale of a trauma like this is hard to imagine today. Of the 289 census tracts in the Bronx, some estimates suggest that 7 lost 97% of their buildings and another 44 tracts lost more than 50% during the decade. This defining narrative of the Bronx was brought squarely into the public consciousness during game two of the 1977 World Series, when television cameras captured a burning elementary school building just blocks from Yankee Stadium, and Howard Cosell spoke the much-quoted phrase, "There it is, ladies and gentlemen, the Bronx is burning [12]."

This history of trauma resulting from poverty and economic inequality in the Bronx continued in numerous ways over the decades that followed. In the 1980s, the Bronx saw disproportionate deaths and mass incarceration resulting from the crack cocaine epidemic and the related war on drugs. As Superintendent Alvarez reminded us, the opioid epidemic is playing a similar role in the Bronx today, devastating families in his community, as it ravages communities across America. High population density and poor construction practices have continued to kindle some of the largest fires in the city, even compared to the arson crisis of the 1970s. In 1990, the infamous Happy Land Social Club fire killed 87 people; and in the deadliest fire in NYC since then, 17 people perished in an apartment building fire in January 2022 [13]. Because a large number of essential workers—first responders, hospital staff, grocery and maintenance workers, and transportation personnel—live in the Bronx, the community also experienced large loss of life during the terrorist attacks of September 11, 2001, and in the early days of the COVID-19 pandemic, continuing a cycle of vicious trauma [14, 15].

Through all these challenges, when the world framed the narrative of the Bronx as an embattled urban desert, local residents and community organizations found ways to work together to thrive and rebuild. The Bronx has developed a strong cultural identity as a place of hope and opportunity for immigrant families, and the home to a thriving art and music scene that birthed cultural phenomena such as hip-hop and salsa [16]. The borough has also been a haven of political and community activism and advocacy, with local residents banding together to address long-standing challenges and revitalize their neighborhoods. Superintendent Alvarez shared:

> *You have to realize you can't do it by yourself. And what I've seen across the country from [superintendent] colleagues, is that a lot of districts were left to figure it out by themselves and didn't think about the resources that are in their own backyards that could have supported them had they worked collaboratively to move that work.*

Bridging together non-profit organizations, labor unions, and faith-based resources [17], the communities of the Bronx embody a culture of empowerment and collaboration that was clearly visible in the pandemic response of CSD #7.

The Moving Target of Pandemic Trauma

The long history of navigating adversity and addressing trauma as a community was especially important during the pandemic because the nature of the challenge evolved dramatically over time. The moving target of trauma required educators in Bronx CSD #7 to pay close attention, continuously reassess and reprioritize needs, and leverage a range of resources to support their students and families. In the early days of the pandemic, the number of unknowns related to the virus, its rapid spread through the community, and the devastation of illness and death required district personnel to harness incredible psychological and emotional resources. The loss of life was devastating. Superintendent Alvarez was open about how difficult it was for him, even with his years of military service:

> *That was a tough one, because I've had to see quite a few things that were very difficult as a superintendent. I think I went to every single funeral for any staff member or student in my district, and that was tough for me to do. And I have tough skin.*

He was also clear when we spoke to him in the spring of 2021 that he did not believe this would be the most traumatic part of the pandemic for his district. As schools fully reopened and students and school personnel returned to the buildings and classrooms where principals, teachers, staff, and students they had lost were no longer present, the true scope of the district's tragedy would sink in:

> *Think about the fourth grader who's now going into sixth grade, middle school, who missed fifth grade, did it virtually, but now is going to a new environment, maybe not knowing some of the kids. Think about the student who lost the teacher who never got to say goodbye or lost a friend who wasn't able to say goodbye. When students come back, the emotional tension that's going to rise from that experience is gonna be overwhelming.*

Superintendent Alvarez considered the difficulty that those returning to in-person learning for the first time would face as they experienced the empty desks or offices of those lost during the pandemic. So many additional mental health supports would be needed for students and adults alike, to ensure a positive outcome.

As the lockdown wore on, the trauma of ongoing isolation and the potential harm to students who disappeared from districts in large numbers became a primary concern for school-level leadership. Between March and October of 2020, approximately three million K-12 students disappeared from schools across the country, and while a return to in-person learning brought those numbers down, far too many students remained unaccounted for [18]. Principal Sorden considered the difficult balance that would have to be struck between keeping everyone safe from further spread of the virus (and the likely fears of infection everyone would have) and the desire to make returning comfortable in a school setting again:

> So, it goes back to the culture piece. Something that was important to me was that the children that were coming back in September, that we didn't freak them out, and that we try to keep our interactions with them as normal as possible. It would be like if a child sneezes, don't lose it! Let's just be real. It's okay if they sneeze or cough. We will take care of it, but how can we make sure that they still feel like this is a safe place and that they still want to come in and are happy to learn?

While the nature of the concerns varied from the district office to school building, the resilience of the educators was apparent in how they centered student well-being in their thought process.

ADAPTING TO TRAUMA WITH RESILIENT RESPONSES

Ultimately, adaptation and resilience remained the goal of the educators we spoke with at every turn, even while facing down the deadliest outbreak of COVID-19 in the United States. In discussing the responses they undertook at the district, school, and classroom level, it became apparent there was a deep commitment to a strengths-based understanding of the Bronx and its rich cultural history, as well as a centering of many trauma-informed education practices in the district to help students and school personnel thrive in psychologically taxing times [19]. By focusing on creating a sense of psychological safety, communicating through a democratic process, validating a diverse range of stakeholder voices, and advocating for socially responsible decision-making, district personnel created a true sanctuary in the midst of dark times [20]. These efforts required a great deal of compassion and empathy from all educators, and strong, equity-minded leadership to guide adults and students, alike, in bringing forth their best at each turn. In large part, the Bronx CSD #7 team consistently adhered to the understanding that students would not be able to stay adequately engaged and learn if their most human needs for safety, shelter, and sustenance were not being met. While they planned online instructional units quickly to allow for the smooth transition to emergency online learning, it was clear in our conversations that when Superintendent Alvarez said, "Please keep in mind that for a district like seven, it wasn't just about instruction," he meant it.

Leveraging Community Assets

There were few statements made by Superintendent Alvarez in our time together that explained what motivated his leadership approach and his district's response to the pandemic more than his claim that as superintendent, "it is very important that you're not thinking about just your school district, but you're thinking about the community at large." The relationship between school and community was clearly bidirectional in Bronx CSD #7, with the school acting as a hub for a range of essential services for community members, and the community also funneling resources back through the school to ensure they reached families in need. This interaction between educators throughout the district, students and their families, and local government, nonprofits, and businesses created an intricate, but interconnected, web of shared responsibility and outcomes that contributed to a holistic and efficient support system for community members. Leveraging community resources in creative ways that stayed responsive to the changing needs on the ground helped create the positive adaptations that led to resilience.

The coordinated efforts between the district office and the building and classroom levels evolved with the changing needs of students and families. As the transition to societal lockdowns and emergency online learning began, two issues emerged quickly. First, even if the district could quickly move curriculum online and send home devices, far too many students lacked an internet connection. Second, as home to many essential workers, many students would be left unsupervised at home during remote learning if safe spaces could not be set up for their care. A multi-pronged approach would be needed to address these complex community needs.

At the building level, principals and teachers started leaning on their strong relationships with families their schools served and assessing their needs. Principal Sorden, who had always had an open-door policy with her families, developed alternative ways to stay connected. A weekly survey helped her track COVID infections among her students' families, but also allowed her to uncover evolving needs for internet connections, school supplies, and groceries. While more systematic arrangements could be made by the district, her teachers made hard copies of curriculum, sent home materials, and made sure students' homes were stocked with libraries for reading. By distributing books and materials they had on hand in their classrooms among their students before they left for spring break, teachers ensured that students would at least be supplied for learning from home in the short term. Principal Sorden also encouraged teachers to do regular check-ins with each other and with their students and parents. Initially, daily phone calls alerted the school to issues such as the need to adjust expectations when students were sharing devices with multiple siblings or did not have a private space to take part in an online class. Ms. Cruz was a vigorous advocate for her students, taking up donations for families, and delivering additional resources to their homes if they could not afford them or did not have access to them. While doors could not stay open for parents and students to drop in to make a need known, teachers dedicated time to being on Google Hangouts to eat lunch with their students and remain accessible to keep the lines of communication open.

At the district level, Superintendent Alvarez set about addressing more systemic issues. While the early days of the pandemic and the move to remote learning brought focused attention to the long-standing issues of inequality related to internet access in America, much of the national attention stayed on rural communities. But unlike the 4.6 million rural households without broadband access, where issues of access are often related to the limited footprint of broadband services, the lack of access in 13.6 million households in highly connected urban centers is often a question of affordability [21]. Understanding the disproportionate impact this would have on his district, Alvarez worked with internet providers to arrange free internet access during the lockdown, so all students could engage in remote learning. While this could help increase access for many families, the offer was only open to those who paid past due bills and brought their accounts up to date with providers. Recognizing that many had lost jobs during lockdown, and this was often the cause for the unpaid bills, Alvarez also sought support from local politicians and non-profit organizations to arrange sponsorships for families to receive free Wi-Fi hotspots. This community support allowed students to have internet access in their homes, even if they were in temporary housing, creating a vital lifeline to school.

To address the second immediate challenge of providing care for the children of essential workers during remote learning, New York City set up 93 Regional Enrichment Centers (REC Centers) in school buildings that were empty once remote learning began. These supervised spaces provided three hot meals, instructional spaces for remote learning, emotional support, and activities to engage the children of essential workers in the city throughout the day. True to his ethos of community engagement,

Superintendent Alvarez even ran one of these centers so firefighters, police officers, healthcare workers, grocery store employees, and so many others who helped run essential services during the city's lockdown, could go about saving lives with the knowledge that their children were cared for and safe. He explained:

> *As we thought about the rewriting of the narrative of the South Bronx, being able to be inclusive of the community and their thoughts, and decisions, and minds collectively, helped us get through this pandemic. Wholeheartedly, without the help of the NAACP, United Way, My Brother's Keeper, local pantries, local supermarkets, I'm not necessarily sure we would have been able to get through the majority of it in this particular area. So that would be the greatest success is tapping into the local resources and utilizing them to the fullest potential.*

Bronx CSD #7 showed its community spirit in this endeavor, with not only Alvarez taking on immense responsibility for running a REC Center while leading the district through a crisis, but with substitute teachers, volunteers, and even parents coming out to lend a hand to their community's essential workers. This spirit of collective effort and mutual respect was a central part of the new narrative that the community was shaping for itself.

Psychological Safety

The coordinated efforts of Bronx CSD #7 educators across district leadership, school leadership, and teachers also presented themselves as an asset when dealing with the overwhelming psychological impact of COVID-19. To respond to the many facets of trauma that their community was experiencing—grief, loss, isolation, and fear—district personnel leveraged their community resources, but also brought to bear their abundant creativity. Once again, Superintendent Alvarez used his organizational strengths to reach out to Lincoln Hospital, located just two blocks from the district office, to arrange mental health services for anyone in the district who might be in need. He also worked with the local Child Protective Services to provide grief counseling to those experiencing loss. By utilizing local resources to provide psychological supports to students, families, and staff alike, Alvarez was able to shore up the most vulnerable members of the community quickly.

Consistent with the deep compassion for families that was evident in our conversations with district personnel, Alvarez also highlighted the social experiences that were developed to support family members of CSD #7 students through the extreme isolation of lockdown. As part of New York City's Department of Education, Bronx CSD #7 benefits from services provided by the Office of Family and Community Empowerment. The district's team of parent coordinators, school support staff, leadership, parents, and community organizations worked together as engaged members in each child's educational experience. These coordinators provided vital capacity to plan and execute community-building activities during the most severe part of the city's lockdowns. With a holistic view on building healthy environments where students can thrive, coordinators went to great lengths to deliver materials to families that would allow them to do "I paint, You paint" activities online, or virtually enter the superintendent's kitchen and do a healthy cooking class with him. As restrictions eased a little, families were invited back to the school in safe ways, including a socially distanced salsa dancing class for parents that took place on a school athletic field.

While the district provided many organized activities, the strong school-family relationships at the individual schools allowed principals and teachers to stay meaningfully connected with their students and their families during virtual schooling. Principal Sorden insisted, "The greatest success, really, were the teachers because they maintain that culture in the classroom." But her own strong connection with families was also apparent. To help students and parents maintain their connection to school, and to remain present in their daily lives, she recorded read-aloud videos on YouTube and asked parents to share them with students at bedtime. Through the sometimes-lonely experience of lockdown, students and their parents could hear a bedtime story, and continue to engage in essential literacy practices that would support ongoing learning.

As students returned to in-person schooling around the world, the significant negative impact of isolation during the pandemic lockdowns on child and adolescent mental health overwhelmed mental health service providers across the country. Reports indicate that more than 140,000 children in the U.S. lost primary or secondary care providers during this time [22], and while there was a high concentration of these losses in New York City in the early days of the pandemic, the educators in Bronx CSD #7 were aware that the dangers to the psychological health and safety of their students were more complex. Lockdowns also meant that vulnerable students lost regular connections and safety checks that were built into their lives through school. Adults in lockdown were also potentially experiencing greater stress due to illness, job loss, or having to support their children's learning at home using unfamiliar technology.

As mandated reporters, teachers, and principals in CSD #7 felt an acute responsibility to ensure their students remained safe, but also that they had opportunities to process the traumatic experiences. They learned quickly that there was limited privacy in many students' homes, and some did not feel comfortable discussing their feelings in front of family members who might overhear their conversations. To facilitate regular, open communication, Principal Sorden took advantage of the same learning technologies that were supporting learning in classrooms. Students recorded brief Flipgrid videos when they had a moment alone to check-in with teachers and counselors. These were then used to deploy psychological supports to students who needed them. A small but meaningful adjustment that empowered students to choose the time and place of their communication allowed for more regular and efficient check-ins in which students were able to speak freely.

Teacher Cynthia Cruz also described to us how invaluable the relationship between the guidance counselor and teachers in the schools proved to be. Not only was the counselor able to lend a hand to teachers doing daily check-ins with their students, but they also served as an essential thought partner in determining how to address unique situations that arose. In fact, Ms. Cruz felt that more counselors were needed in schools because there was more work to be done than one counselor could possibly manage. But this need did not mean that teachers in her school did not feel supported through this challenging experience. Principal Sorden had strong relationships with her students and their families, and she created the conditions to ensure that her teaching staff could build similarly supportive relationships. Ms. Cruz described the trust that the district office and the teachers at CVES had in principal Sorden, and her unique way of getting the job done:

> *She has a very open-door policy. So, if we ever need her support we just reach out and she's the type that will drop whatever she's doing and go for it. In terms of district level, they were involved here and there. But because our school has it under control compared to other schools in our district, I think we were at the bottom of their list. Like they got it. I don't need to get involved. I'm not even bothering. Let me focus on this other school that might need our support a little*

more. Well, we understood it wasn't anything like oh, wow, you guys are not checking in on us. I think they knew that Sorden being Sorden, she had it under control out there in Sorden's way.

The mutual respect shared between the members of the Bronx CSD #7 reflected in this dynamic between the district office and school leadership was mirrored in many different relationships that district personnel discussed in our interactions with them. It was also clear that this egalitarian and democratic approach to decision-making and communication was an important part of the leadership style espoused by Superintendent Alvarez.

Democratic Communication Practices

In times of great upheaval, so much of the successful implementation of any plan hinges on clear and consistent communication; as the complexity of the situation increases, so too does the need for good communication. As the leadership and teachers of Bronx CSD #7 navigated the complexities of their COVID-19 pandemic response, the importance of communication was never far from their thoughts. Ensuring that communication practices not only spoke to specific stakeholder groups in meaningful and understandable ways, but also reflecting the voices and ideas of those same stakeholders was important for building trust and providing mechanisms for shared meaning-making. Described by Superintendent Alvarez as leading "with moral purpose," the underlying guiding principle was simply put, "what impacts you, impacts me. What impacts me, impacts you." In this time of large-scale, shared trauma, where the community's well-being depended on the contributions of all members, the district took a democratic approach to communication that served it well.

While engaging a diverse, multicultural community was not new to Superintendent Alvarez, the large volume of communication that students and their families needed during the pandemic required careful thought. Starting from a point of humility, Alvarez recognized that for the numerous new approaches the district employed during the pandemic to work for everyone, he would need to hear directly from those being impacted by the district's decisions. At the onset of the pandemic, he met daily with the district's instructional leadership team, ensuring that all school leaders were aware of ongoing developments and could communicate emerging concerns. As the experiences of remote learning and lockdowns unfolded,

Alvarez leaned on the counsel of a wide range of advisory groups, including a principal advisory, assistant principal advisory, teacher advisory, parent advisory, and even a student advisory that included representation from third through twelfth grade. His openness to a diverse range of voices uncovered issues that may have otherwise gone unnoticed.

Having been empowered to raise concerns to the district through the advisory structure, students were able to communicate the incredible strain of hours spent in online classes without the naturally occurring and developmentally necessary opportunities to have social interactions with peers that occurred during a regular school day. In addition, the isolation of the pandemic left them with few opportunities to process the challenges of remote learning with peers. To address this important social-emotional need for connection, students proposed the development of a student-led district newsletter in which they could share their ideas. They also helped start supervised online spaces called "team talks," where they could connect with elementary or middle and high school peers. Students also developed podcasts where they explored common challenges for students their age. This collaborative approach between educators and students showed a clear view of diverse voices as cultural assets for the community, and emerging research suggests that similar programs were used by other districts across the country to help students make sense of their experiences during the pandemic [23].

Thoughtful communication also supported the parents' experience in Bronx CSD #7 through a time of great upheaval and unfamiliar, new responsibilities. For Principal Sorden and Ms. Cruz, the process of democratic communication was ultimately grounded in relationships in the context of their school. For Sorden, this meant taking her hands-on approach and open-door policy to a new level. Parents had to know that their communication was welcome. For Ms. Cruz, it was about communicating a desire for collaboration in the best interest of their child. Parents needed to trust that even if they did not always agree on the direction to take, they were headed to the same destination and driven by the same goal: the learning and well-being of their children. In practical terms, this meant that as students learned from home, parents needed guidance on how to support them. Once again, the district leveraged the instructional technologies already being employed for remote instruction to greater purpose. Providing teaching strategy videos for parents that aligned with each unit of study online meant that parents would not only have a better understanding of the content students were learning, but that this information could be automatically translated to 180 languages, more effectively meeting the needs of the linguistically diverse population of the Bronx.

Socially Responsible Decision-Making

The culture of fairness and equity did not just extend to the communication practices of Bronx CSD #7, rather it permeated much of the decision-making in the district through structures, practices, and priorities. Superintendent Alvarez summed up clearly how these ideals are codified in the very structures he uses to lead the decision-making processes in the district:

> *The way I divide my district up is to ensure that there's equity in voice and empowerment of the schools, and the school leaders, and the community. Our district comprehensive education plan is aligned to how we run meetings across our district. So, there's a team for every goal that we're trying to address as a district. And on every team, there's parent representation, student representation, administration representation, district representation, and our central office's representation. And during those meetings, we plan a scope and sequence for the year, as to how we're going to address meeting that particular goal.*

As if extending from the historical bedrock of the district, and connecting the rich experiences of the diverse community, a deep drive toward socially just and culturally responsive educational practice seemed to motivate important decisions throughout the pandemic experience.

At Concourse Village Elementary School, this drive for fairness appeared in academic and social decisions alike. As with many schools during the pandemic, teachers at CVES learned quickly that remote learning could not just be a replication of the in-person school day via Zoom [24]. Not only could students not stay engaged this way all day, but there were also limitations on access resulting from slow internet connections or shared devices in homes, problems that required creative thinking. "So, in the spirit of being fair and giving everybody what they needed, we needed to customize our expectations and not hold everyone to a one-size-fits-all model," reasoned Principal Sorden. While Sorden leveraged the willingness and expertise of parent coordinators to drive to students' homes and support technology issues, and sent home hard copies of assignments, she also realized that some expectations could be reasonably adjusted in ways that honored the unique needs of individual families yet provided a quality education to all students. In many ways, this realization opened many doors.

Once freed to think in terms of equity rather than sameness, teachers were able to provide students with more choices, differentiating assignments based on interest and the materials students had access to at home. Not only did this empower students and "put them in the driver's seat," as Sorden described it, but it also increased motivation and engagement. Ms. Cruz found her students asked more questions and genuinely seemed to display greater interest in assignments. Some students started to advocate for themselves by suggesting additional ways that they wanted to show their learning, from video recordings to written responses, and from art projects to acting out the responses in a creative performance. New opportunities to engage, Ms. Cruz suggested, even brought quieter students out of their shells, and allowed others to display their creativity while presenting their content understanding. The greatest testament to the success of this new approach was her decision to keep these new pedagogical approaches in her arsenal once the school returned to in-person instruction.

Not all socially responsible educational practice during remote learning was without risk in the Bronx. Teachers had to contend with having their classrooms open to anyone in the room where a child was engaged in remote learning, and a certain amount of trepidation went into some of the more challenging classroom discussions that took place during this time. While navigating the psychological traumas of sickness, death, and isolation, students at CVES, like the rest of the world, confronted the brutal killing of George Floyd at the hands of Minneapolis Police Officers. Less than two weeks later, a peaceful protest held in support of George Floyd in the Mott Haven neighborhood of the Bronx ended in a violent crackdown by police, resulting in numerous injuries and the detention of over 100 protestors [25]. To ensure that students and staff had safe opportunities to work through the trauma of racial unrest that they were seeing on television, and possibly experiencing in their own lives, Principal Sorden arranged for the school to make a YouTube video to share with families where staff members had the option to participate. While not in the building together, she understood that her community needed to heal and have open dialog about the traumatic events taking place around them. Was this a risky undertaking for the school leader? Perhaps, but it was a risk that paid off. When asked if there was an important lesson from the pandemic experience she wanted to share with the field, Ms. Cruz summed it up well:

> *Don't ever doubt the ability of your students. They can do it. Just believe in them. And I would say, it doesn't matter their home situation. If you're able to build that connection and that bond with your students that shouldn't matter.*

As we saw time and time again in CSD #7, educator decisions were driven by a trust in their community, each other, and in their students. They had created a culture that invested in and valued relationships, and these deep connections allowed them to approach solving each problem collaboratively from a place of trust.

Lessons Learned from the Bronx

Throughout our conversations with educators in the Bronx, it was apparent that the pandemic quickly shifted the ideas and thinking on how to provide education. As Ms. Cruz said, "When the pandemic started, we tried to recreate the whole school day. We tried to do everything exactly as we would in school. That was a big flop. I would not do that again. I would never suggest anyone do that again." Indeed, Bronx CSD #7 and CVES had to radically reimagine education, not just to ensure students still learn but also to ensure their mental, physical, and emotional safety. While many changes to education emerged throughout the pandemic, the Bronx provides three lessons for all exploring how to reimagine and improve education.

Connect to Community

As Superintendent Alvarez showed us, in times of trauma, focusing only on students while they are in the school building neglects so much of what affects a student's education. Trauma extends beyond school walls, and the whole community, not just students, were experiencing pandemic traumas. The relationship between the school and community was mutually beneficial: the school served as a hub of essential services, but the community also rallied together to support families in need. The story of the Bronx is so much more than mutual support, though; it highlights how important it is for school leadership and all those involved in education to truly be a part of the local community [26]. The coordinated efforts of nonprofits and Superintendent Alvarez would not have been possible without his knowledge of existing groups in the community. Ms. Cruz and Principal Sorden would not have been able to help track COVID infections among students' families and deliver groceries to their doors without intimate knowledge of the community and the families they served. Regardless of the purported purpose and design of schools, they are not isolated buildings at which students go to learn. Rather, when they are fulfilling their purpose, schools are the center of a community, a conduit to the knowledge, culture, and empathy that are so critical to today's educational needs.

Relate and Represent

Bronx CSD #7 also showed us the importance of uplifting different voices and perspectives to create a sense of trust and understanding. Throughout our discussions, this idea of listening to students, families, and community members was constantly present. As Principal Sorden said, *"relationships are everything."* Ms. Cruz took time out of her day to eat lunch with students over Google Hangouts and talk with them about their issues. Principal Sorden surveyed families and used this to determine needs for school supplies and food. Superintendent Alvarez created an advisory team that included leaders and students from third through twelfth grade. Every intentional effort ensured all voices and perspectives were heard. And it was this feeling of being heard, understood, and appreciated, that bolstered the trust to navigate through a time of crisis together. One of the lessons Principal Sorden said the community learned is, "we're definitely stronger together. We are each other's assets." No one has all the answers, but by ensuring representative voices are in the room, we can collectively make the best decision. As Superintendent Alvarez said,

> *It sounded like I had all the answers, Faiza, but I promise you, I didn't have all the answers at the time. It was through collaboration, communication with my team, and the pushing of thoughts between principals, assistant principals, parents, students. They came up with the answers. I just made the final decisions based on those answers.*

Think Developmentally

As the site of some of the most critical and intentional practices devised to support human development, it is always surprising when education professionals forget to consider students, parents, teachers, and school leaders as developing human beings. Yet very little highlights that the individuals belonging to these groups are all living, breathing, growing humans than the ever-present, ever-increasing loss of life that defines a pandemic. Perhaps the most important lesson we can take away from the resilient educators in the Bronx, who managed to not only survive, but even find moments to thrive, in the midst of immense trauma, is the importance of centering each other's humanity in our educational practice.

Superintendent Alvarez leaned on his understanding of developing human beings in two critical moments early in the pandemic that set the tone for much of what would follow in the district office, and at CVES. First, when members of his student advisory committee explained that entire days of lecture-style classes on Zoom were not working, he asked himself the important developmental question: why do we have middle school? A reflection on the important socialization aspects of school that had been lost in the transition to virtual learning resulted in the robust array of socially engaging activities for parents and students that bolstered connectedness and psychological safety in the community. With this foundation in place, educators could focus on preventing learning loss.

Superintendent Alvarez shared his second important developmentally oriented decision with us when he selected Principal Alexa Sorden and her school to be the focus of our work in CSD #7. While Principal Sorden had a stellar professional résumé, boasting multiple national awards for her school, it was her resilience through personal challenges and not her successes that Alvarez wanted to represent his district. During the pandemic, Sorden, struggling to balance her role as principal of an award-winning school, the completion of a dissertation for her doctorate, and her own health and well-being, had approached Alvarez with the intention to leave her position as founding principal of CVES. Convinced that she should not have to leave something she had worked so hard to build in order to achieve her next academic goal, Alvarez personally mentored Sorden, providing flexibility and support to help her meet all her goals. In hindsight, the investment in the development of an irreplaceable principal not only proved invaluable for CVES during the pandemic, but also highlighted another example of "leading with moral purpose." Through this choice,

Alvarez passed on the important lesson to Sorden that guided Bronx CSD #7 through the pandemic: she did not have to do it alone because she was a part of a community that had her back.

> **Reflect and Discuss**
> We invite you to consider what you have read in this chapter and apply it to your own community context. Use the following questions as a starting point for your personal reflection and for discussion with education stakeholders in your community.
>
> 1. How did the district context of The Bronx impact educators' responses to the pandemic?
> 2. What aspects of your local context influence the response of area schools in times of trauma and hardship?
> 3. How does generational trauma affect the abilities of students to learn in the today's society? How does this look in your local context?
> 4. How did education leaders provide support for students' psychological safety in the Bronx?
> 5. What lessons can be applied to classrooms in your context today so future generations of students are able to learn in psychosocial safety?

References

1. Pattakos, A. (2010). *Prisoners of our thoughts: Viktor Frankl's principles for discovering meaning in life and work.* Berrett-Koehler.
2. The WNET Group. (2021). History of Brooklyn: Early and colonial years. Retrieved April 1, 2023, from https://www.thirteen.org/brooklyn/history/history2.html
3. Census Reporter Profile page for Bronx County, NY. (2021). *American Community Survey 1-year estimates.* U.S. Census Bureau. Retrieved April 1, 2023, from https://censusreporter.org/profiles/05000US36005-bronx-county-ny/
4. The District One Community Education School. (2021). *Governance structure.* The District One Community Education School. Retrieved April 1, 2023, from https://cec1nyc.org/resources/school-governance/

5. New York State Education Department (2021). *Student Information Repository System: Enrollment Data.* New York State Education Department. Retrieved August 2, 2023, from https://data.nysed.gov/enrollment.php?year=2021&instid=800000046647
6. Sorden, A. (2021). *Principal's Message.* PS 359 Concourse Village Elementary School. Retrieved April 2, 2023, from https://www.cves359.com/apps/pages/principal
7. Katella, K. (2023). *Omicron, delta, alpha, and more: What to know about the coronavirus variants.* Yale Medicine. Retrieved April 2, 2023, from https://www.yalemedicine.org/news/covid-19-variants-of-concern-omicron
8. Cowley, S., Das, A., Haag, M., McKinley, J., Shapiro, E., & Tully, T. (2020, March 15). New York City to close schools, restaurants, and bars. *The New York Times.* https://www.nytimes.com/2020/03/15/nyregion/nyc-schools-closed.html
9. Roby, M. (2008). The push and pull dynamics of white flight: A study of the Bronx between 1950 and 1980. *Bronx County Historical Society Journal, 45*(1/2), 34–55.
10. Jonnes, J. (2002). *South Bronx rising: The rise, fall, and resurrection of an American city.* Fordham University Press.
11. Gonzalez, E. (2004). *The Bronx.* Columbia University Press.
12. Flood, J. (2010, March 16). Why the Bronx burned. *New York Post.* https://nypost.com/2010/05/16/why-the-bronx-burned/
13. Gross, J. (2022, January 10). The fire was the deadliest in New York City since 1990. *The New York Times.* https://www.nytimes.com/2022/01/10/nyregion/happy-land-fire.html
14. Bronx COVID-19 Oral History Project. (2023). *Project description: More about us.* Bronx African American History Project. Retrieved April 2, 2023, from https://www.thebronxcovid19oralhistoryproject.com/what-we-do
15. Hu, W., & Schweber, N. (2020, June 16). When rich New Yorkers fled, these workers kept the city running. *The New York Times.* https://www.nytimes.com/2020/06/16/nyregion/mount-hope-bronx-coronavirus-essential-workers.html
16. Rodriguez, S. (2018, December 12). How the Bronx was branded. *The New Inquiry.* https://thenewinquiry.com/how-the-bronx-was-branded/
17. Wolfe, N. K. (2015). *A community at war: The Bronx and crack cocaine.* Fordham University Press.
18. Litvinov, A. (2021, July 8). Finding the Lost Students of the Pandemic. *NEA.* Retrieved April 2, 2023, from https://www.nea.org/advocating-for-change/new-from-nea/finding-lost-students-pandemic
19. Blitz, L. V., Anderson, E. M., & Saastamoinen, M. (2016). Assessing perceptions of culture and trauma in an elementary school: Informing a model for culturally responsive trauma-informed schools. *The Urban Review, 48*(4), 520–542.

20. Esaki, N., Benamati, J., Yanosy, S., Middleton, J. S., Hopson, L. M., Hummer, V. L., & Bloom, S. L. (2013). The sanctuary model: Theoretical framework. *Families in Society, 94*(2), 87–95. https://doi.org/10.1606/1044-3894.4287
21. Porter, E. (2021, June 2). A rural-urban broadband divide, but not the one you think of. *The Wall Street Journal.* https://www.nytimes.com/2021/06/01/business/rural-urban-broadband-biden.html
22. Vestal, V. (2021, November 8). COVID harmed kids' mental health—And schools are feeling it. *The Pew Charitable Trusts.* https://www.pewtrusts.org/en/research-and-analysis/blogs/stateline/2021/11/08/covid-harmed-kids-mental-health-and-schools-are-feeling-it
23. Borrero, N. E., Yeh, C. J., Dela Cruz, G., & Collins, T. (2022). The COVID-19 pandemic and emerging cultural assets, equity & excellence in education. *Taylor & Francis Online, 55*(4), 328–341. https://doi.org/10.1080/10665684.2021.1992603
24. Kelly, H. (2020, September 4). Kids used to love screen time. Then schools made Zoom mandatory all day long. *The Washington Post.* https://www.washingtonpost.com/technology/2020/09/04/screentime-school-distance/
25. The Human Rights Watch. (2020, September 30). "Kettling" protesters in the Bronx: Systemic police brutality and its costs in the United States. *The Human Rights Watch.* https://www.hrw.org/news/2020/09/30/us-new-york-police-planned-assault-bronx-protesters
26. Torres, L. E. (2023). *The six priorities: How to find the resources your school community needs.* ASCD.

CHAPTER 4

Education in a Time of Danger: A Story of Choice

> *We are a port in the storm. That is all we are. We are safe harbor.*
> —Jack Purkeypile, Principal, Monterey High School

Danger has taken so many forms in U.S. schools over the decades, but never has the definition of danger been so widely debated, nor were the safety needs of students and teachers as polarizing an issue as they were through the first two years of the COVID-19 pandemic. The pandemic brought with it danger of a new kind, ill-defined and hard to understand, as it took on a life of its own. It seemed to be the *unknown* and the *unknowable*. At a time with the most advanced medical science in human history, having to depend on fluid and emerging scientific information was an unusual and uncomfortable experience for many. The danger of the pandemic also created a wide variety of experiences over time, with the acute threat of the virus ebbing and flowing based on where someone was located in the nation. Texas, like much of the southern United States, experienced a summer COVID surge in 2020, and unlike New York, was shielded from the earliest phase of the pandemic. This resulted in a different set of variables and unknowns with which to contend.

Even when the danger in a school takes the form of a visible and violent armed intruder, reaching consensus on a likely course of action to provide a safe learning experience can be difficult. The history of failed attempts at

© The Author(s), under exclusive license to Springer Nature Switzerland AG 2023
F. M. Jamil, J. E. Siddiqi, *Public Education in Turbulent Times*, https://doi.org/10.1007/978-3-031-43237-8_4

stricter gun control legislation after school shootings over the last few decades suggests that consensus can be difficult to come by even in situations defined by shocking tragedy and loss of life. When the danger is an invisible virus, and even the experts are not exactly sure how it spreads—droplets that only spread through close physical contact or airborne particles that can permeate a room—decision-making becomes even more easily influenced by feelings over facts. When we do not have broad scientific consensus on how the danger is defined and how people can protect themselves from it, the cultural context tends to play a larger role in informing and guiding communities in their response. In the case of the COVID-19 response in the United States, the level of danger the coronavirus posed was so deeply obscured by political rhetoric and a parallel pandemic of misinformation, especially in the early stages of the pandemic, that it made any consistent risk assessment difficult to undertake for communities, schools, and individuals alike.

Differing responses to danger that occur as everyone is struggling to chart a course to safety for themselves and their loved ones can sow discord and division within a community. The educators and leaders at Monterey High School, part of the Lubbock Independent School District in Lubbock, Texas, were able to cut through the volatile discourse taking place across the country by listening to stakeholders and providing students, and their families, with the opportunity to make choices that best suited their needs. The district provided students the opportunity to switch between virtual and in-person learning multiple times throughout the 2020–2021 academic year. This availability of choice provided students, families, and community members the flexibility and stability they needed to navigate through the danger that was the COVID-19 pandemic and provided the rest of us a possible approach to addressing the ever-present and ever-changing dangers that exist within education. It does appear that when there is a great deal of variability in individual levels of risk tolerance, providing more options for education stakeholders to choose from results in more students ultimately having their needs met in schools. At the end of the day, it was meeting the needs of students and the local economy that helped the educators in Lubbock ISD chart a course through the shifting landscape of education in a time of danger.

The District Context of Lubbock

Situated in the northwestern part of Texas, Lubbock County sits in the middle of a region known as Llano Estacado (translated in English to Staked Plains). This large mesa, the largest in North America, rises over 5000 feet above the surrounding Texas and New Mexico landscape and is home to several counties, including Lubbock [1]. Once occupied by the Comanche Nation, Lubbock County was founded in 1876, and shortly after, a small town, known as Old Lubbock, began to grow [2]. In 1890, this town merged with Monterey, another small town in the area, becoming what we now know as the city of Lubbock. The city was officially incorporated in 1909, the same year the first railroad line arrived [3].

Lubbock, the county seat of Lubbock County, is nicknamed the "Hub City" given its role as the economic, educational, and public health hub for numerous counties that surround it. This is in large part due to the numerous colleges and industries located in the areas, including Texas Tech University. Home to over 310,000 residents, 51% of Lubbock County's residents identify as white, 38% as Hispanic or Latinx, 8% as Black, 2% as Asian, and 2% as multiracial [4]. The estimated per capita income in Lubbock County is $28,880 dollars, slightly lower than the U.S. average of $35,600. Further, roughly 16% of Lubbock residents live below the poverty line, and 21.5% of children experience food insecurity [5].

As you will discover in the rest of this chapter, Lubbock is constantly navigating unique political and social dynamics. These complex social structures can either enhance the community by bringing together a rich tapestry of cultural thought or hinder it through political gridlock. For the education leaders in Lubbock, it was important to separate these politics from the decisions made for students. This "depoliticizing," as Principal Jack Purkeypile called it, allowed leaders to be a "reasonable, rational voice that, if not embraced and accepted from both sides, was at least tolerated." By providing information and "depersonalizing" decisions, Lubbock leaders empowered students and their families to make informed decisions that worked best for their families. It is that navigating through the middle—understanding dangers and possible outcomes to choices—that helps us draw lessons from which we can reimagine future education, not just in Lubbock, Texas, but across the nation.

Understanding the District Structure

There are over 1000 public school districts in Texas, each one self-governing and with its own leadership. While they are accountable to state and federal laws, these independent school districts are separate from any municipality or county in Texas and have their own taxing authority [6]. Lubbock Independent School District [Lubbock ISD], one such school district in Texas, encompasses the city of Lubbock and surrounding areas in Lubbock County. Lubbock ISD serves nearly 26,000 students annually, across 28 elementary schools, 10 middle schools, and 5 high schools.

While the demographics in Lubbock County are predominately white, that is not the case for Lubbock Independent School District. Of the over 25,000 Lubbock ISD students enrolled, 78% identify as a person of color, with 60% of students identifying as Latino/Hispanic, 14% Black, 2% Asian American/Pacific Islander, 2% multiracial, and 1% American Indian compared to the 22% of students that identify as white. Further, it is estimated that 72% of students served by Lubbock ISD are economically disadvantaged.

When Superintendent Dr. Kathy Rollo took over the helm of Lubbock ISD two years before the COVID-19 pandemic, she had little idea of the dangers and decisions that lay ahead. A graduate of Texas Tech University (Bachelor's, Master's, and Ph.D.), Superintendent Rollo has been in education for more than 30 years in the same school district that cultivated her love of education. She began her career as an elementary school teacher before being named assistant principal and later principal. She moved from the school level to the district level when she was selected to establish and run Lubbock ISD's professional development department, where she developed training for teachers and administrators to increase their depth of instruction and guide their use of data.

Throughout each role she held, Superintendent Rollo followed three pillars to guide her: value data, love people, and develop leaders [7]. She brought this leadership philosophy with her when promoted to associate superintendent in 2013 and superintendent in 2018. In our conversations with Superintendent Rollo, it was clear that all three pillars of her philosophy were critical in her leadership during the pandemic, especially in determining how to overcome the dangers that presented themselves. She also acknowledged that success did not come through her leadership alone. The partnerships between school leaders and the community were critical to her district's success, she claimed, "I'm really pleased and proud of the grit and determination of the people in this community, and the overwhelming support ... that helped us get through the year."

One of the integral pieces of that support for Superintendent Rollo was the principal of Monterey High School (MHS), Mr. Jack Purkeypile. Purkeypile had been principal at MHS, located in downtown Lubbock, since the 2012–2013 school year, which had allowed him to develop a working relationship with Superintendent Rollo over the previous decade. Having formerly served as Assistant Principal at MHS, Purkeypile was uniquely experienced with the challenges and dangers that MHS faced daily. While the COVID-19 pandemic was a completely new danger, Principal Purkeypile was able to draw from previous experiences to ensure students had a quality education, regardless of virtual or in-person modality.

Monterey High School enrolls over 2100 students yearly. Roughly 64% of students identify as Hispanic, 22% as white, 11% as African American, and 2% multiracial. Nearly 70% of students are classified as economically disadvantaged and 5% are English Language Learners [8]. The unique culture and politics of Lubbock have created instances of disagreements, but compromise and honor have always been a part of the culture of MHS since its founding. MHS was named in honor of the former community of Monterey, which agreed to combine with the town of Old Lubbock. This merger required the community of Monterey to take the Lubbock name, in exchange for townspeople of Old Lubbock relocating to the site of Monterey, and the ideal that secured that compromise is still present today. Compromise is not always pretty, but it is important to moving forward and navigating through challenges. As Principal Purkeypile said:

You know? Our school colors are blue and red. That's purple now. Not everyone would agree with me on that, but that's where we live. You know we're just trying to navigate the middle. I love the middle, actually. It's a beautiful place.

This community value of compromise was reflected in every conversation we had with educators in Lubbock, and clearly permeates the culture.

While Principal Purkeypile led MHS through the dangers of reopening during the pandemic, he frequently acknowledged that none of it would have been possible without the work and support of his 137 teachers. One of those teachers, Ms. Sarah Williams, a high school teacher at MHS, navigated the dangers gracefully in her classroom. Teaching high school during the pandemic offered its own unique challenges and dangers. Unlike younger students, high school students had more autonomy and independence. While still considered minors, high school students held the responsibilities of their own choices, and an expectation that they would have agency in important aspects of their schooling experience. However, these choices were not always based in reality, especially as social media made it more difficult to discern fact from fiction. As Mrs. Williams noticed, "everything they bring to the table [in discussion] comes from social media. Everything they are reading. Everything they are doing. And it's not always backed up factually." Rather than shy from the various stories and discussions that take hold of society through social media, Mrs. Williams embraced them and used them to engage students and exemplified the MHS's mission of "Real School. Real Kids. Real Success [9]."

> *[Social media] was kind of a challenge. So, a lot of it is just explaining to them that you need to be more educated in what you're reading, what you're doing. And we integrated that with school. Like we're not going to dismiss it, let's include it, so we can ask those hard questions, and accept multiple perspectives.*

Apparent in Mrs. Williams's approach to teaching, this idea of providing information, context, and perspective to decision-making played an important role in how Lubbock ISD navigated the dangers of the pandemic. As you will see in the rest of this chapter, everyone experiences danger differently, and the choices one makes are based on the calculations related to that danger.

The Evolving Experience of Danger

Much like the educators we spoke with in the Bronx, the team at Lubbock ISD navigated dangers that changed, grew, and revealed new complexities through the first year of the pandemic. While the middle path that Principal Purkeypile favored was an important guide for calibrating their decisions, we heard repeated references in all our interviews to an aspect of cultural and historical identity that was not only a source of great pride, but also formed a foundation of quiet confidence for district personnel. The people of West Texas, it appeared, were no strangers to experiencing danger, and whether those dangers emerged from nature or were man-made, they expected to get on with the business of living, learning, working, and thriving. Superintendent Rollo described them as "very determined and very persistent people," who expected there to be instructional continuity, even as they expected the district to keep their children safe and secure. It is difficult to truly understand the full weight of these words by Superintendent Rollo without giving them some further historical context.

The determined nature of Texans in the western part of the state lives in its history, its lore, and in its landscape. In many ways, it represents a deep respect toward the land and the people who have chosen to make it their home over many generations. From the members of the Comanche tribe, who used their newfound dominion over horses to move into the Great Plains and establish their homeland of the Comanchería in this area, to the European settlers who followed the promise of property and trade to settle the Llano Estacado and establish Lubbock, residents of Lubbock and their ancestors have faced danger while working toward future prosperity—this has served as their defining ethos. While the dangers look different today, when the European settlers that founded Lubbock arrived in West Texas, they were facing their own dangers, establishing a town in the heart of the Comanchería, where the Comanche had waged war on the Apache tribe for over 100 years to establish their empire [10].

The reputation of the Comanche as fierce hunters and warriors was even captured in their name. While they referred to themselves in their own language as *Nermernuh*, or "the people," the name *Comanche*, given to them by outsiders, derived from the Ute word meaning "anyone who wants to fight me all the time" [11]. The early European residents of Monterey, and then Lubbock, were aware of the dangers of the life they were choosing when they moved to West Texas. Their choice is reflected in a spirit of independence and an abiding respect for working through adversity.[1] This attitude was articulated by Principal Purkeypile:

> *Texas is a beautiful state ... but this is a rugged part of the state. [It] is barren and dry and dusty, and we tie our hats on tightly around here. And so that's it ... I mean we're open for business right now.*

---

[1] Acknowledging the truth of our histories' intersections is critical. In describing the deep connection between the people of West Texas and the land of the Llano Estacado, we must also remember that Lubbock Independent School District sits on the occupied, unceded territories of the Comanche and Mescalaro Apache Peoples, the original stewards of what is now Lubbock and was once the heart of the Comanchería. The foundation of Lubbock came at great cost to the Indigenous peoples whose lands the city was built upon. We pay our respects to them and the legacies of violence and displacement they have endured.

While on the surface this connection to the distant past may seem to be a stretch, the drive to overcome dangers, both natural and man-made, have continued to be reflected in more recent events in Lubbock's history.

A History of Danger and Thriving

The landscape of Lubbock has played an important role in its history. From supporting the buffalo herds that drew the Comanche to its environs, to providing later European settlers with ample land for farming and ranching, as well as a suitable site for a railroad hub. As reflected in the words of Principal Purkeypile, the land continues to be an important character in the story of Lubbock. But as residents of Lubbock have learned over the years, their natural environment can be a challenging adversary as well. One of the most powerful tornadoes ever documented in the United States was the 1970 Lubbock Tornado, which on the evening of May 11, swept through about one-quarter of the city's downtown, claiming 26 lives, injuring over 1500, and causing over $100 million in damage [12]. The devastation caused by the tornado was so severe that it was mapped by meteorologist Ted Fujita to inform the development of his rating scale for tornado intensity, a version of which is still used today. The Lubbock Tornado was given the designation of F5 on the Fujita Scale, the rating reserved for the most powerful and damaging tornadoes [13].

While this tragedy displaced hundreds of families and resulted in devastating property loss, subsequent studies of the area have found that rebuilding efforts undertaken by the city government and citizens of Lubbock actually helped revitalize what was, at the time, a flagging economy, and ushered in a period of sustained economic growth for the city [14]. While the city rebuilt from this event, severe weather continues to be a part of everyday life in Lubbock. With risks for drought, wildfire, and devastating storms continuing to increase because of climate change [15], the residents of Lubbock continue to navigate these dangers with an eye toward solving complex problems efficiently and supporting the economic well-being of community members through their decisions.

Another danger that continues to be a part of life in Lubbock is crime. In fact, Lubbock has consistently been listed among the most dangerous cities in the state of Texas. While other cities in West Texas tend to see more violent crimes, high levels of property crimes and robbery brought Lubbock close to the top of that ranking in 2015, as the second most dangerous city in Texas [16]. Over recent years other cities in Texas have become relatively more dangerous, dropping Lubbock down to being the seventh most dangerous city in Texas in 2021, but when examining the violent crime rate in the city, it is apparent that this is not because Lubbock has become safer: the violent crime rate in the city has increased by roughly two-thirds in the last seven years [16]. Sadly, this increase in violent crime and homicide has swept across the nation in the last few years, with 2020 having a higher crime rate than had been recorded in the previous twenty-five years. Lubbock has been no exception: the homicide rate jumped 182% from 2019 to 2020 [17].

For places like Monterey High School, this ever-present danger is coupled with an environment of increased risk, because communities that have growing income inequality and high poverty rates tend to also have a higher likelihood of experiencing mass shootings [18]. Understanding the qualitative nature of the poverty many of his students experienced gave Principal Purkeypile a new awareness of the problem. As Lubbock ISD switched to emergency virtual learning, the first challenge was ensuring all students were able to get online. Delivering hotspots to student homes provided an opportunity for greater understanding:

> *And then we spent time and I just drove around in my little red pickup and delivered hot spots and got a real clear understanding of the children that we serve. I had a real good understanding of it, but it was a reminder of, "I'm taking Wi-Fi hotspots to houses that don't have furniture." And I'm serving the absolutely poorest of the poor, which is a lot of people in Lubbock, Texas ... Because I can look at an economically disadvantaged data point and see that 70% of my students are economically disadvantaged. But there's a truth. There's a difference between economically disadvantaged and abject poverty. And abject poverty is what I was confronted with ... Wi-Fi shouldn't be a privilege. It should certainly be at least as easy to get online to do school as it is to buy a gun in the state of Texas.*

While the pandemic afforded new opportunities for Principal Purkeypile and his teachers to connect with the real-world experiences of his students during lockdown, how the educators, parents, and students of Lubbock ISD thought about danger evolved over the course of the pandemic, as it has evolved for communities across the world.

The Moving Target of Pandemic Danger

The novel coronavirus that began spreading in late 2019 appeared to be a problem that was isolated to big cities and to the coastal parts of the United States in the early days of the pandemic. In fact, many southern states went relatively unscathed during the spring of 2020 when educators in New York City faced their most devastating losses. The dangers of coronavirus infection would not be truly experienced by the Lubbock ISD community until the summer months of 2020 [19]. Perhaps it was the regional nature of how the pandemic unfolded across the country that reassured the school board and many community members that the decision to return to in-person education on the originally planned start date in the fall of 2020 was the right choice. Or perhaps it was the fact that, like many districts around the country, they never did completely shut down their operations, rather repurposed empty school buildings into care centers for the children of essential workers. For the community in Lubbock, a regional medical hub, the early days of the pandemic were especially busy for the healthcare workforce.

As two major hospital systems in Lubbock relied on the medical workers in the community to support the public health response to the pandemic, Lubbock ISD converted elementary schools into childcare centers, and hired its paraprofessionals to help run the centers. This not only provided extra financial support to paraprofessionals at a time when many families were coping with lockdown-related income loss, but also allowed the district to develop and practice safety protocols for when classes would resume in person. The new COVID protocols would be put to the test very quickly, because as Superintendent Rollo reminded us:

> We were one of the few states that actually opened schools. And we were the largest district in Texas that opened on time, so really people were more looking to us [for answers], than we were looking to them, because they weren't in school.

Lubbock managed to stave off some of the economic downturn ravaging the rest of the country during 2020 by keeping people working; the service that the school district provided to the community was a point of pride for Superintendent Rollo.

While the educators at Monterey High School shared this pride in supporting their students and their families in such a difficult time, they also reiterated how central the safety of their community was as they worked through the complexities of in-person schooling in the middle of the summer COVID surge in 2020. Establishing trust and respect between all community members was the key to a safe return. Principal Purkeypile understood that part of ensuring safety for his students was bringing them back to school where they had access, not only to learning resources, but to nutritional and mental health support as well. If his students were receiving this support at school, their parents could be at work, affording the families financial stability. To achieve this, he needed to have the trust of their parents. "All about developing trust and having them trust us. A promise, you know. We just had to be safe. We had to be a port in the storm and man, it was stormy," he explained. At the same time, Mrs. Williams focused on how once students were in school, the key to keeping them there was respecting the discomfort and fear many might be experiencing, especially if they had vulnerable family members at home who they feared they might expose to the virus. This balance between community and individual needs was a recurring theme in our conversations with educators in Lubbock.

It was also not lost on any of the educators that while the return to in-person schooling would increase student safety through greater connections and access to resources, the congregation of so many individuals in the absence of a vaccine would also increase the potential health risk to teachers and students. A comprehensive strategy of rigorous safety protocols included masking, social distancing in the cafeteria, adding QR Codes to lunch tables to enable contact tracing, free testing locations, and, once possible, vaccine clinics. The community bought into the approach: if students wanted to learn in person, they had to follow the protocols. Their mask was their *ticket to ride* or their *entry ticket*. The message was clear and consistent. Fortunately for Lubbock ISD, when Rollo had started her tenure as Superintendent, one of her first big achievements was updating the emergency response protocols in the district, making her a trusted leader in this area. There was also an unforeseen benefit of the new protocols—the extended lunch period allowed Principal Purkeypile to connect with students more meaningfully throughout the day, once again reiterating the much-needed sense of trust in the high school.

But as it did across the country, the pandemic and people's risk assessment regarding the coronavirus evolved in Lubbock over the course of the 2020–2021 academic year. With pandemic fatigue setting in, state and local governments pushed for fewer restrictions in public settings, and Texas was no exception. As the fall of 2021 approached, schools across the country started ending virtual learning options that had been available to students through the pandemic [20], and simultaneously, masking policies in schools were allowed to expire, or in some cases, were even banned [21]. While these policy changes were often made on the basis of changing vaccination and infection rates, and an increasing appetite for returning to normal around the world, in many places, these changes reflected an increasingly polarized political environment rather than available data and science-based expert recommendations. The changing choices available to students and parents also created new complexity in schools. As Principal Purkeypile explained:

> As bizarre as last year was, we had a plan. We had a ticket. We had a mission. We had a vision. We had a rock to stand on that we could sell to our public ... This year we didn't have that ... didn't feel as solid. That sounds counterintuitive, because last year should have been the debacle year ... but this year, I actually feel more loose threads or more split hairs than there were last year, because, whether we agreed or disagreed, I was able to communicate that message super effectively.

The consistency of the protocols and the message during the previous school year had facilitated trust between the school district and families. While many families and district personnel welcomed the increased flexibility and freedom that accompanied reduced COVID protocols, the new choices came with a need for new leadership approaches. Even as the menu of choices that Lubbock ISD has been able to offer its community members at different times during the pandemic changed, certain leadership principles were consistently applied to help educators in the district manage the complex dangers their students faced.

Addressing School Danger Through Choice

Like all school districts in the United States, the educators at Lubbock ISD were trying to keep students and adults safe during the return to school. It was clear in speaking to individuals playing different roles in the district that, across the district, school, and classroom levels of the system, a shared leadership ideal of tolerance and pluralism guided decisions. Just as the old cities of Monterey and Lubbock were initially built on the edges of empires, requiring constant negotiation between diverse people to coexist, the modern communities that make up Lubbock, Texas represent a wide range of the political spectrum where people with broadly divergent goals and beliefs share public spaces and thrive. Community and school district leaders represented the interest of these diverse groups throughout the pandemic, relying on the clear communication of data to support individual decision-making among their students and families. They also tried to find flexible solutions that responded to changing situations, and while this sometimes meant not fully satisfying anyone, it also allowed community members with very different needs to have their needs met. Ultimately, the priority was student learning and well-being, and by keeping that priority in focus, the district was able to walk the narrow path in the middle to which Principal Purkeypile so often referred.

Leading Through the Political Noise

Leadership in a time of political fracture, especially in a situation that requires the application of rapidly emerging scientific knowledge, requires cutting through political rhetoric to isolate facts. Since the start of the COVID-19 pandemic, numerous studies showed that the parallel pandemic of misinformation that occurred increased virus spread and loss of life [22]. The more politically noisy the situation became, the less people turned to shared sources of trusted knowledge. And once leaders were relying on conflicting or *alternative* facts, reaching consensus on a course of action became impossible. The educators at Lubbock ISD understood this and leaned on several approaches to increase the likelihood of consensus.

At the district level, bringing together policy leaders to devise a shared strategy and message was an important part of gaining public trust. Superintendent Rollo described the value of the district's collaboration with the city government from the very beginning of the pandemic, including its work with the public health department and the mayor's office, in gaining community support. While the politics of the pandemic, including the relationship between individuals, society, and government, remained divisive issues across political lines, the leaders in Lubbock relied on localized public information campaigns and role-modeling by officials to promote a shared set of facts and solutions [23]. If they could work together, regardless of their political leanings, and promote that same collaborative approach to their community, they could navigate the pandemic.

At the school level, Principal Purkeypile described this strategy as *depersonalizing*, an approach he and his teachers had been promoting among their diverse student body as a path to thriving in a socially complex setting. He explained:

> *And it helped us to kind of depersonalize and depoliticize the whole thing. And it enabled us to be thinking, "Okay, we're doing this with nothing but kids in mind. And we all know that kids being in school is going to be the best way for*

> them to learn. So how do we make that happen?" So really, in this little reddest of the red part of the state, there was a group of people that did a great job of being a reasonable, rational voice that was, if not embraced and accepted from both sides, was tolerated from both sides.

While he admitted that the idea of depersonalizing things at school, where success and thriving depend on positive relationships, seemed counterintuitive on the surface, the message he and his teachers consistently shared was that code-switching between private and public spaces was important to maintaining a respectful and pluralistic culture at school. While the members of the school community were free to cultivate their own systems of values, beliefs, and opinions, how those ideas were shared in private settings carried different social responsibilities than how they were shared in public settings. School was a shared space that needed to allow all members of the community to coexist without fear of judgment.

To support the maintenance of this shared ideal, educators even role-played with students in each incoming class at Monterey High School, to help their acculturation into the shared space. Much as teachers of young children must help students learn to differentiate their *inside voice*, appropriate for the classroom, from their *outside voice*, appropriate for the playground, the educators at Monterey High School helped their students differentiate their *private voice* from their *public voice*. Both practices ensured every individual's right to free speech, while simultaneously facilitating everyone being heard. In essence, the communication skills needed to explore the problems and solutions related to a return to school in a pandemic were already in place for educators at Monterey High School to build on as they navigated the early dangers of in-person schooling.

Making Unpopular Decisions for Popular Outcomes

Even with a supportive culture in place, the educators in Lubbock knew that as the pandemic wore on, keeping school safe for their students would require a willingness to make many unpopular decisions. As Principal Purkeypile explained, "probably a third of our population wants to know why we're not mandating masks, and the other two thirds is promising to boycott school if we do." As the vaccines became available and state mask mandates expired, much of the political noise that the district had kept at bay during the 2020–2021 school year came rushing back. While state and local laws governed the options the district had for maintaining safety protocols, they prepared to manage the aspects of the situation that were in their control.

Interestingly for Mrs. Williams, the second pandemic school year still felt calm and safe, and perhaps even more so than the first. With the vaccine now available, and all her students returning to in-person learning with the end of a virtual schooling option, more was in her control. As much as the return to school in the fall of 2020 had been governed by reasonable voices and strong leadership, the return to school in 2021, and the personal and professional choices it presented her, meant that one of those reasonable voices could be her own. While the administration and the State would establish safety protocols for the community, in her classroom, she was free to assess her risk tolerance and focus on student learning needs. For example, as a young woman with no children of her own at home, and parents who lived in another city, Mrs. Williams was not as concerned as many of her colleagues with families that she might contract COVID from her students and infect a vulnerable family member at home. On the other hand, she was very concerned that her mask had been an impediment to communicating clearly with many of her students the previous year. She reflected:

> *The moment you spend eight hours a day projecting your voice [from behind a mask], you realize, honestly, how many kids look at your mouth when you speak [to understand you]. And for them, it really blocked their voice, which was challenging. I felt like, as students, their voices were hidden because they could hide behind the mask.*

To support the varying needs in her classroom, Mrs. Williams replicated the district's strategy of personal choice and empowered her students to take masks on and off based on their comfort and move around the room to achieve the social distance needed to safely complete their current activity. She also reinforced an important social contract with them: as part of her classroom community, they would respect and support each other's choices.

Principal Purkeypile focused his return-to-school energies on two areas that were clearly under his purview, and where he had the power to make a real difference: student attendance and teacher morale. He understood that if student learning were the priority, then students and teachers would have to be present and engaged. In the earliest days of the pandemic, this meant ensuring internet connections. The fall of 2020, as students and teachers returned to the Monterey High School campus, this meant everyone having their *ticket to ride*, their face mask:

> So, we decided if we're going to have something that's going to be a money drain for us, let's make it these little five-cent masks that we can give away like candy. And so, we gave those away like candy, so that we could uphold our end of saying, "this is your ticket." And if you've lost your ticket, I've got another one for you today, tomorrow, the next day and every day for 181 days if that's the case. I probably ordered more masks than any school in our district. But it worked, and it was a pittance compared to losing those children for attendance.

Once students were in the building, then Principal Purkeypile could ensure that contact tracing, testing, and quarantine procedures were followed to keep as many of them attending as possible. And while it was not always popular, the no-nonsense approach that year worked. Principal Purkeypile proudly shared that his school warded off the significant learning losses that so many schools in the country were contending with.

For his teachers, Purkeypile was not just their boss, but an important advocate and coach. When political discord or tensions with students and parents over safety protocols emerged, he reminded them, "Don't forget last spring when you were considered heroes and on the front lines of everything that you're doing. Now, you're truly on the front lines. So don't lose that and don't get consumed by the nothing." Sometimes these simple reminders could uplift weary spirits and refocus frayed nerves. At other times, more serious discussions about self-care and mental health were needed. Mrs. Williams explained how teachers were encouraged to use the free counseling sessions provided by the school district—they were told to take the time they required to stay healthy themselves so that they could be there to support their students. At a time when schools faced a plague of resignations as burnt-out teachers abandoned the field for safer careers with higher pay, Lubbock ISD's teacher turnover rate remained fairly steady.

Communicating the Danger to Inform Choice

Because safely managing the return to school at Lubbock ISD relied on individual choices, initially with the option to remain online or return in person, and then on the decision to wear a mask or not, success of the approach required individuals to make accurate personal risk assessments.

In order to do this successfully, the district needed to clearly communicate relevant information in a timely manner. While this was important in all districts across the country, and we saw communication strategies leveraged successfully in our conversations with Bronx District 7, the stakes in politically polarized Lubbock were especially high and required balanced leadership from all levels of the system. Broadly, this balance was achieved in two important ways. First, when communicating about the actual dangers of the virus, across district, school, and classroom, educators focused conversations on specific aspects of the issue that aligned clearly with their role and expertise. Second, the educators communicated a broader picture of the dangers that students faced, coupling information about the danger posed by COVID infection with the dangers of learning loss and mental health challenges that students faced during lockdown and virtual learning. To make well-informed personal choices, students and their families could weigh each of these dangers for themselves.

Sharing the changes in coronavirus infection rates and vaccination rates provided the solid backbone for the district's strategy for data transparency. As a strong advocate for data-driven decision-making, Superintendent Rollo started her efforts of collaboration with city health officials early, establishing the trusted sources for information for herself and her district. At the school level, Principal Purkeypile could trust that information about the virus was being communicated by the experts, and he could focus on clearly and consistently sharing how Monterey High School's safety protocols would keep students and staff safe if they were followed. Initially, this communication was used to establish buy-in for the school district's mask requirement. As the pandemic entered a new phase and masking became a choice, the goal of the communication leaned more heavily toward encouraging personal safety and respect for the choices of other community members. For Mrs. Williams, communication in her classroom focused heavily on differentiating facts and opinions and learning to identify reliable sources of factual information. At a time when so many students relied on social media to understand the world around them, these efforts focused on respecting different perspectives on situations, while seeking a shared set of facts. While this may not have been a coordinated effort, per se, it positioned the educators in the district to navigate the complex situation more successfully. It also aligned well with their attempts at depoliticizing and focusing on the spaces they controlled.

An important aspect of the Lubbock ISD communication strategy included a multidimensional understanding of danger. While many other districts focused entirely on the dangers of COVID, the educators in Lubbock also kept students and parents informed about the dangers present during emergency virtual learning to empower individuals to make a personal risk assessment. One major danger that most districts faced was learning loss during virtual schooling. The educators at Lubbock ISD were cognizant that students in virtual learning were suffering significant learning losses across the state [24], with many low-income students lacking consistent access to the internet, and families too often struggling to provide supervision for students going to school from home while keeping up with work responsibilities. Superintendent Rollo reiterated, "Our board felt very passionate about having [in person] school, so we had summer school for some small groups of students who we knew were behind and had a hard time connecting digitally." With a successful summer of safe, in-person schooling behind them, the district could forge ahead sharing data with the community about the benefits of the return to school and its ability to keep students safe.

In many ways, the return would not be an academic return to normal, but rather, a dive into a new and improved blend of traditional learning with the value added of new, technology-enhanced approaches. With her students back in the classroom, Mrs. Williams intentionally incorporated the many new learning tools and technologies that she had relied on during virtual learning to enhance their in-person learning experience:

> *I really think that there's a lot of value in online learning. I just don't think it needs to be the full answer. It definitely needs to be a blend, but I'm excited to use the tools and resources that we have now and mix it. I can do stations now in a group setting and then I can go back and have them write a reflective piece online.*

In this way, she reinforced the balanced communications that originated from the district office and her own building-level administration, using all the resources at hand to support student learning.

Lubbock ISD's pragmatic approach also demanded attention to and honest communication about another danger that grew as pandemic lockdowns and virtual learning continued. With a growing mental health crisis in the summer of 2020, opening schools was as much a question of safety for Lubbock ISD as virtual learning had been the semester before. The isolation of lockdown was difficult for students and adults alike. With internet access already a challenge for so many who lived in poverty in the community, limited availability of mental health services in the city increased the risk for community members. Lubbock's 6.9 psychiatrists per 100,000 residents were about half the national average [25]. Bringing students back to school could alleviate feelings of isolation and provide much-needed support to learners of all ages. Perhaps Principal Purkeypile described it best when he said, "We are a port in the storm. That is all we are. We are safe harbor." And this sentiment was clearly reflected by Mrs. Williams as well. School was the safe space in the lives of many of her students, and if student safety was the top priority, it needed to include physical safety, but they could not overlook mental health and emotional safety. Lubbock ISD taught the whole child, and as such, it needed to protect the whole child from the dangers of the pandemic.

For Superintendent Rollo, the fact that the district was able to provide the in-person schooling option for every student who wanted it in the 2020–2021 school year was a great point of pride, and what she determined to be its greatest success. She also understood that pushing right into summer school to help those who had suffered learning loss, and then bringing the entire student body back to in-person learning for the 2021–2022 school year was going to be a big lift for the district's teachers. When asked what she would go back and change in that critical year of pandemic schooling if she had the power, she relied on the data once again for the answer, but allowed herself to, perhaps, look beyond it:

> *We tried to reduce the stress and workload on our teachers. But it was tough on them, and I wish we could have just found, maybe, some other ways that we could have helped reduce that stress. But fortunately, they did not quit, and they said they would come for summer school. We have no more turnover than what we normally do in any other year, so I think teachers recognized that we were all doing the best we can, and we extended lots of buckets of grace.*

At a time when schools across the country were plagued by staffing shortages, with teachers fleeing the profession due to low pay, politicization of curricula, and physical and psychological burnout [26], Lubbock ISD used thoughtful leadership to keep the politics out and stay sensitive to the financial needs of some of its lowest paid employees. Superintendent Rollo's compassion for the toll it took on teachers was clear in our conversations. Their heroic efforts came at a cost, and the final tally was still becoming clear as the world slowly emerged from the pandemic into a new normal that had not yet fully revealed itself.

Lessons Learned from Lubbock

Throughout our discussions with educators in Lubbock, it was clear that education decisions are not made in a bubble. They are not confined to the classroom, or Monterey High School, or even the Lubbock Independent School District. Rather, they are a part of a larger set of choices and decisions that every student, parent, guardian, and community member must make daily. As Mrs. Williams said, "we still have a way to go ... but the good thing is we made it through the hardest part, which was making a decision. Now from there, we can adapt and do." It was through attention to these choices and understanding the dangers that persisted with each decision from which we can glean lessons to improve and reimagine education.

Leave Politics at the Door

In the early stages of the pandemic, little was known about the science of COVID-19. There was a danger in being exposed to the virus, but as seen through this chapter, there was also a danger to student learning and mental health associated with virtual learning. As we saw across the nation, conversations around in-person versus virtual learning took a hard turn from discussing science and research to shouting political slogans and ideology. The leaders in Lubbock ISD chose to leave the political noise at the door and focus on the facts presented, or as Principal Purkeypile said, "separate the politics from the science." The leadership team and Lubbock ISD collaborated from the very beginning with the mayor, city council, public health department, and even the police chief to ensure all perspectives were taken into account. Superintendent Rollo credited this collaboration for their ability to present a united message that cut through the politics. Not everyone agreed with every decision the leadership team made, but by removing politics and making data-informed decisions as a team, the leadership could stand confident that their decisions were made with the best interest of students in mind.

It is important to note, this did not mean that the educators at Lubbock ISD did not help their students find their voices about issues that mattered or did not take a stand in order to teach students about important issues when the need arose. On the contrary, they empowered them to have a voice and use it thoughtfully. When students wanted to protest and support the March for our Lives initiative after the school shooting at Marjory

Stoneman Douglas High School in Parkland, Florida, Principal Purkeypile supported the conversations, saying:

> And so, what we had to let our teachers understand is these kids are, for the first time, feeling called to have their voice. And they saw that from Stoneman Douglas, and it carried over with George Floyd. And it's okay for them to have an environment where they can voice that somehow.

But he also worked with his teachers to achieve this nuance in a way that made sure that tolerance for multiple perspectives was not confused with moral relativism—school needed to be a safe place for all students and that meant not all voices could be always public voices:

> And so how do we deal with that as a school? And are we gonna let these kids wear BLM masks? And the answer to that is, yes. Yes, we are. And well, then, what about a confederate flag mask? Are we gonna let them wear that? No, no, we're not. Well, how is that any different? Well, they're different.

It was clear from all our conversations with district personnel that "depoliticizing" was not an approach taken out of avoidance, but an intentional choice that focused the conversation on creating a safe learning environment for all.

Communicate Facts to Support Choice

Another key lesson derived from our conversations in Lubbock revolved around the idea that choices come through flexibility. As seen above, there were unique concerns expressed about the choices to continue virtual education as well as to return to in-person learning. Dangers lurked behind every choice, and in a situation like that, flexibility and resilience are needed. What the educators of Lubbock ISD realized was that by providing flexibility and adaptable structures, they could empower families to make the choice that was best for their situation. Further, Lubbock ISD leaders realized that circumstances could change, and they provided students the opportunity to switch between virtual learning and in-person learning multiple times throughout the 2020–2021 academic year. This empowerment through choice and flexibility had dual results. First, teachers and administrators became more comfortable with online learning, allowing students who thrived in it to continue, and finding ways to incorporate it into in-person learning. They chose to see this new technology as a way to connect and instill flexibility in educational delivery. Second, they empowered students and families to make the decisions directly related to their education, resulting in more trust in the leadership across Lubbock ISD. People's choices may have differed, but it was this empowerment to make the choice that united individuals across divides. As Mrs. Williams stated:

> *You can be friends with somebody who thinks differently, feels differently than you, and you can still empower them ... I think the blend [of different choices and decisions] makes everyone stronger.*

This pluralistic approach emerged in many ways across our conversations with Lubbock educators but was clearly a powerful guiding principle in a politically and demographically diverse community.

Know Your Priorities

A once-in-a-lifetime event, such as a pandemic, can upend long-standing traditions, create new routines, and even call one's priorities into question. One theme that permeated every discussion with Lubbock's leaders was that they knew their priorities—namely, academic achievement—and that they would strive to do their best to continue them, regardless of the situation. They also understood, though, that the roadmap to achieving their goals must change with the world around it. At that moment, students did not need tests on multiplication tables and lessons on chemistry; they needed mental health support, food security, access to Wi-Fi, and other basic needs. The priority was still academic achievement, but the means by which to achieve that shifted drastically, and so did the services that Lubbock ISD provided. By keeping their vision focused on their priority, they could provide flexibility and care that moved students toward their goal of academic success.

The focus on priorities by leadership provided students and families stability and motivation, even in a time of chaos, doubt, and uncertainty. Nowhere was this clearer than in how Principal Purkeypile explained his school's approach to what was coming next:

> *We are absolutely hitting reset at Monterey High School. There is not one system, not one program, not one way of doing business that is not on the evaluation*

> *table ... A lot of what goes on around Monterey High School is about the art of education, and what it brings outside of the science of education ... We are evaluating everything that we do. And exactly what that's gonna look like—I don't know. It's all on the big board. And we're slowly crossing off things on the big board as we discuss, OK, is that truly a priority? Or is that something that can be down the line? And so, I think what it's done is made us recognize that we can't continue business as usual. Otherwise, we're a wonderfully air-conditioned museum with outdated practices of education and traditions. We have to be careful, because tradition is the positive way to see outdated practices if you're not careful. And so, we're really evaluating all those traditions and ways of doing business so that we don't become a museum.*

Ultimately, the district would reflect and rely on a strong cultural value that had been a part of Lubbock for generations: a determination to do what was needed to achieve its prioritized goals. If the pandemic disrupted everything, then everything would have to be reimagined, because progress is not possible without an acceptance of risk and an openness to change.

Reflect and Discuss

We invite you to consider what you have read in this chapter and apply it to your own community context. Use the following questions as a starting point for your personal reflection and for discussion with education stakeholders in your community.

1. How did the district context of Lubbock impact conversations around student physical and mental health and safety?
2. What aspects of your local context influence the response of area schools in times of danger?
3. How do education leaders today effectively communicate information about student physical and mental health needs? How does this look in your local context?
4. How do local, national, and global politics affect the ability of educators, school leaders, and students to do their job?
5. What lessons can you draw from Lubbock to navigate tough political conversations in your professional position?

References

1. Leatherwood, A. (2023). *Llano estacado*. Handbook of Texas Online. Retrieved April 2, 2023, from https://www.tshaonline.org/handbook/entries/llano-estacado
2. Comanche Nation. (2023). *Our nation: About us*. Comanche Nation. Retrieved April 15, 2023, from https://comanchenation.com/our-nation/about-us
3. Hill, R. (2011). *Lubbock*. Arcadia Publishing.
4. U.S. Census Bureau. (2021). *QuickFacts Lubbock City, Texas: Lubbock County, Texas*. U.S. Census Bureau. Retrieved April 2, 2023, from https://www.census.gov/quickfacts/fact/table/lubbockcitytexas,lubbockcountytexas/PST045221
5. Feeding America. (2017). *Food insecurity in Lubbock County Texas*. Feeding America. Retrieved April 2, 2023, from https://map.feedingamerica.org/county/2017/child/texas/county/lubbock
6. Petre, M., & Venkat, P., (2019). Funding, investment, and wealth equalization across Texas public school districts. *SSRN*. https://doi.org/10.2139/ssrn.4033332
7. Lubbock ISD. (2018). *Dr. Kathy Rollo*. Lubbock ISD. Retrieved April 2, 2023, from https://www.lubbockisd.org/domain/137
8. The Texas Tribune. (2018-2019). Monterey High School. The Texas Tribune. Retrieved April 2, 2023, from https://schools.texastribune.org/districts/lubbock-isd/monterey-high-school/
9. Monterey High School. (n.d.). *Mission*. Monterey High School. Retrieved April 2, 2023, from https://www.lubbockisd.org/Domain/744
10. Walbrick, S. S. (2021, November 22). *New Group Aims to Honor Llano Estacado's Native American History*. KTTZ. https://radio.kttz.org/2021-11-22/new-group-aims-to-honor-llano-estacados-native-american-history
11. Lipscomb, C. A. (2020, October 9). *Comanche Indians*. TSHA. Retrieved April 15, 2023, from https://www.tshaonline.org/handbook/entries/comanche-indians
12. U.S. Department of Commerce (1970). *The Lubbock, Texas Tornado May 11, 1970*. U.S. Department of Commerce, Environmental Sciences Services Administration. Retrieved April 2, 2023, from http://lubbocktornado1970.com/pdf/ESSA_SurveyReport.pdf
13. Fujita, T. T. (1970). The Lubbock tornadoes: A study of suction spots. *Weatherwise*, *23*(4), 161–173. https://doi.org/10.1080/00431672.1970.9932888
14. Carlson, P. H., & Abbe, D. R. (2008). *Historic Lubbock County: An illustrated history*. HPN Books.

15. Environmental Protections Agency (2016). *What climate change means for Texas*. Environmental Protections Agency. Retrieved April 2, 2023, from https://www.epa.gov/sites/default/files/2016-09/documents/climate-change-tx.pdf
16. Solomon, D. (2015, January 22). The FBI's list of the most dangerous cities in Texas. *Texas Monthly*. https://www.texasmonthly.com/the-daily-post/the-fbis-list-of-the-most-dangerous-cities-in-texas/
17. Stebbins, S. (2020). *Homicide is soaring in the Lubbock, TX metro area*. 24/7 Wall St. Retrieved April 2, 2023, from https://247wallst.com/city/homicide-is-soaring-in-the-lubbock-tx-metro-area/
18. Kwon, R., & Cabrera, J. F. (2019). Income inequality and mass shootings in the United States. *BMC Public Health, 19*(1147). https://doi.org/10.1186/s12889-019-7490-x
19. New York Times. (2023). Tracking coronavirus in Lubbock County, Texas: Latest map and case count. *New York Times*. Retrieved April 2, 2023, from https://www.nytimes.com/interactive/2021/us/lubbock-texas-covid-cases.html
20. St. George, D., & Strauss, V. (2021, June 15). Virtual learning is the new fault line in education: It's either on the way out or on the rise. *The Washington Post*. https://www.washingtonpost.com/education/virtual-school-learning-future/2021/06/14/63763532-c2f5-11eb-8c18-fd53a628b992_story.html
21. Decker, S. (2021, August 20). Which states banned mask mandates in schools, and which required masks? *Education Weekly*. https://www.edweek.org/policy-politics/which-states-ban-mask-mandates-in-schools-and-which-require-masks/2021/08
22. Bursztyn, L., Rao, A., Roth, C. P., & Yanagizawa-Drott, D. H. (2020). Misinformation during a pandemic. *National Bureau of Economic Research*.
23. Vergara, R. J. D., Sarmiento, P. J. D., & Lagman, J. D. N. (2021). Building public trust: A response to COVID-19 vaccine hesitancy predicament. *Journal of Public Health, 43*(2), 291–292.
24. Waller, A. (2021, July 9). New Data: At schools across Texas, students of color returned to in-person learning at below-average rates. *The 74*. https://www.the74million.org/article/new-data-at-schools-across-texas-students-of-color-returned-to-in-person-learning-at-below-average-rates/
25. Ellingson, K. (2020, September 3). Coping with the pandemic: Lubbockites talk mental health. *NPR*. https://radio.kttz.org/news/2020-09-03/coping-with-the-pandemic-lubbockites-talk-mental-health
26. Gaudiano, N. (2022, February 22). One ex-teacher in Memphis said she had 194 students during virtual classes because a colleague quit, and it shows why so many teachers are burned out and fed up. *Business Insider*. https://www.businessinsider.com/teachers-burnout-staffing-shortage-pandemic-quitting-schools-education-2022-2

CHAPTER 5

Education in a Time of Need: A Story of Community

In ordinary times, we're trying to do three things. We're trying to help students learn. We're trying to provide that safety net for working families. And we're trying to take care of the people who work in our schools, because they're the ones who do those other two things.
—Austin Beutner, Superintendent, Los Angeles Unified School District

Large urban centers often lure many from their homes in other parts of the country, and the world, with the promise of economic opportunity. With the exchange of ideas and goods that is created by this large concentration of people, there exists the possibility of a loss of culture and identity in sacrifice to efficiency and growth. Los Angeles and Los Angeles County, California, are a vast metropolis with the second largest school district in the country. While Los Angeles is the most well-known city, Los Angeles County boasts a wide and diverse population with over 88 incorporated cities within its borders and many more unincorporated areas. With the vast cultural and ethnic diversity, so too exist steep wealth inequalities that impact how people experience real-world events. L.A. Unified School District is a microcosm of this cultural and economic

© The Author(s), under exclusive license to Springer Nature Switzerland AG 2023
F. M. Jamil, J. E. Siddiqi, *Public Education in Turbulent Times*, https://doi.org/10.1007/978-3-031-43237-8_5

diversity, which presents challenges and affordances for sustaining education in a time of need.

While the COVID-19 pandemic brought tremendous pain and fear from the virus, it also presented a unique economic challenge unlike one experienced ever before. Roughly 9.6 million U.S. workers ages 16–65 lost their jobs within the first nine months of the pandemic, but these losses were most notable in the arts, entertainment, and recreation industries [1]. Los Angeles County, a place known for its entertainment, movie and television sets, and beautiful beaches, suddenly ground to a halt. Over 437,000 Los Angeles residents lost jobs in 2020, accounting for nearly 5% of total job losses in the nation [2]. Each of those 88 cities and the numerous unincorporated areas of Los Angeles experienced the adversity that emerged from the economic outcomes of the COVID-19 pandemic. Instantly, there was a tremendous amount of need that left citizens looking to neighbors, governments, and schools to fill. The story of Cudahy, California, and Ellen Ochoa Learning Center illuminates the way one community, a school, and its community neighbors came together to support one another through this intense time of economic hardship and found richness and opportunity by harnessing community cultural wealth—a type of wealth often overlooked in today's economic system.

THE DISTRICT CONTEXT OF LOS ANGELES

Spanning from the beaches of Malibu and the Santa Monica Pier to the outskirts of the Mojave Desert, and encompassing numerous cities and neighborhoods such as Compton, Belair, and Hollywood, Los Angeles County encompasses over 4000 square miles, four times the size of Rhode Island. With nearly 10,000 million residents in 2022, it is the most populous county in the nation [3]. Los Angeles County was one of the original counties of California, created at the time of California's statehood in 1850, but the history and culture starts well before that with the presence of the native Tongva peoples, and later the establishment of a Spanish settlement in the area [4, 5]. This Spanish influence on culture in the area continues to this day, in large part due to its thriving Hispanic and Latin American immigrant population. Ethnically, over 49% of Angelenos identify as Hispanic or Latino [6]. In terms of race, 70% of residents identify as white, 9% as Black or African American, 15% as Asian, and 3% as multiracial [6]. This rich tapestry of cultural diversity, makes the area a popular destination for transplants from within the United States and immigrants from around the globe, but also results in vast inequalities of income in the area. While Los Angeles County had a median household income of over $71,000 in 2020, this income level varied greatly across the county. The Los Angeles Times ranked 272 Los Angeles County neighborhoods according to median household income, and the results were staggering, ranging from a median household income of over $200,000 in some neighborhoods to numerous others that reported a median income of less than $30,000 [7]. These large economic differences result in incredibly different experiences of hardship during the pandemic.

Nestled in the heart of downtown and surrounded by some of the wealthiest neighborhoods in the county, the city of Cudahy ranked near the bottom of the LA Times rankings, seeing a median household income of $46,000 in 2020 [8]. Cudahy is the second smallest city in Los Angeles County but is also one of the most densely populated cities in the country. The city also has one of the highest concentrations of residents identifying as Hispanic at 96% [9].

The area was farmland for hundreds of years, but in 1908, the town namesake, Michael Cudahy, sold his shares of the Armour-Cudahy meat packing plant in Omaha, Nebraska, and used his fortune to buy a 2777 acre ranch in east Los Angeles [10]. He subsequently divided the ranch and sold it in one-acre lots, which fundamentally changed the composition of the community. As the population in the West grew, there became greater incentive to build meatpacking facilities near population centers. The meatpacking industry of the 1920s brought in a new wave of workers to Cudahy, primarily immigrants from Mexico and other Latin American countries. The workers were often paid low wages and worked in hazardous conditions because these were frequently the only jobs available for immigrants. The economic inequality in Cudahy, and Los Angeles at large, only worsened during the Great Depression, as many of the meatpacking plants closed [11]. This left large numbers of workers unemployed, leading to widespread poverty in the community.

The economic boom post-World War II led to the development of new steel, automobile, and aerospace industries, which provided new opportunities for jobs and wealth. However, the benefits of this economic growth were not shared equally, and white business owners profited, while Latin American immigrants faced wage and housing discrimination. Even as the rest of L.A. County prospered around Cudahy, its residents were left struggling. As factories closed and white residents fled to the suburbs in the 1970s and 1980s, the residents of Cudahy were again left fending for themselves, while watching McMansions being built in neighboring communities like Hollywood and Bel Air. During the next twenty years, the sprawling tracts of land once used for ranching in Cudahy were turned into apartment complexes, and low-wage workers moved into the area seeking affordable housing in L.A. County [12]. By 2007, Cudahy had become the second most densely populated city in California, and home to one of the largest populations of undocumented residents in the nation.

All in all, Cudahy, while not seen as an economically wealthy city, is a prime example of what it means to harness community cultural wealth to enrich all residents. While the individuals living in the wealthier neighborhoods of L.A. County might rely on access to influential social networks or shared cultural norms to navigate institutions such as school or the workplace, and create opportunities for their future, the residents of Cudahy have leveraged different, collective assets to overcome structural inequality [13]. Community cultural wealth refers to an array of skills, knowledge, and experiences that are shared by a marginalized group of people that, together, creates a way of knowing and being. As you will see in the rest of this chapter, the residents of Cudahy leveraged this community cultural wealth in unique and successful ways to overcome the educational and economic disruptions of the pandemic [14].

Understanding the District Structure

Covering over 710 square miles, including most of the city of Los Angeles, and all or portions of another 25 cities and unincorporated areas of L.A. County, the Los Angeles Unified School District (LAUSD) is the largest school system in California, and the second largest in the nation (with the New York City Department of Education ranking number one) [15]. Boasting a nearly $10 billion budget in Fiscal Year 2021–2022, LAUSD is the second largest employer in L.A. County, employing over 73,000 people, including over 25,000 teachers, 3000 administrators, and over 42,000 support personnel [15].

Over 4.8 million people live within LAUSD's boundaries, and the district thus serves more than 500,000 K-12 students across 1424 schools. Nearly 74% of students in LAUSD identify as Hispanic/Latino, 10.5% as white, 7.6% as Black or African American, 5.9% as Asian or Pacific Islander. Additionally, 59.9% of students are on free or reduced lunch programs and 28.0% are English Language Learners [16]. An educational organization this big requires a leader willing to think boldly and imagine a better future, something which Superintendent Austin Beutner promised to bring when taking over LAUSD in 2018.

Son of German immigrants, Superintendent Beutner was born in New York and raised in Grand Rapids, Michigan [17]. Beutner used his extensive experience from a successful career in finance, and subsequent leadership positions as a member of the Clinton Administration, the first deputy mayor of Los Angeles, and the Superintendent of LAUSD to usher the district through the challenges of the pandemic [18]. As the son of a public school teacher, he knew first-hand how important education was, especially for economically disadvantaged families. When Austin Beutner started his tenure as Superintendent of Los Angeles Unified School District in May 2018, he knew his first act would be to assess the school district's organizational structure and to center the community in that structure. Any organization as large as LAUSD requires a centralized leadership structure with the ability to adapt to different conditions that might present themselves across the diverse organization.

Beutner knew how important it was to organize around the community, and this leadership philosophy led him to undertake a full restructure of the LAUSD governance system. Previously, LAUSD had split its schools into various smaller districts based on either grade level or geographical location. Beutner transitioned the district to a feeder system structure that gave teachers a more direct role in instruction and local managers more familiarity with their campuses and staff [19]. This restructure was essential to providing services to communities during the COVID-19 pandemic. Superintendent Beutner summarized the reorganization and subsequent benefits best, saying:

So, when I started it was a top-down, one size fits all organization. And [LAUSD] is now organized around 44 nimble local teams. And it turns out, by the way, that's the best way to provide service to the community in a crisis like [COVID]. So, what we've been doing organizationally, there was no better proof point of what that reorganization was about in terms of the support to the community.

In order for this reorganization of the school system around communities to be successful, though, local leaders had to be willing to serve as that conduit between the school and community.

Marcos Hernandez, principal of Ellen Ochoa Learning Center (EOLC) in Cudahy, CA, was one of the leaders that Superintendent Beutner highlighted as that bridge between the community and school. As a former local leader, Principal Hernandez had a passion for improving education in Southeast Los Angeles. He used his migrant experience to teach students how to overcome generational challenges and reap the benefits of an excellent education. When he took the job at EOLC, he was aware of the challenges the students and the community faced, but never expected to encounter as much need as he did when the COVID-19 and the subsequent economic recession hit. Luckily, his previous experience in community organizing and building partnerships prepared him to thrive in this role.

Given the economic status of Cudahy, roughly 95% of the 1250 students enrolled at EOLC are identified as economically disadvantaged. Further, there is a strong sense of shared cultural identity in the community, as 99% of students identify as Hispanic/Latino [20]. When the pandemic began and the service, entertainment, retail, and construction industries closed, students at EOLC and their families were drastically affected. Principal Hernandez knew from his previous work and life experiences that in a time so fraught with fear and isolation, the antidote was community and togetherness. He understood that students and families would struggle if they were left to fend for themselves, and he used this knowledge to direct his leadership response, saying:

> We understand that we have to serve the entire family, that we have to serve the entire community. We understand that we cannot just do everything in isolation—like teach literacy—and then have rent or other things impact the family. We have to address all the pressures that families have.

As you will hear in the rest of this chapter, Principal Hernandez utilized his skills in building relationships to create numerous partnerships that were beneficial to the community. From organizing community backpack drives, to bringing vaccine clinics to the school, Hernandez found ways to connect residents to available services. The school quickly emerged as that essential connection point, because Principal Hernandez knew that it took a well-trained, energetic, and committed staff for his school to be the community support, the solid rock, that he wanted it to be. From the numerous full-time counselors to the teachers, to the community organizers funded through grants, each individual played a role in the greater community's success.

Elida Lozano was one of the teachers who were integral to the success of EOLC. Ms. Lozano was a first-grade dual language teacher and the arts coordinator at EOLC. A proud mother of four, Ms. Lozano had spent the past 20 years being a fierce advocate for students, working tirelessly to secure resources and funds to support the students, families, and communities that she served. When the pandemic and recession hit Cudahy, Ms. Lozano knew that the teachers were already prepared for the support that their community would need, even if support had not been provided at such a large scale before.

> *In our community ... [teachers] are there to serve not only as educators, but as activists. We are always fighting for resources to be placed in our school, so that we can have a library, so we can have a community park. That's the beauty of where I teach. I feel like we are very unique in the sense that all the teachers are committed to helping out.*

Ms. Lozano quickly realized that while much of the need and distress in Chaudhry stemmed from economic challenges, the community was rich with other forms of capital, and by harnessing this capital, she could improve the lives of her students. Along with Principal Hernandez and other educators, Ms. Lozano went out into the community and used their social and cultural capital to uplift community members. From organizing virtual winter arts nights to inviting Superintendent Beutner to come to Cudahy and see their issues, EOLC educators pooled their vast knowledge and resources to support students.

Ms. Lozano openly admitted that teaching during the pandemic was difficult, expressing "how hard it is to keep the attention of 25 students at a time," especially virtually. Once she accepted that she could not recreate the in-person experience online, she was able to adapt and meet the students where they were. Moving away from whole group instruction, she worked in small groups and focused on first addressing social and emotional needs. She even administered assessments individually to be able to fully understand how student learning needs were evolving. As an experienced teacher, Ms. Lozano was also able to share this learning and provide the guidance and advice that many less experienced teachers needed to persevere through the chaos. At the end of the day, though, she credits the success of their work to the teamwork and leadership at EOLC, saying:

> *You know you can't do this alone, so you rely on your team, either your grade level team or your administrative team … to talk when it is needed, and this helps us stay connected as a school and identify what is important to us.*

The importance of relationships and connection for teachers, students, and parents, alike, was reiterated in many of our conversations with educators in LAUSD.

In summary, chaos, uncertainty, and need impact every person, family, and community differently. As you will see in the rest of this chapter, Cudahy and EOLC experienced an immense amount of need because of the various challenges faced in 2020, but thanks to the work of a bold group of educators, they were able to pool community resources, utilize all forms of wealth, and challenge inequity.

THE EVOLVING EXPERIENCE OF NEED

The interviews with educators in L.A. began with the same panged expression and heavy exhale that so many others began with; almost as if it were the first time they could hang up the superhero capes they had been donning for so long, and, even if for just a moment, reflect on what they had been carrying for the past year and a half. Interviews abounded with various examples of need. The immediate needs for students were similar to those in Lubbock and the Bronx, like providing food and a safe place for those whose parents were front-line workers. Once those physiological needs were met, or at least systems were created to meet these needs, efforts shifted to items such as expanding Wi-Fi and creating engaging virtual programming to meet academic needs and keep students learning during lockdown.

What emerged from these conversations, though, were themes of a more encompassing definition of need. As one of the largest employers in L.A. County, and now one of the most stable employers in a pandemic-stricken economy, the employees and leaders of LAUSD and EOLC knew they were cornerstones in the community, and they were not new to this role. As Superintendent Beutner told us:

> *Think of schools as their own community that you can label as a city, county, state, whatever you wanna call it. But you better be prepared to have the broadest conversation. You'd better be prepared to solve the problem there because that's where it's gonna come and that's where our next generation resides. And*

that's where we have trained people who are well equipped to be that support for their students or family.

There had been numerous instances before when the community had come together to overcome unique needs, and the tripartite challenges that started in 2020, only activated and elevated support systems and community networks that had been evolving and growing for years. Traits such as resilience, aspiration, and familial ties all highlighted the immense community cultural wealth present in EOLC and the community of Cudahy around it.

Understanding the history of the unique challenges, and assets, that the people of Cudahy possess, provides perspective on how they responded to 2020 and plan to not only survive, but thrive moving forward. Too often, communities and schools are counted out because they do not seem rich in economic capital, but to do this ignores the richness of so many traits that students, faculty, staff, and community members bring to the table.

Historical Experiences of Economic Inequality

The industries employing the largest number of Cudahy's residents were the ones most affected by the COVID-19 pandemic, namely retail trade, manufacturing, and construction. In an instant, families and a community were thrown into the unknown, not knowing when, if ever, they could go back to work. In May of 2020, residents of Cudahy were living through a 20% unemployment rate, almost 7% above the national average [21]. Even worse, residents of one of the most densely packed communities in the nation were asked to isolate themselves from one another to avoid transmitting a deadly disease. In a city where it is not uncommon for multiple families to share a home, social distancing was a challenge even in one's own residence. Living in close quarters also meant that challenges were more likely to be met through collective action, and no one was on their own.

While nothing could prepare a community for what was experienced in 2020, an unfortunate string of government corruption and environmental racism scandals had prepared the people of Cudahy to care for one another, because they could not count on others to do so. In 1922, the Exide Battery Plant opened and was one of the largest producers, distributors, and recyclers of lead-acid batteries, which were often used in automobiles and other motorized devices [22]. For the next century, Exide smelted recycled batteries to extract materials. However, smelting plants are known to be dangerous to communities. During the heating and melting process, heavy metals were sent into the air, which would blow throughout the area and fall onto the land and water. For nearly 100 years, the toxic dust contaminated over 10,000 homes, many of which housed working-class, Latino families [23]. And this is just an example of one company's misdeeds in an area full of industries rife with toxic waste, left to contaminate communities perceived to be too poor and powerless to fight back.

Schools have not been free from environmental racism in Cudahy either. Park Avenue Elementary (PAE) experienced far worse and more visible repercussions from toxic poisoning. Opened in 1968, PAE sits along the edge of the Los Angeles River. From the moment it opened its doors, reports came of substances oozing throughout the school yard [24]. Reports of a toxic environment were constantly made to the appropriate authorities but save for some short-term school shutdowns and temporary fixes, the school continued to operate in unsafe conditions. More recently, in 2020 a Delta Air Lines jet dumped 15,000 gallons of fuel over the community of Cudahy. While making an emergency landing at Los Angeles International Airport, pilots were forced to dump fuel to reduce the plane's weight before landing. At least 20 students and 11 adults at Park Avenue Elementary were injured by the fuel dump. In a community already plagued by environmental and racial injustice, this was just another example of harm toward a community of color where many lived in poverty.

The need for justice in Cudahy has only been further exacerbated by a history of political corruption that has plagued the government's ability to respond to a series of crises. When California legalized medical cannabis in 1996, few systems were set up to govern the licensing and opening of new stores. What resulted were bribery schemes that incriminated former elected officials, the mayor, and city employees in Cudahy. Principal Hernandez noted:

> *Remember, school is the center of the community ... because to have services, it has to run through a trusted organization because, you know, our communities have been taken advantage of for a long time. They're very skeptical of the corruption we've had with the government.*

Criminal investigations eventually led to convictions in 2012, but by this time public trust and confidence in local government had been eroded. In many ways the unequal protection provided by the legal and government systems that so many take for granted has been the catalyst for developing psychological resilience and proud interdependence that the community of Cudahy relies on.

As Principal Hernandez said, "we're used to fighting, we're used to struggling, but by all of us coming together, we are one, and you really have to be mentally strong." The community of Cudahy, and EOLC, have only used these injustices to strengthen their resolve and ability to support one another, outside the traditional structures. It is by exploring the community cultural wealth present in Cudahy that we can fully appreciate their response to the evolving needs that presented themselves throughout 2020 and beyond.

Meeting Need with Community Cultural Wealth

Traditional measures of wealth in capitalist theory focus on the accumulation of assets and resources that essentially translate to multi-generational power and security. This building of wealth is essential not only to current wealth holders, but wealth accumulation sets future generations up for success. In other words, financial wealth begets more financial wealth [25]. However, the history of America is less than stellar when it comes to bringing communities of color into the economic fold of wealth creation. As a result, generational wealth gaps continue to widen in America [26]. White Americans hold approximately 86% of the overall wealth in the country, while only accounting for 68% of households. In contrast, Black and Hispanic households hold only 3% of the wealth in the country each, while accounting for 16 and 11% of the U.S. population, respectively [27].

Superintendent Beutner understood that leading LAUSD, with its immense wealth gaps, would require creative solutions for moving resources from the places where they were accumulated to the places where they were needed for greatest effect. He put his efforts toward ensuring that the communities within the LAUSD meta-community were connected and taking care of each other. As he told us when we interviewed him:

> *And one of the things that this crisis reminded us of is we have to meet students where they are. … We brought in Snapchat and Alicia Keys and Russell Westbrook for our high schoolers because we said, well, let's do something around books. And the first question Ms. Keys asks, "What book do you want me to recommend?" I said, no, no, no, no, this is you. They meet you, or whatever the*

> *right phrase is on Snapchat, because it's authentic. It's got to be a book you're reading. ... And then we brought in foundations and philanthropists and individuals, and we made it free, where we brought in the other entertainment. The James Cameron class on the voyage of the Titanic is captivating, and it's real school. There's literacy, math, science. You take it for credit. But we had to find ways to engage students. ... Most of the viewing was a student or a child and a family member. So, again, even in that time of need, we found a way to build a community for that family.*

Beutner clearly understood that within the broader LAUSD community, there were plenty of resources that could be leveraged to support learning and engagement in the time of great need, and he was responsible for supporting those efforts.

While much can and should be done to close these economic gaps that limit opportunity for too many students, stopping here would offer a narrow, deficit-oriented view on "wealth" that might negate many positive attributes and assets that communities of color hold and can leverage to live empowered lives of contribution to society. Even when cultural assets and traditional or folk funds of knowledge [28] have been considered as valuable resources for producing prosperity, they have often been framed from a Eurocentric perspective, usually emblematic of the white, middle-class values and relations [29]. However, when expanding the definition of cultural wealth to explore communities of color, it is clear that they bring many forms of capital that are often not counted in today's economy but serve as valuable resources that promote thriving.

Dr. Tara Yosso, a critical scholar whose work focuses on how education can serve as a tool for liberation, proposes a model of community cultural wealth that demonstrates the array of knowledge, skills, and abilities that communities of color possess and use to operate and survive in today's society in the face of the daily injustices [30]. This framework for understanding wealth is key in identifying the types of resources and assets that members of communities of color, like the residents of Cudahy, bring to bear in lieu of financial wealth. The six forms of capital as outlined by Yosso contribute to the overall wealth of the community and extend beyond the economic measures of income:

- Aspirational capital—supports the maintenance of hopes and dreams for the future, even when faced with barriers, real or perceived.
- Linguistic capital—includes the additional social and intellectual skills people of color gain from experiences in more than one language or dialect.

- Familial capital—stems from the connection to community history, memory, and culture that is gained from individuals who are considered family.
- Social capital—is the emotional or instrumental support accessed through the individual's network of people and community resources.
- Navigational capital—relies on skills to maneuver through social interactions that do not make affordances for the lived experiences of communities of color in mind.
- Resistance capital—the understanding and skills that are developed through opposing inequality.

These various forms of capital are not mutually exclusive, but rather are part of a dynamic process that builds upon itself, as a community grows, adapts, and experiences life in an evolving society. As experienced in Cudahy, each form of cultural capital was present and utilized for the ever-evolving needs that were present in 2020 and beyond.

The Evolving Needs Created by 2020

The long history of resilience and navigating shifting needs of the community had uniquely prepared Cudahy and its residents to weather any storm that came their way in 2020. It was clear through our interviews that community members had built up an immense amount of cultural wealth in response to the challenges that had already come their way. For example, in 1998 when teachers at Park Avenue Elementary school were experiencing a sudden bout of miscarriages and students had terrible asthma, parents and neighbors believed this was related to the toxic environment on which Park Avenue was built. However, it was not until a group of moms who called themselves the "Dynamite Mothers" harnessed their social and resistance capital to make noise that the situation concerned LAUSD. It was their aspirational capital, though, that kept them fighting and believing in a better future for their children, that finally led to the closure of the school in 2001; they continued to fight when the school was reopened in 2004.

When the Delta plane fuel dump happened in 2020, the community quickly jumped into action, using their familial capital to check on people and understand who had been taken to the hospital for medical treatment. They harnessed their resistance and social capital to push for answers and hold people accountable. While no outcome has been determined, local residents leveraged their social and navigational capital to sue for damages caused by the fuel dump. We saw this same concern as Principal Hernandez, who himself arrived to Cudahy as an undocumented immigrant from El Salvador at the age of eleven, rallied the community around its most vulnerable members. From raising funds to help students' families pay for funerals of family members lost to COVID, to coordinating with teachers to get devices to students stranded in Mexico due to visa complications, Principal Hernandez leveraged his social capital to solve each unique problem as it emerged. Through it all, he relied on the trust he had built with over 300 home visits with students' families since becoming the principal at EOLC, telling us, "The key to us is just having that trust, creating those spaces."

So, with the onset of the pandemic, and subsequent economic hardship, particularly for this community full of service and trade workers, Cudahy and its residents were prepared to utilize their various forms of cultural capital wealth to support one another. Navigational capital quickly came into play, as people looked for a place to centralize support and services. Ellen Ochoa Learning Center (EOLC) emerged as a sanctuary, as it always had. Through community partnerships, joint ventures, and inclusive thinking, educators and community leaders in the area banded together and utilized the school building and its resources to support those most in need. Elida Lozano, teacher at EOLC, noted that EOLC was already serving as a hub for the community, and the pandemic only heightened that need. As she best puts it, "Luckily, we [at EOLC] have had the mentality that we are a resource for the community, or part of the community. We open our doors to anyone in our community."

Immediate Needs at the Onset

At the onset of the pandemic, and subsequent job loss for millions of Americans, the level of need in the Cudahy community hit all-time highs. Principal Hernandez knew how important it was at that moment for his team to stand strong. With increasing need for food and support, along with a heightened fear of death and sickness, Principal Hernandez knew that the focus had to be the familial capital of the community saying, "[families] will never let you forget if you let them down now during a pandemic. Forget reading and writing and all the other stuff that we want to cover. We wanted to make sure we were there for them."

Superintendent Beutner, Principal Hernandez, and his team kicked into high gear to provide food. In a community where nearly 40% of the population is undocumented, and an overwhelming majority of the population works in contract work such as construction, they knew it was important to not just think about the students, but also about the entire family. "We understand that we have to serve the entire family, that we have to serve the entire community," said Hernandez. They quickly rolled out a food bank to ensure every student had access to meals. When they realized that some parents and students were unable to travel to the food bank's central location, they also implemented a system where teachers and school administrators would take turns delivering food.

Soon, the food bank became more than a food bank: it became a community center. Families with all sorts of needs knew that while the food hub might not have what they needed, the people there would have the knowledge and wherewithal to point them in the right direction. This social and navigational capital was critical to getting support services to the community quickly. Principal Hernandez described it like this:

> *[Community members] could come, and then of course the food bank grew into other basic needs. We didn't even have masks, if you remember, so through the food bank, they could get masks. They could get supplies. They could get diapers and other basic needs that they had, so I feel like that just helped us to again calm down a little bit. So now, we had a plan for learning, and now we had the basic necessities.*

Along with supplying basic needs, instruction also had to continue. Suddenly, schools and education systems were navigating the challenges of broadband connectivity. Computers and Wi-Fi hotspots were distributed to students. These devices not only supported students, but they also provided families a way to further navigate the intricate social systems created to provide relief funding to so many unemployed. Further, the distribution of the devices provided teachers and educators with another touch point for families, allowing for mental health check-ins and discussions about the importance of virtual learning. Teachers were able to utilize their linguistic and familial capital to engage families from all backgrounds and did a better job providing services than most local governments could do.

Superintendent Beutner reminded us at the end of our interview, "We should be more forceful about the role schools can play in food relief and other things. We should be more forceful about how schools are the proverbial last mile with connecting people who are on the wrong side of the digital divide." As was clear in Cudahy, the school sat at the center of the community, and by tapping into its immeasurable amount of cultural wealth, the residents of Cudahy and students of EOLC were better off.

Responding to the Changing Needs and Concerns

As the pandemic wore on, stimulus checks and other emergency relief funding were pumped into the national economy. While this arguably helped fight off, or at least shorten, the economic fallout from the pandemic, not all communities were affected in the same way. In communities like Cudahy, with its large population of undocumented immigrant families, access to emergency funds to offset financial hardship was not easily achieved [31]. At the same time, students and their families were wrestling with how to make the most of remote learning. At first, teachers were frantically printing out packets of materials for students. But as mobile hotspots and devices were distributed, teachers were able to leverage their shared culture to connect authentically with students. However, many of the necessary academic resources for students were still not available.

Ms. Lozano recalled that as a dual language teacher, she always had problems accessing quality Spanish materials. With the pandemic that became even more difficult, as most digital resources were in English. Ms. Lozano and her fellow teachers utilized their linguistic and familial capital to go online and converse with teachers in Mexico to obtain Spanish materials for students. Time and time again, we heard similar stories of teachers and administrators going above and beyond, not only for their students, but their communities as a whole. This is in large part thanks to the community connectedness that teachers and administrators had cultivated. Without leveraging the community's cultural wealth, amid economic inequity, teachers would not have been able to so effectively support their students.

As the pandemic progressed, new challenges continued to present themselves. The racial conversations that were brewing across the nation reverberated loudly in Los Angeles, especially in Cudahy, with its rich history of social activism. At first, teachers were hesitant to speak about race in class, especially now in a virtual capacity where anyone could be listening. Ms. Lozano mentioned that teachers were aware of the "social contract of school and education, and the role [teachers] play in that, so those [conversations] were hard to have." Principal Hernandez, quickly acknowledging the nervousness, leveraged his navigational and social capital to provide his teachers "different models or different tools and different opportunities so that we could have these [race] conversations because we're sometimes scared to have them." With their principal's support, teachers were empowered to have conversations about race and equity in their classrooms. During our conversation, Ms. Lozano recognized the teachers who were able to provide culturally responsive teaching, leveraging their cultural and familial capital to engage in tough, but needed, conversations. They served as role models for their colleagues as much as their students in navigating the nuanced landscape of classroom discourse on race and ethnicity.

In sum, the need seen in Los Angeles, Cudahy, and Elon Ochoa Learning Center was constantly evolving throughout the pandemic and 2020. A community that by many standards would be considered economically disadvantaged, showed that there is so much more to wealth than just income. Community cultural wealth was a driver of this tight-knit population, even before the onset of the pandemic, but the magnitude of need that emerged at the intersection of virus spread, economic recession, and racial upheaval required the community to assemble and deploy all its assets in a truly unprecedented manner in 2020. The issues in Cudahy have not magically melted away as we emerged from the pandemic, but it remains a community with a rich history of resilience that is prepared to take on the challenges that lie ahead.

Lessons Learned from the LAUSD and Cudahy

Along with opportunities for economic and social advancement, capitalist societies can also create incredible levels of economic inequality. It is the responsibility of the government, and of the people, to counteract these challenges of economic inequality with humanizing policies and ethical decision-making. We use economic models and data to inform policy decisions; but those data cannot paint the full picture of how economic shocks affect people and their communities. As the central hubs of communities, public schools can serve as important connection points between community members and community assets. While we discussed social and psychological assets to support a community through trauma in the Bronx, and informational and democratic resources to support choices for safe in-person schooling in Lubbock, we saw cultural assets coming together in the school community in Cudahy. The interaction between the community cultural wealth the residents could rally to support each other was also enhanced by the economic power of LAUSD, which was also able to call on industry partners in wealthier parts of the massive district to direct additional opportunities to Cudahy.

The economic recession of 2020 pushed Americans across the nation, including those in L.A. County, to the brink, especially during the period of intense lockdowns when industries experienced significant job losses. While economic capital was sparse, the challenges of the economic recession provided an opportunity for cultural and social capital to take center stage. Those communities that utilized these other forms of capital were able to better support students, families, and their communities, and this was apparent in Cudahy. The lessons drawn from their work offer us a way to reshape and reimagine how we understand educational institutions and their relationship with the communities that surround them.

Consider All Forms of Wealth

As we see in Cudahy, the economic numbers do not paint the complete picture of the vast cultural assets present in a community. Educational systems have viewed students in economically disadvantaged communities from a deficit perspective for far too long, ignoring the richer and more complex understanding of the world that these students develop when they navigate different cultures at home and at school. Drawing on additional perspectives, traditions, and shared experiences, the students and families in communities like Cudahy can approach learning in multiple, flexible ways, if provided with dignity-affirming spaces in which to learn [32]. By framing their work from an asset mindset, the educators of Cudahy were able to capitalize on the cultural wealth present, focusing not on the baggage that students brought with them, rather on the experiences that formed them. Neighbors helped neighbors by creating food banks. Teachers held tutoring sessions for parents about using Zoom. When policy conversations around education devolve to focusing solely on funding, we neglect the other forms of wealth and capital that exist in each and every one of our neighborhoods. Turning this cultural capital into realized wealth is critical as we reimagine education. This does not mean that we should not resource schools in ways that will support thriving and success, especially after the pandemic. Instead, we must invest to create more wealth of all forms. As Ms. Lozano said,

What every school is going to need? You're going to need to have specialists there to help deal with the trauma that was created by these pandemics. You know, social unrest, especially if you're working in a community where it's directly impacted. Where they're actually hearing the noise going on outside, then the unrest happening. It does affect the students and so we need more of those social workers in our classrooms to help the students and then also the teachers.

Share Responsibility for Educating All

The unique structures of Los Angeles' city and school system create the juxtaposition between Cudahy and its neighbors, as discussed earlier in this chapter. While the smaller communities can operate with enough independence to serve the unique needs of the student populations they serve, being a part of a large, wealthy school district also creates economies of scale and opportunities to drive investment from wealthier parts of the district to the parts that need it more. Superintendent Beutner eloquently defines the problem saying,

> *Public education in Los Angeles historically was the haves and the have nots. So, most of the have nots are in public schools in Los Angeles. Most of the haves, the Hollywoods, the Silicon Valley, the Stanfords, the UCLAs, they're on the other side. And they haven't historically been as engaged in public education.*

Within the problem, he also found the solution. The wealthy residents of L.A. County have built their fortunes in industries that rely on a workforce that likely learned how to read, write, add, and subtract in a public school in LAUSD. The safety and stability of their neighborhoods depend on the health and prosperity of the communities around them. They are all in it together, so they need to help each other along. Superintendent Beutner reminded us:

> *And I took this (pandemic) as an opportunity to drag them in. And most answered the call to serve. ... Los Angeles can be an archetype; we have to bring the whole community back into public education. Because whether or not you have a child in your neighborhood school, you have a stake in what's happening in that school because that's the future of your community. Whether you know that or not, whether you liked it or not, that is the future of Los Angeles.*

Our shared responsibility for the future of education should not only be a concern for Los Angeles County. Equitable schools with robust community support are important for the rest of America as well. If the pandemic years taught us anything, it is that viruses do not care about borders, our economic fates are ultimately connected to each other, and social unrest travels at the speed of the internet.

Invest in Homegrown Talent

One of the reasons that community engagement was so successful was Principal Hernandez's history in the community. As he stated, his homegrown roots allowed him to cut through the noise. Educational research consistently shows that students, especially students of color, experience greater academic growth when they learn from teachers who share their racial and ethnic background and can relate to their lived experience [33]. One way to support this type of teacher-student match is investing in Grow Your Own (GYO) programs that recruit and train future educators from within the school district. Unfortunately, this can be very challenging in districts where high housing costs drive teachers further and further from the schools where they teach. Across the nation, educators struggle to live and work in the communities that they serve [34]. Whether it's the need to leave for postsecondary education, salary challenges, a lack of affordable housing, or numerous other reasons that people choose not to teach in their home communities, the connection to the school community, history, and culture is slowly diminished.

Teachers who come from the communities they serve have lived experiences that allow them to understand their students' needs, as well as how to use the various available forms of community cultural wealth to fulfill those needs. They also have the trust of the community, based on their shared experiences, and try new things when they see the need. Ms. Lozano was happy to have her students back in her classroom when school reopened for in-person instruction, and she was able to recognize how the time in lockdown impacted her students. She was also able to use her deep understanding of them to adapt to new needs:

> *Although school conditions are not ideal at the moment, our students are, without a doubt, the happiest to be back. We can see their smiles in their eyes because they're wearing masks, and that brings us such joy. My six- and seven-year-old first graders tell me at the end of the day that they don't want to go home because they love school and being with their friends. It is evident that schools continue*

to be safe havens for many of our students. As teachers, we feel the pressure of mandates from the district as they continue to push professional development in math, reading, and science down our throats, but I will not apologize for slowing down and even stopping my teaching to provide a moment of SEL [Social Emotional Learning] through meditation, yoga, role play, and the arts, when I see that my students have that need.

Intentional investments by Cudahy helped support homegrown talents that truly understood the cultural context and history of the neighborhood. Both from a state and local level, policymakers should continue to explore ways to incentivize educators to give back to the community that shaped who they are. Along with the different forms of community cultural wealth that supported the students at EOLC, the amazing educators who cared so deeply about their community were clearly an incredible asset that sustained learning in a time of great need.

Reflect and Discuss
Use the following questions as a starting point for your personal reflection and for discussion with education stakeholders in your community.

1. How did the history of economic inequity in L.A. affect the way students, educators, and the community experienced the economic recession?
2. What aspects of your local context influence the response of area schools in times of financial hardship?
3. How do education leaders leverage community cultural wealth to meet the needs of their students? How does this look in your local context?
4. How did role of schools in supporting students and their families overcome financial hardships evolve over the course of 2020 and beyond?
5. What lessons on the role of cultural capital in community thriving can you bring to the schools in your area? How can culturally competent educators support your efforts?

REFERENCES

1. U.S. Bureau of Labor Statistics. (2022). Labor Force Statistics from the Current Population Survey. *U.S. Bureau of Labor Statistics.* Retrieved April 15, 2023, from https://www.bls.gov/cps/effects-of-the-coronavirus-covid-19-pandemic.html
2. Sedgwick, S. M., Girard, A., Ramsey, J., Larson, J., Lori, S., & Laferriere, T. (2020, December). *Pathways for economic resiliency: Los Angeles County 2021–2026.* Los Angeles County Economic Development Corporation: Institute for Applied Economics. Retrieved April 15, 2023, from https://wdacs.lacounty.gov/wp-content/uploads/2021/02/Pathways-for-Economic-Resiliency-Condensed-Report-FINAL.pdf?utm_content=&utm_medium=email&utm_name=&utm_source=govdelivery&utm_term=
3. State of California, Department of Finance. (2022, May). *E-1 Population estimates for cities, counties and the state with annual% change—January 1, 2021 and 2022.* Retrieved April 15, 2023, from https://dof.ca.gov/Forecasting/Demographics/Documents/E-1_2022PressRelease.pdf
4. Los Angeles Almanac. (2023). *History timeline, Los Angeles County, 1848 to 1865.* Los Angeles Almanac. Retrieved April 15, 2023, from http://www.laalmanac.com/history/hi01c.php
5. Discover Los Angeles. (2022, December 31). *Historical timeline of Los Angeles.* Los Angeles Tourism & Convention Board. Retrieved April 15, 2023, from https://www.discoverlosangeles.com/things-to-do/historical-timeline-of-los-angeles
6. U.S. Census Bureau. (2022). *QuickFacts Los Angeles, California.* U.S. Census Bureau. Retrieved April 15, 2023, from https://www.census.gov/quickfacts/losangelescountycalifornia
7. Los Angeles Times. (2023). *LA median income for its 272 neighborhoods.* Los Angeles Times. Retrieved April 15, 2023, from https://maps.latimes.com/neighborhoods/income/median/neighborhood/list/index.html
8. Data USA. (2020). *Data USA: Cudahy, CA.* Data USA. Retrieved April 15, 2023, from https://datausa.io/profile/geo/cudahy-ca/#:~:text=The%20largest%20industries%20in%20Cudahy,%2C%20and%20Information%20(%2438%2C475)
9. U.S. Census Bureau. (2022). *QuickFacts Cudahy City, California.* U.S. Census Bureau. Retrieved April 15, 2023, from https://www.census.gov/quickfacts/cudahycitycalifornia
10. City of Cudahy. (2023). *About the city.* Cudahy City Hall. Retrieved April 15, 2023, from https://www.cityofcudahy.com/201/About-the-City#:~:text=Named%20for%20its%20founder%2C%20meat,part%20of%20a%20large%20metropolis

11. Hise, G. (2009). Industry, political alliances and the regulation of urban space in Los Angeles. *Urban History, 36*(3), 473–497.
12. Schneider, J. (2008). Escape from Los Angeles: White flight from Los Angeles and its schools, 1960–1980. *Journal of Urban History, 34*(6), 995–1012.
13. Edgerton, J. D., & Roberts, L. W. (2014). Cultural capital or habitus? Bourdieu and beyond in the explanation of enduring educational inequality. *Theory and Research in Education, 12*(2), 193–220. https://doi.org/10.1177/1477878514530231
14. Tichavakunda, A. A. (2019). An overdue theoretical discourse: Pierre Bourdieu's theory of practice and critical race theory in education. *Educational Studies, 55*(6), 651–666.
15. Los Angeles Unified. (2022). *Fingertip facts 2021–2022*. Retrieved April 15, 2023, from https://achieve.lausd.net/cms/lib/CA01000043/Centricity/Domain/280/Fingertip_Facts_2021_2022.pdf
16. US News and World Report. (2019). Los Angeles Unified School District. *US News and World Report*. Retrieved April 15, 2023, from https://www.usnews.com/education/k12/california/districts/los-angeles-unified-106440
17. Williford, S. (2011, November 2). Austin Beutner speaks softly and plans to carry a big city. *Our Weekly Los Angeles.*. https://ourweekly.com/news/2011/11/03/austin-beutner-speaks-softly-and-plans-to-carry-a/.
18. Kahn, G. (2011, May 1). The unpolitician. *Los Angeles Magazine*. https://www.lamag.com/article/the-unpolitician/.
19. Blume, H. (2019, April 9). L.A. schools chief Austin Beutner says no major restructuring is in the works. *Los Angeles Times*. https://www.latimes.com/local/lanow/la-me-edu-beutner-details-lausd-reorg-plan-20190409-story.html
20. US News and World Report. (2021). Ellen Ochoa learning center. *US News and World Report*. Retrieved April 15, 2023, from https://www.usnews.com/education/k12/california/ellen-ochoa-learning-center-232062#:~:text=Overview%20of%20Ellen%20Ochoa%20Learning%20Center&text=The%20school's%20minority%20student%20enrollment,enrolls%2095%25%20economically%20disadvantaged%20students
21. Homefacts. (2022). *Cudahy, CA unemployment rate report*. Homefacts.com. Retrieved April 15, 2023, from https://www.homefacts.com/unemployment/California/Los-Angeles-County/Cudahy.html
22. Cook, T. (2020, December 17). A toxic mess in Cudahy. *Los Angeles Education Examiner*. Retrieved April 15, 2023, from https://la-edex.org/a-toxic-mess-in-cudahy/
23. Barboza, T., Poston B. (2017, August 6). What we know about California's largest toxic cleanup: Thousands of L.A. County homes tainted with lead. *Los Angeles Times*. https://www.latimes.com/local/california/la-me-ln-exide-what-we-know-20170806-htmlstory.html

24. Behringer, A. (2021, October 28). LA's toxic secret. *KCRW*. https://www.kcrw.com/culture/shows/bodies/toxic-contaminated-schools-community-remediation/las-toxic-secret-full-transcript
25. Bourdieu, P. (2011). The forms of capital (1986). *Cultural Theory: An Anthology, 1*(81–93), 949.
26. Toft, M., & Friedman, S. (2021). Family wealth and the class ceiling: The propulsive power of the bank of mum and dad. *Sociology, 55*(1), 90–109.
27. Aladangady, A., & Forde, A. (2021, October 22) *Wealth inequality and the racial wealth gap*. Board of Governors of the Federal Reserve System. Retrieved April 15, 2023.
28. González, N., Moll, L. C., & Amanti, C. (Eds.). (2006). *Funds of knowledge: Theorizing practices in households, communities, and classrooms*. Routledge.
29. Oliver, M. L., & Shapiro, T. M. (1995). *Black wealth/white wealth: A new perspective on racial inequality*. Routledge.
30. Yosso, T. J. (2005). Whose culture has capital? A critical race theory discussion of community cultural wealth. *Race Ethnicity and Education, 8*(1), 69–91.
31. Mengesha, Z., Alloun, E., Weber, D., Smith, M., & Harris, P. (2022). "Lived the pandemic twice": A scoping review of the unequal impact of the COVID-19 pandemic on asylum seekers and undocumented migrants. *International Journal of Environmental Research and Public Health, 19*(11), 6624.
32. Moll, L., Amanti, C., Neff, D., & Gonzalez, N. (2006). Funds of knowledge for teaching: Using a qualitative approach to connect homes and classrooms. In *Funds of knowledge* (pp. 71–87). Routledge.
33. Redding, C. (2019). A teacher like me: A review of the effect of student–teacher racial/ethnic matching on teacher perceptions of students and student academic and behavioral outcomes. *Review of Educational Research, 89*(4), 499–535.
34. Perry, A. (2019, June 20). Too many teachers can't afford to live near their schools. *Brookings*. https://www.brookings.edu/blog/the-avenue/2019/06/20/too-many-teachers-cant-afford-to-live-near-their-schools/

CHAPTER 6

Education in a Time of Change: A Story of Justice

> *My goal is to create conditions for success for all our students and staff.*
> *And whatever we accomplish will outlive my tenure and anyone else's.*
> *And it will be the foundation of what is right in public education.*
> —Ed Graff, Superintendent, Minneapolis Public Schools

At a time of seismic shifts in human experience, when the global population underwent dramatic changes in so many aspects of daily life, perhaps the largest cultural inflection point was brought on by the murder of George Floyd, a 46-year-old African American man, in front of the Cup Foods grocery store at the intersection of East 38th Street and Chicago Avenue in Minneapolis, Minnesota. This tragic event was caught on cell phone cameras and made public for the world to see. For months to come, the horrific scene of his tragic and unnecessary death would play out on newscasts and social media over and over again, enraging people with its brutal injustice. The videos illuminated issues of race and police violence, sparking protests around the United States and across the world. But as the people of Minneapolis will tell you, this was nowhere near the first time something like this happened in their community, it was just the first time it was caught on camera.

Today, Minneapolis remains one of the most racially segregated cities in the United States [1]. Inequality has been exacerbated by systemic

© The Author(s), under exclusive license to Springer Nature Switzerland AG 2023
F. M. Jamil, J. E. Siddiqi, *Public Education in Turbulent Times*,
https://doi.org/10.1007/978-3-031-43237-8_6

discrimination and structural barriers, including policies and practices that have perpetuated racial and economic disparities over time. The renewed focus on racial injustice came at a time when communities in Minneapolis were already struggling with the COVID-19 pandemic and subsequent economic fallout. As community members coped with the various issues of 2020, a clear voice of justice permeated every decision. The educators and leaders in the Minneapolis Public Schools (MPS) and Patrick Henry High School (PHHS) stayed steadfast in their mission to serve all students and meet everyone's specific needs. Through our interviews, it quickly became clear that educators across the city were already aware of the structural inequities in their community, and they were doing the tireless work of creating a more equitable and just society through their education systems. It was only now in focus because of the tragic events the world had borne witness to in 2020.

The story of MPS and PHHS is one that not only shows a community's desire to support one another through the COVID-19 pandemic, but the story of a school system that has been making brave, intentional choices to address the root causes of its inequities. By committing to address the structural causes of educational inequities and holding every member of the educational workforce accountable for the success of its efforts, MPS seeks justice, equity, and opportunity for this generation of students and many generations to come. By investing in the future, creating accountability, and empowering schools to empower students, MPS provides an example of how to navigate tough conversations and keep all eyes focused on equity.

The District Context of Minneapolis

Minnesota, known as "The Land of 10,000 Lakes," is home to the source of the Mississippi River. Situated in the southern half of the state and along the western banks of the upper Mississippi River stands the "City of Lakes," also known as Minneapolis. The "Twin Cities" of Minneapolis and St. Paul are the population hubs of the state, with St. Paul also serving as the State Capital. While the two cities have an interconnected metro area, they each have their own distinct history and character. European settlers first arrived in St. Paul, on the eastern side of the Mississippi river, but Minneapolis eventually grew into the larger city, driven by its thriving mining industry. The cities grew into each other through urban sprawl, resulting in today's moniker of the "Twin Cities [2]."

The Dakota Sioux were the sole occupants of the land of present-day Minneapolis until French exploration in the region began in the late 1600s. Soon European settlers began to arrive in the area, as the population of the 13 colonies continued to grow and expand westward. The end of the Revolutionary War and treaties with the British granted the United States government all British-controlled territory east of the Mississippi river. This treaty put the "lands" of a young American country at the edge of the Dakota Sioux territory [3]. The philosophy of American Manifest Destiny, which was the belief that white settlers were divinely ordained to settle the North American continent, and the Louisiana Purchase of 1803 drove more American expansion and settlement in the area. The building of Fort Snelling by the U.S. Army on the south side of present-day Minneapolis further incentivized American advancement [4]. The presence of the military created a sense of security for settlers, bringing traders, fur trappers, and merchants to the area. It also served as a reminder to the Dakota Sioux of settler colonialism and the US policy of assimilating native peoples into European-American society.

As America charged ahead into the Industrial Age, Minneapolis became a powerhouse for lumber and flour milling [5]. The region's many waterways were useful for transporting logs and other goods via boat. Development of the railroads only further positioned Minneapolis as a jumping off point to the West for American settlers. This continual expansion led to clashes with the Dakota Sioux. The U.S. government signed numerous treaties that often limited the right of the Dakota people to hunt and live on certain parts of the land. In exchange, the Dakota people would keep a part of their homeland and the U.S. government would provide goods and yearly payments [6].

In the following decades, these treaties were very seldom honored, and the Dakota people faced many hardships. When the U.S. government faced a budget crisis during the Civil War, payments for Native treaties across the nation were ignored. In 1862, a group of Dakota Sioux declared war on this injustice and killed several settlers. Americans in power swiftly responded, arresting and expelling the Dakota people from the area. In total, nearly 400 Dakota men were tried for murder, and robbery, and 83 ultimately sentenced to death and hanged. To this day, it is still known as the largest mass execution in America, and one of the most violent ethnic conflicts in the history of the country [7]. The trial also provided an opportunity for white settlers to stake claim to Dakota land once and for all. As the Dakota were being expelled because of the war and trial, white settlers quickly began to lay claim to the lands. Minneapolis was officially incorporated as a city in 1867. Over the next century and a half, Minneapolis continued to grow as a lumber and grain milling hub.

Today, Minneapolis is a diverse city with a population of approximately 430,000 people [8]. While approximately 60% of the residents are white, the city has a significant population of people of color, with approximately 18.4% of residents identifying as Black, 1.3% as Native American, 5.7% as Asian, 6.9% as multiracial, and 9.8% as Hispanic/Latino. The largest ethnic groups in the city are African Americans, followed by Hispanic/Latino, Hmong, and Somali. These different cultures and ethnicities make Minneapolis a vibrant and diverse community, but also one with stark contrasts in access and opportunity.

In terms of economics, Minneapolis is, on one hand, a city with a thriving economy and a relatively low unemployment rate and a median household income of $70,000 [9]. However, there are significant disparities in income and wealth, with many communities of color experiencing poverty and economic insecurity. Minneapolis also has a long history of racial tension and segregation, with many communities facing systemic discrimination and barriers to economic and social opportunities. The poverty rate for Black and Native American residents in Minneapolis is nearly three times higher than that of white residents, and Hispanic residents face nearly twice the poverty rate of their white peers [10]. Further, there are significant disparities in access to affordable housing and other resources needed for residents to lead safe and stable lives conducive to thriving and future prosperity.

Minneapolis has also been grappling with very public issues of racial justice and equity, particularly in the wake of the murder of George Floyd by Minneapolis police officers in 2020. However, racial inequities have been present throughout the city's history. Minneapolis was not a particularly segregated city when the first racial covenants restricting residents of color from living in certain parts of the city were passed in the early 1900s. But the city became highly segregated as it developed. As with so many other cities in the United States, newly arriving, non-white residents settled in a small number of racially and ethnically homogeneous neighborhoods and enclaves—sometimes by choice, but more often, because they had no alternative [11]. Even when civil rights legislation was passed in the 1960s, introducing equal housing protections, Minneapolis remained a deeply divided city as segregationists found other ways to ensure the city was still divided. During the 1980s and 1990s, Minneapolis saw an influx of immigrants and refugees from Southeast Asia, Somalia, and other parts of the world [12]. While these communities brought new energy and diversity to the city, they also faced significant challenges, including discrimination, poverty, and inadequate access to education and other resources [13].

Minneapolis Public Schools (MPS) is the largest school district in Minnesota, serving over 35,000 students from diverse backgrounds. Approximately 41% identify as white, 34% as Black, 5% as Native American, 5% as multiracial, 5% as Asian, and 14% as Hispanic or Latino, making the student population incredibly diverse [14]. Over 20% of students are English language learners, and 20% of families live below the poverty line [15]. The 96 schools that make up MPS employ over 2100 teachers and another 2280 full-time staff. The district has a long history of grappling with issues of racial justice, dating back to the early twentieth century when it was a segregated school system.

In 1954, the landmark *Brown v. Board of Education* decision declared segregation in public schools unconstitutional, leading to efforts to desegregate schools in Minneapolis and across the country. These efforts had little impact on structural challenges, and decades of segregation in Minneapolis continued. In the 1960s and 1970s, MPS began to implement busing programs and other desegregation efforts aimed at achieving more racial balance in schools. In 1970, the State of Minnesota required that no school could have more than 30% enrollment of students of color, which prompted dozens of schools to enroll white students at rapid rates, while others quickly enrolled underrepresented students. In 1971, the National Association for the Advancement of Colored People (NAACP) brought a class action lawsuit against the district on behalf of three students. The plaintiffs in *Booker v. Special School District No. 1, Minneapolis, Minnesota*, asserted that MPS was knowingly engaging in structural policies that were keeping schools segregated: assigning schools based on home address, employing less experienced teachers in schools with more students of color, and inequitably maintaining school buildings. As a result of this case, MPS created a new desegregation plan that prioritized the elimination of racially isolated schools, and the replacement of obsolete school buildings [16]. However, many white families, particularly in the northern part of Minneapolis, strongly opposed the new plans. The result was a protracted battle over school desegregation that lasted for decades, ultimately resulting in a federal court order mandating busing and other measures to achieve greater racial balance in the district, which was maintained through semi-annual reports to the court until the district was deemed to have reached compliance with the law at the end of 1981 [17].

Despite reaching compliance with the court order from the *Booker* case, MPS continued to struggle with issues of racial justice in the decades that followed. In the 1990s and early 2000s, the district experienced rapid demographic changes, with an influx of students from immigrant and refugee communities, quickly resegregating schools absent consistent oversights. A new generation of students faced challenges, including language barriers, poverty, and discrimination, leading to persistent educational disparities. A second civil rights case, *Minneapolis Branch of NAACP* et al. *v. State of Minnesota* et al. brought directly against the state in 1995, resulted in five years of debates and negotiations, but eventually led to Minneapolis Schools instituting a new plan for educational equity. Guided by the idea that learning in contexts with high concentrations of poverty leads to lower academic outcomes, the new plan gave students of color access to increased suburban transfers, access to new magnet schools, and options for school choice that could potentially have brought them out of under-resourced and underperforming schools, and into public schools in more economically advantaged communities. As with so many other efforts by the district over the years, the results were mixed [18].

In recent years, MPS has taken steps to address these challenges and promote racial justice within the district. This has included initiatives aimed at improving academic outcomes for students of color, promoting equity in school discipline, and increasing diversity among district staff and leadership. Increasingly the district has focused on leaving students in their communities to learn but moving the school zoning boundaries to place students from different racial and economic groups into the same schools. However, the district continues to face significant challenges, including persistent disparities in academic outcomes, high levels of student mobility, and ongoing racial tensions within the community. As Minneapolis continues to grapple with issues of racial justice and equity, the future of MPS will remain a critical part of the conversation.

Understanding the District Structure

The structure of leadership within Minneapolis Public Schools (MPS) consists of a Superintendent who serves as the chief executive officer of the district, overseeing all aspects of the district's operations. The

Superintendent is appointed by the Minneapolis Board of Education, which is made up of nine members who are elected by the public to four-year terms [19]. During 2020, Ed Graff was serving as superintendent. Graff came to MPS from his superintendent role with Anchorage, Alaska School District. He earned his Bachelor's Degree in Elementary Education from the University of Alaska and his Master's Degree in Education Administration from the University of Southern Mississippi [20]. Unlike other Superintendents we spoke with, who had arrived to their position by way of leadership experiences in industry or the military, Graff was a teacher first, and a district leader second—his experience in the classroom clearly informed his leadership perspective and his approach to the job:

> *I have an educational background and a passion for public education, and giving our students the opportunities for success, both academically and socially. In Minneapolis Public Schools, I saw it as an opportunity to take what skills I felt I had as an educator and align them to what I felt was needed for the district.*

Throughout our conversations, it was clear that Superintendent Graff was dedicated to doing what was best for all students and strived to meet each student's individual needs. His interview illuminated how the contentious racial history permeates every facet of life in Minneapolis, but that with the proper structures in place, MPS could strive toward a better future. As Graff noted, "What we're trying to develop here are structures and supports and conditions for success that will outlast any fad, any trend, any shift in leadership—because they are foundational."

Superintendent Graff's leadership team was responsible for overseeing many of the day-to-day operations of the district, including curriculum development, student support services, human resources, finance, and facilities management. In particular, the Office of Accountability, Research, and Equity was instrumental in providing guidance and leadership through all aspects of 2020—from ensuring that the education during lockdown not only maintained its robust quality, but that in a time when equity issues were exacerbated across the country, all decisions at MPS continued to be guided by the district's commitment to equity. Explaining how the leadership team approached their work after pandemic lockdowns and the murder of George Floyd, one member of the leadership team commented:

> *We show up more human. We talk about our feelings more. We share our passion more. The whole model of how you're supposed to lead is different. And so, I*

think that's a positive change. When people are harmed or hurt, they're expressing that now. And I think it creates more authentic, honest dialogue.

This mindset not only supported students, but more than 4000 teachers and staff in almost 100 schools that were the backbone of MPS as it navigated the pandemic.

One of those schools within the MPS family is Patrick Henry High School (PHHS). PHHS is one of the largest and oldest high schools in MPS, founded in 1926. It was named after the Founding Father and first governor of Virginia, Patrick Henry, the famous American patriot best known for his "Give me liberty or give me death" speech. PHHS is in the northwestern part of Minneapolis, in the Hawthorne neighborhood. The school has a diverse student population, with approximately 49% of students identifying as Black, 31% as Asian or Pacific Islander, 14% as Hispanic, and 7% as white. The school also has a significant population of students from low-income households, with nearly 70% of students eligible for free or reduced-price lunch. The school has played an important role in the education of thousands of students from diverse backgrounds, and its commitment to racial equity was highlighted publicly in a recent decision to change the school's name to one that better represented its student population. Because Patrick Henry, like many Founding Fathers, was a slave owner, the school has made multiple attempts for a name change, a decision that was finally approved in August 2022 [21].

Leading up to the pandemic, Patrick Henry High School had faced significant challenges, including declining enrollment and persistent academic outcome gaps between different groups of students. However, the school had also made significant progress in addressing these challenges, with initiatives aimed at improving outcomes for all students, promoting equity and inclusion, and increasing community engagement. In particular, Principal Yusuf Abdullah took over the helm in August 2015 and provided a mission of a school focused on an unwavering pursuit of liberation for scholars, educators, families, and the broader Minneapolis community [22]. Principal Abdullah made it clear he knew that true justice and equity would only come from a new approach to how the work was done. "You miss 100% of the shots you don't take," he said as we asked about the way he approaches innovation and new ideas. He sought to empower his teachers and students and emphasized the need for accountability measures to truly assess the effectiveness of their work.

One of the teachers Principal Abdullah recognized for being a leader during the trying times of 2020 was Nafeesah Muhammad. Ms. Muhammad began her teaching career in a neighboring Minneapolis High School before beginning her tenure at PHHS in August 2019 as a Project Based Learning/English Language Arts teacher. In just a few short months, Ms. Muhammad and her colleagues would experience the same tripartite challenges that her colleagues across the nation were facing. Soon she realized it was her responsibility to step up as a leader for her fellow teachers and students, and her community at large, and she stressed how this experience had built her confidence in her skills and purpose, sharing:

> *Having to step up as a leader and model online learning engagement, what that could look like—centering joy in identity in my classes—now there's just a big conversation around it ... It really affirmed my assets as a professional, and as intellectual, and as an activist and youth advocate.*

Like other leaders in MPS and PHHS, Ms. Muhammad faced the challenges of 2020 head-on and sought to build a more just society. Her students would not just survive the setbacks of that traumatic year. She set out to ensure they came out of it with stronger voices.

THE EVOLVING EXPERIENCE OF STRUCTURAL INEQUALITIES

Minneapolis, like many cities in the United States, has a long history of racial and economic inequities. As described earlier in the chapter, these inequities are deeply rooted in the city's history, dating back to the nineteenth century when Minneapolis was a booming industrial center, and even earlier to colonization and its legacy of stolen lands. During the era of industrialization, the city's economy was built on the exploitation of workers, many of whom were immigrants and people of color. Despite changes to educational, workforce, and housing policies, however, the city has struggled to address the persistent racial and economic disparities that continue to affect many of its residents.

When the COVID-19 pandemic hit in March of 2020, those systemic injustices were only further illuminated. Asian women, Native American women, and Black women were disproportionately employed in high-risk essential health care, retail, and service jobs in Minnesota. At the same time, layoffs related to the pandemic disproportionately affected Black and Native American residents [23]. This created a compounding effect on underrepresented communities in Minneapolis, as they were the most likely to be exposed to the virus and its horrible health effects while at the same time being the most vulnerable to the economic uncertainty that emerged [24].

Just as most districts had to do, MPS and PHHS quickly began to distribute food and devices for students to do distance learning, but as Superintendent Graff pointed out, roughly 80% of Black and American Indian students needed devices, and many of their communities lacked access to stable internet. Understanding this, Graff and his team did home visits to specific neighborhoods to learn of specific needs and provide services to high-need communities. Teachers quickly converted their lesson plans to virtual lessons. PHHS hosted Google classroom training for teachers, and MPS set up food distribution centers across the city. When parents voiced concerns about making it to distribution centers every day, Graff's attitude of "showing up more human" came through—the district was responsive and began packing meals in sets of five so that families would only have to make the trip once a week. Graff explained the importance of this approach:

> *[We focus on] continuous improvement and conditions for success. The more we are in tune with our students, our staff, our leaders, and our community, the better sense we have of what those needs are, and we can respond and create those conditions for success.*

Leaders at MPS and PHHS also stressed the importance of clear communication with parents and students, as well as with each other. Principal Abdullah echoed the importance of communication, and that once these systems of communication were in place, they started to "see the strength of [their] school." Of course, this communication was most important because it allowed the district to keep improving how educators at MPS served their students.

Just as MPS and its educators were getting systems and policies in place to support students' immediate needs, the Minneapolis community and the world at large were shaken to its core on May 25, 2020, when 46-year old George Floyd was murdered by police in the streets of Minneapolis. A convenience store clerk alleged that Floyd had just used a counterfeit $20 bill, leading to Officer Derek Chauvin kneeling on Floyd's neck for over nine minutes. The following day, videos of the incident became public, inciting outrage and cries for justice. Here is how Superintendent Graff described his complex web of emotions and thoughts.

> *There are definitely competing emotions and competing thoughts. I think to start with, just the raw emotion of murder. Seeing the way that it was presented through the video captured by a young woman, a former student in our district. And just the pain and sadness of that. The humanity. The loss of a life ... And then shifting from that to saying, what does this mean for us? Where do we go?*

At this moment the students, teachers, and community were hurting and grieving, but Superintendent Graff also understood the important role educators had in being that stronghold for students. He knew that for his teachers to support students, they must be supported as well.

> *When [the murder of George Floyd] took place, we really had to go back to being grounded in supporting our leaders and how they were going to show up to support the staff and how they were going to support the students. So really making sure that we had the adult well-being and social emotional supports in place to help address those needs that our students and families, and many of my colleagues, were having from what occurred there.*

Teachers provided spaces for students to grieve and process what was happening. "We created healing circles," said Principal Abdullah. "We're all virtual so we created spaces virtually, and it was to pop in and connect with us."

In subsequent days, protests began to grow, first in Minneapolis, then nationally, to protest the historic racism and police brutality that plagues America. While most protests were peaceful, demonstrations in some cities, including Minneapolis, devolved into looting, and rioting that was met with police in riot gear. By June 3, 2020, more than 200 cities in the U.S. had imposed curfews. As the protests continued, most were peaceful, but became more violent after curfew. In total, more than 1500 businesses were damaged during the protest in the Minneapolis-Saint Paul area. The vast difference in political rhetoric and intense emotions that came with the murder of George Floyd and the subsequent protests created a unique dynamic to navigate in the classroom. But the strong support from district and building level leaders provided teachers with the courage to be vulnerable and compassionate as they approached their students in such an emotionally complex time. As Ms. Muhammad described it:

> *How can I protect them and mitigate the harm as much as possible, and at the same time, give them space and room to be vulnerable. I think it's a balancing act, and I think it comes with ... clear communication and the opportunity to be able to pivot based upon where your kids are ... They deserve something, they deserve to know that there's a teacher who had enough forethought to recognize the real life experience in their humanity and provide them with something to deal with that.*

Nonetheless, the leaders and educators at MPS and PHHS seized the moment and embraced the hard conversations.

In closing his interview, Principal Abdullah stressed how proud he was of his students and the way they have matured and embraced the desire to create a more just society, saying one of his proudest moments was seeing some of his students in their red graduation caps and gowns standing arm-in-arm in protest of the historical inequities that continue to exist today. Interviewed by *Time Magazine* in their graduation regalia, the students, whose graduation ceremony was canceled in 2020 due to COVID social distancing restrictions, leveraged their resistance capital in their own celebration of Black excellence in the wake of horrific racial injustice in their city [25].

Challenging Inequality Through Just Policy

The murder of George Floyd brought renewed attention to long-standing disparities in policing, housing, education, and other areas, sparking protests and calls for change. As Minneapolis continues to work toward greater equity and justice, addressing these disparities will be a critical part of the conversation. Despite these challenges, Minneapolis remains a vibrant and dynamic city, with a diverse population and a rich history that continues to shape its identity and future. The leaders in MPS and PHHS illuminated the ways that Minneapolis embraces its history and seeks to provide justice and equity for all during the critical time of disruption that began in 2020. As we heard from Superintendent Ed Graff

> *Minneapolis Public Schools has been on this journey of addressing the racial inequity, and the idea of equity altogether for, for several years ... We knew that these were areas and specific pieces of work that we had to address prior to the pandemic ... and obviously just saw a heightened acceleration, or a magnification of those inequities through the process.*

The summer of 2020 brought all aspects of racial inequity to the forefront in Minneapolis, as disruptions to all aspects of life made everyone pay attention. And while youth activism used social media tools to drive support toward movements like #BlackLivesMatter [26], and students wore graduation gowns to protests, MPS also continued down a path of consistently just policy making to make structural change.

Addressing these inequities requires more than just individual action, but also the implementation of just policies that can help to promote equity and justice for all. Just policies are those that are designed to address the underlying causes of inequity, and to ensure that everyone has access to the resources and opportunities they need to thrive. These policies can take many different forms, including efforts to promote fair housing, improve access to healthcare, and invest in education and job training programs. They can also involve efforts to address systemic racism and discrimination, and to promote greater equity in areas such as criminal justice, immigration, and voting rights. By challenging inequity through just policies, we can work to create a more equitable and just society, where everyone has the opportunity to live a full and meaningful life. The team at MPS and PHHS stressed that financial investment, transparency and accountability, and student and teacher empowerment through sound policies would prepare MPS for a more equitable future.

Comprehensive District Design

One of the leadership team's biggest investments was the Comprehensive District Design (CDD) that the school Board approved on May 12, 2020. The CDD sought to address issues within MPS related to academics, equity, and fiscal sustainability. Superintendent Graff and his team acknowledged that MPS's current structures and policies deprived students from minoritized backgrounds of the well-rounded education they deserved [27]. When asked about the thought process behind the CDD and the creation of the plan, Superintendent Graff said:

> *We knew that when you are working from a system, there are many different angles you can come at it from. You can come from a technical or adaptive angle. We obviously knew that the technical piece is what many bureaucratic systems fall into, and it becomes the driving force when you're working with a board of education and you're working with policies and things of that nature. That work was already started in our comprehensive district design. And then,*

not to be missed, is the adaptive work with adults. And so again, really putting forward in a consistent and deliberate manner, "What are our values? We often say things, but do we believe them, and can we demonstrate them?"

By addressing much needed policy change, the CDD had the potential to eliminate long-standing policies and practices that disadvantaged students of color and low-income students; to ensure MPS stayed compliant with new federal laws about student access and effective teaching; and to increase achievement through more equitable access to rigorous and relevant coursework [27].

There were two areas within the CDD that truly showed MPS's commitment to investing in a sustainable future. First and foremost, the new plan centered equity throughout. A 2019 equity and diversity impact analysis of MPS showed that current policies around student placement were not leading to further integration of MPS schools over time. As a result, the CDD called for a radical overhaul of school zoning. The district used these "structural equity practices" so that structural inequality could be addressed by dismantling and reassembling structures to be more equitable. They knew the only way to reduce racially and economically isolated schools was to invest in high-quality community schools in every part of the city and support climate improvements to bolster student learning retention and family and staff experiences [28]. Many parents were outraged at the changes that came with school zone realignment which did not grandfather students into their existing schools. New boundaries also changed enrollment numbers drastically, and many schools changed which grades they served. Nonetheless, MPS stayed true to their data-informed decision, and made purposeful structural change.

Part of the investment in a more supportive school climate was an investment in personnel. Money was allocated to create the Chief Equity Officer position, to focus on making the structural changes needed to fix the system. The district invested heavily in data to empower decision makers, but it also understood that this took financial support and commitment. By bringing the areas of accountability, research, and equity into the same office, the district ensured that the planning for educational equity, and the processes that tracked progress, would work in tandem to ensure that changes had the desired impact. Additionally, the district began to practice a new commitment to budget sustainability, ensuring available funding for any policy changes that might require allocated resources over time. This would allow adequate time for policy changes to be fully implemented and have the desired impact.

The district invested in equity training for personnel, knowing they could not just expect people to create equity without first equipping them with the knowledge and skills required. This included adding a line item to the budget for 40 hours of equity training for all personnel to ensure that training would occur on an ongoing basis to keep everyone growing. Given the role of police in the murder of George Floyd, MPS also re-evaluated its contract with resource officers and their purpose within the school building. A member of the district leadership team described this financial investment and rethinking of resource officers as a no-brainer, saying:

> *We hear your voice. We act on it. We align it to the budget so within that year, you see the relationship between what you said needs to be changed, an action plan, and then it's funded.*

This statement clearly echoed the district's decision to enact data-driven policy changes that were supported through budget allocation.

A climate framework was also created to codify a need to assess progress and create accountability. The framework was published and open for all to read. It articulated clear principles to guide understanding of where the district must continue to grow and embrace change and opportunities to practice collective accountability [29]. The plan outlines initiatives along with the budget implications to support it. In particular, *Policy 1304*, which compels every employee to dismantle systems of oppression and inequality, was a drastic change to the way educators had approached equity work in the past. In some ways the policy mirrors "mandatory reporting" policies such as for Title IX and child abuse, by making equity a work requirement. The district also took measures to collect more data, ensuring that data were used to hold the school system accountable to its stakeholders.

While the financial investments for equity and accountability are costly endeavors, Superintendent Graff's team promised that they could implement these transformative changes to MPS for less than 2% of the annual operating budget. The realignment of school districts is expected to save nearly $7 million annually, and changes to start and end times could reduce additional costs [30]. These savings are then able to be reinvested in the schools and personnel to continue to uplift all students.

Empowered Implementation of Change

The implementation of the CDD immediately faced unexpected challenges. Within days of its passage at the MPS school board meeting, the murder of George Floyd plunged the city into chaos. As Superintendent Graff told us, "The challenges of beginning to implement [the CDD] during a pandemic were significant, and ... the upheaval of the unrest we saw [added to the challenges]." However, this also highlighted what Superintendent Graff and his team meant when they said MPS was already working to create a more equitable society. The world was just paying attention to what was occurring in Minneapolis in 2020. They were already working for equity at MPS. In that dark time, with more equitable policies in place, their role was to empower schools to empower students to use their voices and join the call for social justice.

First and foremost, the leaders of MPS knew the events unfolding in their city were not only affecting the students, but teachers and support staff were also coping with the images they were seeing on television and the unrest that was taking place outside their front doors. Students understood this as well. This trust teachers had in their students, and the time they had already invested in building caring relationships, allowed for more honest dialogue and empowered principals and their teachers to lead more authentically. At PHHS, Principal Abdullah provided space for morning meetings to touch base with teachers and check in on their well-being. He provided more grace to teachers and encouraged them to take care of themselves. When asked about how he led during this time, he said, "My leadership—we continue to say, 'showcase grace, showcase grace.'" But he also noted that his teachers had to model grace as well. "If I'm going to show the teachers grace, then why don't you show the students grace?" he asked them.

The ability to lead with a gentle hand, but also to call educators to a higher standard in their responsiveness to students was a cornerstone of Principal Abdullah's approach to leadership. In addition to empowering teachers, he believed in empowering students by ensuring they were brought into the planning and purpose that guided decisions at his school. Principal Abdullah had already built a culture at PHHS:

> *So, we had a strategic plan, we had a mission, a vision. We had a core belief on equity, and we had four pillars that we stood on: caring and supportive environment, college and career preparation, connection to community, and family and cultural responsiveness. We stood on those pillars.*

So, when the murder of George Floyd occurred, students had a framework on which to rely. The school's caring and supportive environment, its connection to the community, and the family and cultural responsiveness with which all the educators were expected to behave came to the forefront.

Ms. Muhammed, a strong proponent of intergenerational learning, focused on the new opportunities that virtual learning afforded to build deeper connections with families. She shared:

> *Okay, the best part is that the parents were going to school with their kids because they were at home ... One of my parents told me after our class ended that it was difficult for her to help her children with their online work. Because of her educational background, she felt these insecurities, and so I thought I will create some curriculum for you as well. I just found some readings and I did some stuff for her around literacy just for her to practice. But she was just so grateful. ... For me, that was probably the greatest gift that parents were able to attend school or attend my class with their kids and find support with me.*

Through this act of service, Ms. Muhammed embraced several parts of the school's framework, extending the caring and supportive environment she had created in her class to parents. Responding compassionately to the learning needs of families, as well as their child, she made a personal contribution to greater educational equity in the community that PHHS served.

It was not that the pillar of college and career preparation was forgotten during the pandemic, rather it was seen in the context of what was happening in the world. When educators provided a space for student identity development, academics also improved. As Ms. Muhammed said, "Between the teachers and the students, to have some place of safety and healing" and be in community, even if it was virtual, was essential in those early days. Students were able to process in numerous ways. Ms. Muhammad pointed out that some of her quieter students thrived in an environment where they could write and express their feelings in other ways. She also told us that the ability to transition to assessments "based upon competency and connection rather than punitive measures and metrics" during the pandemic, naturally dismantled some of the inequities in education, and allowed the teachers to better serve their students. They could spend time focusing on the learning that was urgent in their lives at that moment. As stated earlier, some of the students chose to go to protests in their graduation caps and gowns. Teachers tried not to shy away from conversations, but rather root them in facts. They were also clearly proud of their students, as Ms. Muhammad shared, "They did not cower in the face of injustice. They rose to face it." Students knew they were supported and empowered to express themselves and explore their understanding of the world. As Principal Abdullah stressed, "The thing about it is you're not alone. We have a support system for you to tap into, so that we can all support."

Lessons Learned from Minneapolis

Throughout our conversation with educators and leaders in Minneapolis, it was clear that the fight for equity and justice in schools is never-ending. Just because the cameras were not focused on Minneapolis in 2019, does not mean that injustices did not exist. Earlier in this chapter, we described the historical and cultural context of the city and the school district in which the murder of George Floyd occurred. It did not happen in a vacuum. Nor does it mean that those community and education leaders were waiting for a time when so much attention was on Minneapolis to fight for justice. Rather, the community and education leaders in Minneapolis were actively using their positions of authority to create just policies and right the long history of structural racism and inequality in their community. When the nation's eyes focused on Minneapolis in May of 2020, therefore, these leaders were ready to step up to the challenge. And though the world's attention may have faded once again, the work continues to make Patrick Henry High School, Minneapolis Public Schools, and the Minneapolis community more just and equitable places. Below are lessons to glean from this chapter as we continue to reimagine education and innovate to create a more just education system.

Invest in a Brighter Future

As Superintendent Graff showed us, creating a truly equitable education system takes large-scale thinking and investment in the pieces that are most critical to your missions. In the checkered racial history of Minneapolis, he realized that eradicating injustice would not come with tweaks to the system, but rather a fundamental dismantling and reconstruction of the policies that had been in place for so many years. The CDD was part of that larger investment in a brighter future. As Superintendent Graff put it:

> *What we've done with our comprehensive district design is taken all those areas that were a focus, a desire, or a stated priority over several years and said, "Let's really unpack what is there. What do we need to do to make a difference?"*

While there were critiques of the CDD, it highlighted a deep, system-wide commitment to invest in a different future.

From the budget requests for teacher training and investments in data and assessment, to rezoning all the schools, the leaders of MPS envisioned a more just future and knew that work started now. Specific, mission-aligned, and measurable initiatives were funded, and steps were taken to ensure the fiscal sustainability of changes. MPS and PHHS could have never prepared for what 2020 would bring to Minneapolis, but their investments in educational equity made them more ready to adapt and embrace their brighter future. With the continual budget struggles that school districts see across the nation, it can be easy to focus on the present, without much thought about investing, especially financially, in the future. As seen in Minneapolis, the future is never certain, but investing with purpose in the direction we want to take is something for all to strive toward.

Creat Accountability

Another essential lesson from Minneapolis was the importance of creating accountability. In all facets, MPS knew that investments in the future are futile without continual assessment and evaluation to ensure the outcomes are truly the ones desired. Perhaps, a long history of court-mandated reporting on the outcomes of segregation plans prepared the district to embrace accountability in this way. Perhaps, it is the rapid return to segregated schools it experienced in times when accountability was low. In either case, with a culture of continuous improvement guiding decision-making, it is likely the data will continue to drive the decisions in matters of educational equity.

MPS has invested personnel, funding, and time to better assess not only the academic outcomes of schools, but also the social and cultural outcomes. At the district level, the leadership team analyzed data to understand teacher retention and school climate and culture. At the school level, Principal Abdullah and his team held teachers accountable and provided resources to train in virtual learning. At the student level Principal Abdullah and Ms. Muhammad both expressed the importance of holding students accountable for not only their assignments, but also their words and actions. But as Ms. Muhammed noted, "You can't have high expectations [for students] without support." Principal Abdullah also reminded us that assessment should not be purely test-based, but rather more encompassing of students' talents:

> *[At first,] we didn't shift the way we were thinking in terms of how they're hitting the standards that they should be hitting. We went door to door. We want to be open to understanding and making it seamless. We were still standing in the gaps and if you didn't do what I gave you, [but] I can assess you and, therefore, you earn credit, I think we have to be much more flexible in our thinking when it comes to curriculum and when it comes to standards.*

Educators at MPS spoke with one voice when it came to the understanding that accountability is crucial, but just accountability is even more paramount. Students, staff, and district leaders were all facing an unprecedented number of challenges, including a racial reckoning that started on their doorsteps. The district's response reiterates that just accountability takes into account the world around us to give context to the data we use for decision-making. If we aim to develop more just assessment and data systems, we must commit to contextualizing the data with lived experiences of all involved.

Empower Schools to Empower Students

Last, but certainly not least, our conversations in Minneapolis showed the importance of empowering schools to empower students. Superintendent Graff and his leadership team gave trust and support to school leaders. Rather than using a top-down approach, they trusted in the leaders who were embedded in their communities to know what their schools needed most. As Superintendent Graff said, they "can leverage those connections and the insight and knowledge that they have to not only the community, but to the individuals." Principal Abdullah was empowered by leadership to diversify his teaching staff to be more representative of his students, preparing PHHS to meet the needs of its students in the darkest of times. Principals and teachers met in support groups to empower one another to embrace the current challenges and how to best navigate conversations with students. Teachers empowered students to discuss their feelings and understandings of the current circumstances. As Ms. Muhammed said, "we never have time, resources, permission to do those kinds of things.

Then they became a priority. The messages changed from leadership and the district." These conversations encouraged students to process their emotions, and oftentimes resulted in better outcomes in schoolwork. Ultimately, empowering the leaders of schools to empower their students resulted in the more culturally responsible and justice-oriented learning experiences that students needed.

The work in Minneapolis Public Schools is far from over, and while important progress was made in the pandemic years, there have also continued to be challenges. As in so many districts around the country, the educators at MPS withstood trauma, danger, hardship, and inequality, and supported their communities through the same. The Minneapolis Federation of Teachers (MTF) even called a strike in the spring of 2022, mirroring those that have occurred in school districts across the country since 2020. The success of the district's efforts toward greater structural equity could be seen in the outcome of this strike, with the inclusion of protections for teachers of color during excessing and layoffs being added to district contracts. Because teachers of color are often more recently hired, seniority-based policies disproportionately impact them, and this new policy aimed to address this inequity. This change also served as an acknowledgment of the invisible tax that so many of teachers of color carry in the teaching profession. The invisible tax refers to the extra work Black teachers must do, such as providing unpaid leadership on anti-racism work, or extra support and mentorship to students of color, all while fighting systemic injustices that still exist in the education system [31]. Although difficult, this rigorous engagement of the district's educators and leaders in advocacy and dialog continued to move the education system toward greater justice.

Since the time of our interviews, there have been several changes at MPS. In June of 2022, Ed Graff retired after six years of influential leadership in Minneapolis Public Schools, and a career of over 30 years in the field of education. MPS School Board Chair at the time, Kim Ellison, stated, "Always with students as the focus, Superintendent Graff has brought systemic and transformational change to MPS during an extremely challenging time in our history," and the impact of CDD will continue to live on for decades [32]. Principal Abdullah was appointed Associate Superintendent of MPS, where he could his experience as the principal at PHHS to provide ongoing support and oversight to school building leaders. Ms. Muhammed, an ardent advocate for teachers of color, left the classroom to work for the national non-profit Educators for Excellence, where she could continue her efforts to organize and empower fellow educators. The work in Minneapolis, like the work in school districts across the country, is far from complete. As the nation recovers from the turbulent events that occurred in 2020 and their aftermath, we all must reimagine education for a more inclusive and just future. And perhaps we can find the courage to stand up and speak out for it like the incredible educators we had the pleasure of interviewing for this book. However their stories continue to unfold, there can be no doubt that they gave the best of themselves to the work of education in their communities at a truly unique and unpredictable time in history.

> **Reflect and Discuss**
> We invite you to consider what you have read in this chapter and apply it to your own community context. Use the following questions as a starting point for your personal reflection and for discussion with education stakeholders in your community.
>
> 1. How did the previous history of racial injustice and inequity in Minneapolis impact the district's response in 2020?
> 2. What aspects of your local context influence the response of area schools in times of social instability? What role does the community's history of racial injustice play?
> 3. How do education leaders employ policy to create more equitable communities and education systems? How does this look in your local context?
> 4. How do systemic structures, such as district and school boundaries, unintentionally lead to inequalities?
> 5. What lessons on empowering students and staff to dismantle systems of injustice and inequality can you apply in your context?

REFERENCES

1. Ingraham, C. (2020, May 30). Racial inequality in Minneapolis is among the worst in the nation. *The Washington Post.* https://www.washingtonpost.com/business/2020/05/30/minneapolis-racial-inequality/.
2. Lass, W. E. (2000). *Minnesota: A history.* WW Norton & Company.
3. Risjord, N. K. (2005). *A popular history of Minnesota.* Minnesota Historical Society.

4. Smith, H. (2020). *Confluence: The history of Fort Snelling.* Minnesota Historical Society Press.
5. Glaab, C. N., & Larsen, L. H. (1968). Neenah-Menasha in the 1870's: The development of flour milling and papermaking. *The Wisconsin Magazine of History,* 19–34.
6. Levine, M. (2006). *The Sioux.* Lerner Publications.
7. Wingerd, M. L. (2010). *North country: The making of Minnesota.* University of Minnesota Press.
8. The United States Census Bureau. (2022). *QuickFacts: Minneapolis City, Minnesota; Lubbock City, Texas; Lubbock County, Texas.* The United States Census Bureau. Retrieved April 15, 2023, from https://www.census.gov/quickfacts/fact/table/minneapoliscityminnesota,lubbockcitytexas,lubbockcountytexas/PST045221
9. The United States Census Bureau. (2022). *QuickFacts: Minneapolis City, Minnesota; Lubbock City, Texas; Lubbock County, Texas.* The United States Census Bureau. Retrieved April 15, 2023, from https://www.census.gov/quickfacts/fact/table/minneapoliscityminnesota,lubbockcitytexas,lubbockcountytexas/RTN130217#RTN130217.
10. Minnesota Department of Health. (2023). *Poverty & income: People in poverty.* Minnesota department of Health Retrieved April 15, 2023, from https://data.web.health.state.mn.us/poverty_basic
11. Waxman, O. (2020, May 28). George Floyd's Death and the Long History of Racism in Minneapolis. *Time.* https://time.com/5844030/george-floyd-minneapolis-history/
12. Owen, G., Meyerson, J., & Otteson, C. (2019, August) *A new age of immigrants: Making immigration work for Minnesota.* The Amherst H. Wilder foundation & The Minneapolis Foundation. Retrieved April 15, 2023, from https://www.wilder.org/sites/default/files/imports/MinneapolisFdn_Immigration_8-10sum.pdf
13. Frankenberg, E., & Lee, C. (2002). *Race in American public schools: Rapidly resegregating school districts.* Report by the Civil Rights Project, Harvard University. Retrieved April 15, 2023, from https://civilrightsproject.ucla.edu/research/k-12-education/integration-and-diversity/race-in-american-public-schools-rapidly-resegregating-school-districts/frankenberg-rapidly-resegregating-2002.pdf
14. Minneapolis Public Schools. (2022, February 8). *Minneapolis public schools report of the racial ethnic count of students.* Minneapolis Public Schools. https://studentaccounting.mpls.k12.mn.us/uploads/racial_ethnic_oct1_2021_grades_kg_12.pdf.
15. National Center for Education Statistics. (2016). *District Demographic Dashboard 2016–20.* Retrieved April 15, 2023, from https://nces.ed.gov/Programs/Edge/ACSDashboard/2721240

16. Forbes, P. G., & Cunningham, J. A., Jr. (1995). Desegregation & the Minneapolis public schools. *Hamline Journal of Public Law & Policy, 17*(2), 209–230.
17. Hansen, C., & Diers, B. (2017). Collection on the Minneapolis public schools. *Hennepin County Library*. Retrieved April 15, 2023, from https://archives.hclib.org/repositories/2/resources/317
18. Kraus, N. (2008). Concentrated poverty and urban school reform: "The choice is yours" in Minneapolis. *Equity & Excellence in Education, 41*(2), 262–274.
19. Minneapolis Public Schools. (2023). Cabinet Team. Retrieved April 15, 2023, from https://mpls.k12.mn.us/cabinet
20. Minneapolis Youth Coordinating Board. (2023). Ed Graff. Retrieved April 15, 2023, from https://www.ycb.org/edgraff
21. Edwards, K. (2022, August 17). Minneapolis' Patrick Henry high school to be renamed. *KARE11*. https://www.kare11.com/article/news/local/breaking-the-news/minneapolis-patrick-henry-high-school-renamed/89-8f4f918c-09e1-4ada-98be-dfa965ac72f0
22. Patrick Henry High School. (2023). About Patrick Henry High School. Retrieved April 15, 2023, from https://henry.mpls.k12.mn.us/about_us
23. Hubert H. Humphrey School of Public Affairs. (2022, April 13). *Pandemic sharpens gender and racial inequalities among Minnesota workers*. Minnesota University. Retrieved April 15, 2023, from https://www.hhh.umn.edu/news/pandemic-sharpens-gender-and-racial-inequalities-among-minnesota-workers
24. Bombyk, M., Ewig, C., & Dorman, A. (2020). *COVID-19's unequal impacts on Minnesota workers: A race and gender lens*. University of Minnesota. Retrieved April 15, 2023, from https://www.hhh.umn.edu/sites/hhh.umn.edu/files/2020-12/CWGPP_COVID_Work_Report_Full.pdf
25. Trianni, F. (2020, June 4). Protests instead of graduation, the class of 2020 'Walk the stage of the Streets'. *Time* https://time.com/5848176/graduation-protests/
26. Welton, A. D., & Harris, T. O. (2022). Youth of color social movements for racial justice: The politics of interrogating the school-to-prison pipeline. *Educational Policy, 36*(1), 57–99.
27. Minneapolis Public Schools. (2023). *Comprehensive district design*. Retrieved April 15, 2023, from https://mpls.k12.mn.us/cdd
28. Minneapolis Public Schools. (2023). *Comprehensive district design (CDD)*. Retrieved April 15, 2023, from https://accountability.mpls.k12.mn.us/comprehensive_district_design_cdd
29. Minneapolis Public Schools. (2023). *Equity and School Climate Department*. Retrieved April 15, 2023, from https://equity.mpls.k12.mn.us/

30. MPS Board of Education. (2020, April 14). April 14, 2020, Minutes of Regular Business Meeting. Retrieved April 15, 2023, from https://meetings.boardbook.org/Public/Agenda/1807?meeting=320829
31. King. (2016, May 15). The invisible tax on teachers of color. *The Washington Post.* https://www.washingtonpost.com/opinions/the-invisible-tax-on-black-teachers/2016/05/15/6b7bea06-16f7-11e6-aa55-670cabef46e0_story.html
32. Miska, C. (2022, March 31). Graff's 6-year MPS tenure ends in discord. *MSR.* https://spokesman-recorder.com/2022/03/31/mps-superintendent-ed-graff-announces-plans-to-step-down-following-contentious-meeting/

PART III

On Reimagining Education

CHAPTER 7

The Circle Model

When the system was naturally dismantled, we became better teachers and better servants because of it.
—Nafeesah Muhammad, Teacher, Patrick Henry High School

As we have examined the stories of schools and school districts in times of great societal disruption, one thing has become clear: the future of education will depend on collaborative thinking and collective action. Time and time again, we have seen the strength of communities being the driver of innovation and compassion, with shared values bringing together those within the school and those in the surrounding locale to find the best solutions for children and their families to what often seemed like overwhelming challenges. Whether the threat was perceived to originate from outside, like a virus sweeping across the globe, or from within, fueled by historical trauma and systemic racism, communities *encircled their members with care* and banded together to protect the most vulnerable. It is this circle imagery, and the inherent strength of the circular form, that has inspired the Comprehensive, Innovative, Resilient, and Contextualized Lens on Education (CIRCLE) Model, which we believe can serve as a conceptual framework for reimagining education for new realities and a brighter future.

As we learned from all four school districts we examined in the preceding chapters, the global disruption that started with the onset of the coronavirus pandemic kicked off a series of events around the world that have resulted in a qualitatively different human experience from the one that came before. In this time of vulnerability, communities found that interdependence was the way to survive, and schools were the linchpin around which that interdependence revolved. When families of essential workers in the Bronx needed childcare so they could provide life-saving services, schools *circled* around them and provided safe spaces for children to engage in online learning while their parents worked. When families in Lubbock needed to return to in-person learning due to lack of internet access, the school district and the city's health department operated in a *circle* of trust, depoliticizing virus and vaccine information to provide residents data and facts that they could use to make the best choices for their families. To square the *circle* of massive economic disparities within the district, Los Angeles Unified School District's leadership drew on the immense resources of its wealthy entertainment industry to support schools in communities with high levels of poverty. To strengthen the equitable education policy in Minneapolis, superintendent Graff elevated a range of diverse voices in his inner *circle*. Over and over again, the circle, the strongest structural shape [1], operated as a metaphor for the important role that schools played in challenging times and must continue playing in the future.

Adapting the Conversation to the Times

In this chapter, we will explain the parts of the CIRCLE Model and present a series of propositions aimed at reshaping educational discourse to match the needs of the future. First, we must understand the adaptations to the educational discourse that are needed to reflect the new normal and the challenges that come with it. Renowned pedagogical theorist and scholar of culturally relevant pedagogy, Gloria Ladson-Billings, has called for a "hard reset" to describe the need to take a responsive step forward rather than returning to old ways [2]. While the CIRCLE Model highlights the importance of understanding the necessary changes within the context of each school, its student population, and the community within which it exists, one thing is universally true—going back to a normal that was already not working for too many is not an option. In fact, the disruption of the global pandemic afforded the opportunity to ask questions and make changes that were long overdue. How should "normal" look now that we have experienced the great pandemic disruption? How has the purpose of public education and our understanding of its purpose evolved since the start of the pandemic?

The Purpose of School

The most important challenge that the current moment holds for educators is defining the continuously evolving purpose of schools [3]. The current underpinnings of the U.S. school system, developed for an industrializing nation with an agrarian majority, and the current realities of a globalized society where information drives both civic engagement and commerce appear to be at odds [4]. The rapid exchange of ideas today challenges schools to stay flexible in their contemporary goals, which may be to educate citizens or workers, or which may prioritize something else entirely. As depicted in the ombre shading in the CIRCLE Model figure (see Fig. 7.1), the broader purpose of education will likely continue to evolve in response to global events, flowing seamlessly from one purpose to the next as needed, increasing demands for adaptability and responsiveness in schools over time, and from day to day. This part of the model is

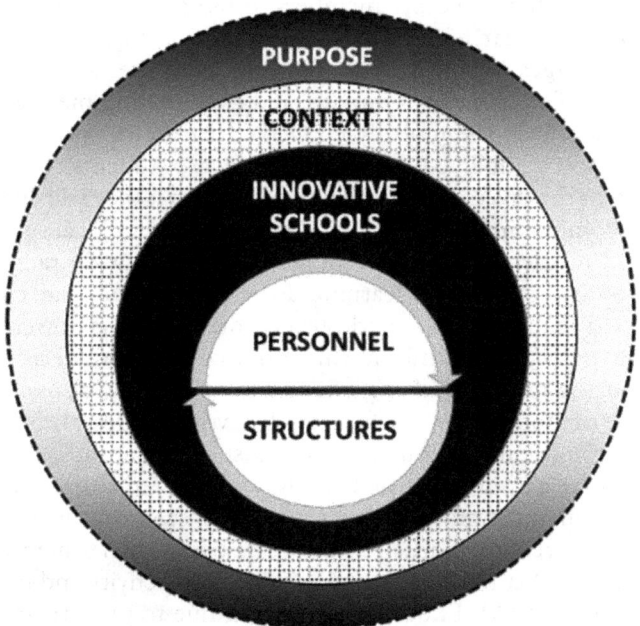

Fig. 7.1 The Comprehensive, Innovative, Resilient, and Contextualized Lens on Education (CIRCLE) Model

also bound by a dashed line, suggesting that the purpose of school will remain porous to the influences of the changing political and economic conditions around the world, and constituents whose understanding of the situation depends on increasingly disjointed information received through social media silos [5]. A complex and diverse society comes with a need for a complex conceptualization of the goal of schools, and with the acceptance that public education will play different roles in the lives of different students, based on their current conditions and aspirations for the future.

As demonstrated in the early days of the coronavirus pandemic, the readiness of schools to serve an evolving and complex purpose will vary based on assets and challenges in the local context—increasing the importance of cultivating local systems of support around schools and leveraging the texture and flavor that every community has the potential to bring to the education of its members. If we are thinking of the purpose of education as being guided by the community in which it is taking place, then we must partner with community members to build a more inclusive educational experience that honors the cultures and lived experiences of our students, leverages local opportunities and expertise, and supports the development of students into thriving and contributing members of their communities. Given the globally connected nature of society that exists today, this means public education must prepare students to not only be well-versed in the diverse ideas and perspectives that they will encounter in their local communities, but also understand how their local surroundings are situated in the world, where individuals with a wide range of lived experiences are interacting, learning from each other, and conducting business on a regular basis: a world where information is power.

Battling the constant misinformation that plagued decision-makers throughout the rapidly evolving crisis of the pandemic also showed that the purpose of schooling in the future will have to address the need for not just workers and citizens, but perhaps most importantly, informed consumers of information. In an increasingly connected world where information can sometimes move faster than good sense, the future of education will have to address the needs not only of a population armed with technology, but one that benefits from equitable connectivity and information literacy to guide it [6]. Educators must continue to push themselves and the field to ask the hard questions. What is the primary purpose of education today? Who do we serve through the work we do? When needs compete, who do we prioritize—the individual students we work with, or the greater societal needs that may be at odds with their interests?

Influences of School Context

The types of resources available to schools to meet their purpose are highly contextualized and should be understood in relation to the cultures, geographies, and economies of the communities they serve. The pandemic disruption showed us that these contextual factors can signal inequities in monetary resources because of substantial economic differences between communities, but they can also signal important cultural and relational capital that stems from shared experiences [7]. Repeatedly over the course of our conversations with school personnel in the highlighted districts in this book, we saw the powerful influence of the local community and context on school personnel, the opportunities they had to offer students and families, and the decisions that they ultimately made. At the surface, and perhaps most obvious level, the socioeconomic context of the school governed the resources available to the district to fulfill its purpose. But in a time of true crisis, schools were able to dig beyond that surface level and reach into their communities in innovative ways, and connections to local organizations and institutions afforded districts with essential partnerships.

For example, teachers in the Bronx were able to receive critical mental health support from a nearby hospital that helped them navigate trauma in their classrooms and personal lives more effectively. In Los Angeles, the district was able to leverage a partnership with Fender Guitars to build a virtual music program that students could engage in during lockdown to learn how to play the guitar. Yet, we also saw how the school context can provide strong connections to a shared history, culture, and ethos that allow school leaders to garner buy-in around difficult decisions. In Lubbock, the strong cultural and historical narrative of facing adversity as a community to secure economic prosperity shaped support for opening schools for in-person instruction long before a vaccine was available. To reflect this nuance, the textured fill of the school context section in the CIRCLE Model depicts the complex nature of the communities where schools are situated. These contexts provide the richness—both monetary and cultural—of the surrounding area, and the inherent assets in the community that must be leveraged to ensure that schools are their thriving center [8]. There are many essential questions that educators must ask in collaboration with community partners to ensure that their school is evolving into a place where students can truly thrive as individuals and as members of their community [9]. Who is invested in this school and its community? What needs are reflected in the community context? What assets exist in and around the school context that can support student thriving? What innovations are needed to garner the greatest positive impact from these assets?

Innovation in Schools

For schools to be the thriving center of any community, they must innovate to meet the needs of their stakeholders. No assets were more powerful during the disruptive years of the pandemic than the unshakable commitment and creativity of school personnel to solve problems. In the aftermath of global lockdowns, communities and families turned to schools to navigate hardship, relying on them for learning resources, but also for food, internet connections, and social interaction during a time of great isolation. In each district and school that we examined, unique challenges had the potential to derail learning, yet teachers and administrators collaborated to develop novel and responsive approaches to face the adversity their students and families encountered. From adopting new technologies to shift learning online in a matter of days, to introducing new types of communication, to hosting social activities in order to strengthen mental health support in unsafe times, the capacity of educators across the nation to innovate was undeniable and necessary. While public education can at times be overwhelmed by bureaucracy, when educators were unleashed and given the freedom to innovate, they worked with extreme efficiency to make changes that had likely been needed long before the pandemic [10].

In the CIRCLE Model, innovative schools are depicted as the weightiest component of reimagining education, because it is this culture of innovation and direct, sustained access to students and families that allows schools to have meaningful and lasting impact on their communities [11]. We learned during our interviews in Minneapolis that innovation can include everything from social justice oriented school programs to recruitment and retention policies and practices that support a diverse and engaged teacher workforce. Since the end of the pandemic, we have also seen schools move with reduced hesitation toward new models to address the learning losses accumulated over the pandemic years, experimenting with year-round calendars and structured time in the school day for more targeted academic support for all students [12]. For this innovation to continue, educators must keep asking probing questions to support it. What are the barriers to solving problems in our school district? What investments would support the implementation of new approaches that center equity in educational opportunities and outcomes? What policy and structural changes are needed to make room for innovative pedagogy and practice that meet the changing needs of our students?

Necessary Structural Change

For innovative pedagogical practices to be employed in public education, schools also have to approach their work with increased structural flexibility, adapting the use of time and space to meet the needs of their students. During the pandemic, we saw schools make rapid decisions to adapt schedules and repurpose spaces. For example, allowing teachers to have common planning time in their schedule with colleagues who had the same students or course/grade level assignments had been recommended by education researchers and practitioners for decades, but complexities of scheduling often made this an unachievable task. Yet during the pandemic, schools reprioritized the well-being of students as an essential component of the educational enterprise, opting to leave space in online schedules for teachers to consult with each other and support students individually or in groups as needed [13].

Structural changes that leverage learning modalities—in-person, virtual, and hybrid—to further the learning goals of the schools and of specific students must also be considered as tools that schools can employ to broadly improve educational experiences, not just as emergency learning supports. Whether this comes in the form of choice-based flexibility that allows students to choose learning modalities that better meet their individual needs, or leverages technologies to improve access to courses that may not be otherwise available to students in a particular school, the same technologies that were rapidly, and sometimes imperfectly, deployed during lockdown out of necessity, now have to be reintroduced more thoughtfully in places where they may garner added benefit. While there is great temptation to roll back the advancements in learning technologies in response to a deep collective drive to "return to normal," no such place exists for us to return to—there is only now. How do current time, space, and organizational limitations prevent us from doing our best work in service of students? How can structural barriers be removed to welcome new ideas and solutions? How do policy structures and personnel in our schools collectively reify existing inequalities or dismantle mechanisms that empower some individuals over others?

Evolving Roles of School Personnel

It became clear during the pandemic that the roles of adults in schools could be far more flexible and responsive to the needs of students than school structures traditionally allowed for. The answer to the question "whose job is this?" became a resounding, "anyone who can get it done!" School bus drivers delivered meals instead of transporting children during lockdown [14], and once schools reopened with driver shortages, school principals drove school buses [15]. As we look forward to how the roles of education personnel must look in the future, it will be important to consider that, within the regulations required to protect and advocate for children's interests, educator roles must provide autonomy to solve problems and act in the best interest of students. Teachers need to have a voice in the development of education policy because they are trained to understand the nuances of enacting those policies with students. In creating a professional culture within the educator workforce where the adults are free to respond to challenges with competence and connectedness to their students, we create schools where children have models for how to conscientiously respond to challenges, and develop a community-oriented, collaborative, and intrinsically motivated learning orientation [16].

The exact nature of evolving educator roles will have to vary based on the needs of the students, the assets within the school and community context, and characteristics of the individuals entering the profession. In the CIRCLE Model, we conceptualize school personnel and school structures as needing to evolve in relation to each other, as pieces of a puzzle that must fit together in ways that address concrete needs within the school. For example, this may mean that if a school with teaching shortages is having to bring in many inexperienced teachers at the same time to meet a workforce need, the personnel structure might have to change with a master teacher mentoring, leading, and sometimes co-teaching with a group of novice teachers, serving as a de facto head teacher for the group. This more hierarchical structure could afford much-needed intensive induction support for new teachers, but also create a significant leadership development opportunity for the more experienced teacher, perhaps allowing for a retention incentive in salary and a future opportunity for advancement.

The pathways to entering the teaching profession, and the qualities required of successful teachers, also require innovative thinking as we transform the profession for the needs of the future. Since the start of the pandemic in 2020, schools have seen a significant rise in the levels of trauma students have experienced and the related increase in mental health challenges being faced by students across grade levels. Yet educators are seldom trained in trauma-informed teaching, and they are not recruited for possessing dispositions, such as compassion, empathy, emotional intelligence, and self-regulation, that would support such teaching practices in the classroom [17]. In applying the CIRCLE Model in schools, we create conceptual space for education leaders and policymakers to consider the personnel needs of schools in conjunction with structural realities and within the broader community context. What dispositional characteristics do new teachers need to possess to meet the specific needs of the school's student population? What new recruitment and retention strategies will help schools address evolving student needs? How do current training and licensure requirements for teachers encourage or impede the development of a teacher workforce that can thrive in the emerging realities of the profession?

THE GUIDING PRINCIPLES OF PROGRESS

The CIRCLE Model provides a nested system of interrelated factors about schools that we believe educators must remain reflective about when responding to education in challenging times. As we face systemic challenges, we must think systemically, embracing complexity of purpose and context to develop innovative structural and personnel solutions. To support the use of this model in creating powerful learning experiences for students, we put forward three propositions that will clarify the model's use in practice. These propositions are based on our learning from the interviews we conducted in the Bronx, Lubbock, Los Angeles, and Minneapolis, as well as examples from our own educational careers. They incorporate what many might consider conventional wisdom or common sense, and as such, serve just as much as value statements as they do advice.

Innovation Occurs from the Outside-In

In the CIRCLE Model, the outside rings of Purpose and Context are essential drivers of intentional innovation in schools, because the broader objectives that innovation serves, and the resources required to enact innovation, often originate from these outer spheres of the model. For example, the need for innovative use of virtual learning tools during the COVID-19 pandemic arose from the pandemic lockdowns that forced learning online. The initial transition to virtual learning was limited by the realities of the community context where the school was located. In communities like Lubbock, where a large proportion of students lived in poverty, schools had to support internet access by delivering internet hotspots or parking buses that served as mobile hotspots in neighborhoods around the district so students could access Wi-Fi for virtual schooling. In addition to responding to contextual challenges, we also saw changes in purpose that drove school structures and personnel decisions through the early days of the pandemic and beyond. Within days, schools turned into day-care centers for first responders, clinics where the COVID vaccine was administered, and hubs for parent education and family entertainment in times of isolation. In essence, during a time of crisis, schools became hubs of community services—a place for connection, collaboration, and contribution—not just for their students, but for the broader communities they served.

As we envision the schools of the future, applying this "outside-in" principle can help schools start their planning with an honest assessment of the needs and assets in their context, so that educational innovations leverage community assets to develop a truly symbiotic relationship between schools and communities. What industries drive the local economy, and how are schools connecting the learning experiences of students to the future opportunities they hold? What investments are businesses and organizations making in their local schools to connect education to economic development? How are learning experiences reflecting and including the different voices present in the community, and how are they meeting the diverse learning needs that are present?

Thriving Emerges Through Interdependence

In many ways, what we are proposing about the important connection between schools and communities is not new, rather made more salient through the lessons educators have relearned during the upheaval of the COVID-19 pandemic. These ideas are grounded in Maslow's hierarchy of needs: before students in schools can fully engage in the pursuit of self-actualization through education, they must have the fundamental needs of living—physiological, safety, love and belonging, and esteem—met [18]. Luis Torres, a former elementary school principal in the Bronx expanded on this idea in his 2023 book, *The Six Priorities*, in which he argued that before families can focus on their children's education, they must address the more immediate needs of food, shelter, safety, health, and access to technology [19]. This reality, and the important role that communities and schools played in addressing these priorities, was evident during the pandemic. Starting in the spring of 2020, students in American schools saw all these basic needs threatened simultaneously. Health and safety needs were threatened by a lethal virus and a floundering economy, as lockdowns created food and shelter insecurity for millions. Access to technology had to be established before emergency online learning could even occur. Feelings of love and belonging faltered in the isolation of virtual learning, and a sense of esteem was shaken for millions more from watching the videos of people dying at the hands of police and protests in cities around the world. And while vaccines, treatments, and virus evolution have reduced the daily number of COVID deaths, schools have reopened, and stimulus payments have helped many families meet food and shelter needs, the trauma from these events has remained with us.

As we look to the future of education, we need to conceptualize schools as places of interdependence between people and their communities to address the human needs that are essential for the thriving of every person, be they student, parent, or community member. For learning to occur in schools, children must have consistent access to nutritious meals, a safe place to go home to at the end of the day, and a sense that they are valued and cared for at school and at home. For communities to thrive, their young must experience positive development so they may grow up to be productive members of the community in the future. Educators must examine the extent to which this interdependence is a part of the experience that students have in their school. How is the value of interdependence being communicated? Do all members of the community have equal access to this mutually beneficial system? Whose needs are not being considered, and what can we do about it?

Complexity Is Valuable in Educational Discourse

As we use the CIRCLE Model to envision the possibilities of more context-specific, partnership-oriented approaches to structuring public schools, we must be cognizant of the complexity this introduces to an already challenging situation. We do not consider complexity to be a negative condition, rather a clear reflection of reality; public schools are complex institutions situated in complex contexts, facing increasingly complex challenges. The problem does not lie in these layers of complexity, but in the lack of complexity that too often defines our discourse about educational issues. The challenges of education occur at the intersection of complex systems—politics, economics, culture, media—requiring decision-makers to think with nuance and start from an understanding that there are no one-size-fits-all solutions in education. As our student population and their needs become more diverse, almost all educational debates that are defined by dichotomies reflect an unnecessary oversimplification of the issues.

Consider the Reading Wars that involved decades of researchers and practitioners taking sides between phonics-based reading instruction and whole language-based reading instruction. The field eventually settled on a balanced literacy approach that combined important aspects of the two approaches in most reading curricula. Subsequent research has revealed that the balance of approaches did not fully align with needs of developing readers, and reading researchers are contending with how the cognitive science behind reading and reading instruction can be harnessed to create more developmentally appropriate learning experiences for a diverse student body. These approaches meet learners where they are at the start of the school year and responsively build from there [20]. As we think about this example, we have to wonder, if the decades spent debating whether phonics-based instruction or whole language approaches were "the right way" were instead committed to understanding how to balance important instructional practices in ways that served the needs of individual learners, would we have served the last generation of school children better?

Taken together, we believe the three propositions above can support a nuanced application of the CIRCLE Model to schools. Embracing interdependence and complex discourse, we believe a school can work from the outside-in, considering its context-specific assets and challenges as they relate to its stated purpose and goals. Considering these contextual factors, schools can and must create innovative solutions to school structures and personnel challenges in order to help their students and communities thrive. In the following chapters we present some promising practices and policies that exemplify this vision, and we propose some new approaches we think might challenge the field to approach education more creatively in the future.

> **Reflect and Discuss**
> We invite you to consider what you have read in this chapter and apply it to your own community context. Use the following questions as a starting point for your personal reflection and for discussion with education stakeholders in your community.
>
> 1. What were your initial reactions with the CIRCLE Model? How does it impact the way you view the broader ecosystem of education?
> 2. What is the role of innovation in education? How might a model like this help inform best practices and innovation for the schools in your context?
> 3. What structural changes might be needed in your local schools to better meet the educational needs of the students in your community?
> 4. How did the role of school personnel in your community evolve during the pandemic? How can this evolution continue to better support students in the future?
> 5. How can you use your voice to support a more comprehensive, innovative, resilient, and contextualized lens on education in the schools in your community?

REFERENCES

1. Ching, F. D. (2014). *Architecture: Form, space, and order.* John Wiley & Sons.
2. Ladson-Billings, G. (2021). I'm here for the hard re-set: Post pandemic pedagogy to preserve our culture. *Equity & Excellence in Education, 54*(1), 68–78.
3. Goodlad, J. I. (1979). *What schools are for.* Phi Delta Kappa Educational Foundation.
4. Spring, J. (2018). *American education* (18th ed.). Routledge.

5. Wihbey, J., Joseph, K., & Lazer, D. (2019). The social silos of journalism? Twitter, news media and partisan segregation. *New Media & Society, 21*(4), 815–835.
6. Meyer, K. R., Carpenter, N. J., & Hunt, S. K. (2022). Promoting critical reasoning: Civic engagement in an era of divisive politics and civil unrest. *eJournal of Public Affairs, 11*(1), 8.
7. Reardon, S. F., Kalogrides, D., & Shores, K. (2019). The geography of racial/ethnic test score gaps. *American Journal of Sociology, 124*(4), 1164–1221.
8. Aidman, B., & Nelson Baray, S. (2016). Leveraging community resources: Creating successful partnerships to improve schools. *The Educational Forum, 80*, 264–277.
9. Community Schools Forward. (2023). *Framework: Essentials for community school transformation.* Community Schools Forward. Retrieved April 2, 2023, from https://learningpolicyinstitute.org/project/community-schools-forward
10. Williamson, B., Eynon, R., & Potter, J. (2020). Pandemic politics, pedagogies and practices: Digital technologies and distance education during the coronavirus emergency. *Learning, Media and Technology, 45*(2), 107–114.
11. Wallace, T. L., & Chhuon, V. (2014). Proximal processes in urban classrooms: Engagement and disaffection in urban youth of color. *American Educational Research Journal, 51*(5), 937–973.
12. Jones, D. A. (2022). Views on modifying the traditional school calendar for a post-COVID world: Could a balanced calendar model mitigate COVID-19 slide? *Journal of Education*, 00220574221112626.
13. Reich, J., Buttimer, C. J., Coleman, D., Colwell, R., Faruqi, F., & Larke, L. R. (2020, July). *What's lost, what's left, what's next: Lessons learned from the lived experiences of teachers during the pandemic.* Retrieved April 2, 2023, from https://edarxiv.org/8exp9
14. Demarest, C. (2020, March 17). Aiken County school district begins daily meal delivery: Distance learning packets ready Thursday. *Aiken Standard.* https://www.postandcourier.com/aikenstandard/news/aiken-county-school-district-begins-daily-meal-delivery-distance-learning-packets-ready-thursday/article_85cabdb1-ca14-55c6-9e54-b1eefc4e9e1b.html
15. Keagy, K. (2021, October 29). *Principal drives school bus due to driver shortage.* WSAZ News channel 3. https://www.wsaz.com/2021/10/29/principal-drives-school-bus-due-driver-shortage/
16. Marshik, T., Ashton, P. T., & Algina, J. (2017). Teachers' and students' needs for autonomy, competence, and relatedness as predictors of students' achievement. *Social Psychology of Education, 20*(1), 39–67. https://doi.org/10.1007/s11218-016-9360-z

17. Brown, E. C., Freedle, A., Hurless, N. L., Miller, R. D., Martin, C., & Paul, Z. A. (2022). Preparing teacher candidates for trauma-informed practices. *Urban Education, 57*(4), 662–685.
18. Maslow, A. H. (1970). *Motivation and personality* (2nd ed.). Harper & Row.
19. Torres, L. E. (2023). *The six priorities: How to find the resources your school community needs.* ASCD.
20. Goldberg, M., & Goldenberg, C. (2022). Lessons learned? Reading wars, reading first, and a way forward. *The Reading Teacher, 75*(5), 621–630.

CHAPTER 8

Reimagine Where Schools Fit: Purpose and Context

> *I'm acknowledging the resilience of the kids, of the faculty, of the staff. I would just want that to be noted. No, nothing is perfect. Yes, we were able to make a really positive impact on such a negative situation.*
> —Sarah Williams, Teacher, Monterey High School

Building off the CIRCLE Model presented in the previous chapter, we will now focus further on the surroundings of educational institutions—the broader societal purpose they serve, and the more immediate community and culture in which they are situated. As we take our learning from the great disruption that began in 2020—the coronavirus pandemic, the ensuing economic instability, and the racial reckoning—we find ourselves wrestling with competing demands that must be reconciled as part of reimagining education for an evolving future. We must teach children in ways that maintain our competitive edge in the global economy and maintain our credibility on the global stage as the birthplace of modern democracy. All the while, we must keep challenging ourselves to be guided by how these competing demands will have to be met in different ways for different students.

The CIRCLE Model's approach to the educational endeavor situates research findings in the local context, values assets and experiences in the local culture, and leverages novel partnerships with surrounding communities as part of school funding solutions. With this in mind, we now explore some successful examples from the field that can inform how we chart a course forward. From partnerships between school districts and non-profit organizations to fund innovation, to models that structure school districts for greater educational equity, education is poised for meaningful change for the next generation of American students. If the turbulence of the global pandemic showed us anything, it is that these more equitable and contextually responsive approaches to education are necessary in the society this new generation of students will build and lead.

The future of education must prepare students to navigate a world where capitalism has a conscience, and innovation relies on interdependence. While socioeconomic variations in school contexts have traditionally been seen as barriers to equitable outcomes, we suggest that with greater investment in the local context, and more intentional connections across schools and districts, partnerships can be mutually beneficial and equity-building. For this outcome to be possible, we may need to re-evaluate how we conceptualize *achievement* and *success*. Ultimately, this always starts with the question of purpose, or as author of the best-selling book, *The 7 Habits of Highly Effective People*, Stephen R. Covey, suggests, as we chart a course forward, we should "begin with the end in mind [1]." What is the primary purpose of education today? Who do we serve through the work we do? When needs compete, what do we prioritize—the individual students we work with or the greater societal needs that appear to be at odds with their interests at times?

Reaching Consensus on School Purpose

At the start of this book, we described the three broad categories from the work of Joel Spring that are often used to explain different ideas on the purpose of education: political, social, and economic [2]. The political purpose broadly grounds the goals of education in developing good citizens for a democratic society. The social purpose of education concerns itself with moral and ethical goals of growing students into positive members of a community. The economic purpose is geared toward producing the members of the future workforce who are prepared to achieve the American Dream. While the exact ways these ideas have been represented in educational discourse over the years, and which ones are being prioritized in educational practice at a given time, have evolved in each update of Spring's work, we believe that the lessons of the pandemic and related disruption call for a simultaneous balancing of all three of these purposes as part of a larger social justice purpose of education.

The current generation of American public school students represents the most economically, socially, and culturally diverse group that has walked the halls of K-12 schools in the country's history. This fact holds within it a great challenge and an immense opportunity for purposeful education. A June 2022 report from the Government Accountability Office to the Chairman of U.S. House of Representatives Committee on Education and Labor [3] stated that while the student population of America's schools has become increasingly diverse, it also remains largely segregated along racial and ethnic lines—14% of students attend schools where at least 90% of students belong to one racial group. Education policy scholar Sean Riordan suggests that the racial and ethnic test-score gaps in the United States result from disparities in parental income and education: students of color have fewer educational opportunities due to high levels of housing and school segregation. This demographic clustering is a result of a history of unequal treatment afforded to members of different racial and ethnic groups in school and in the workplace and represents a multigenerational accumulation of trauma and structural racism [4]. It also hinders societal progress and keeps Americans trapped in political gridlock in ways that weaken our democracy [5].

Designing Districts for Social Justice

To truly ameliorate the lasting injustices of America's history, we must leverage all the traditional goals of education in support of greater diversity, equity, inclusion, and, in turn, social justice. We must develop conscientious citizens who understand how our democracy has resulted in differing experiences and opportunities for different groups over time, and who will work toward the realization of a democracy that gives voice to all its citizens to build a fairer society for the future. How can we exercise our democratic rights and cast our votes in an informed manner if we are not learning in school about the diverse histories and experiences of our fellow citizens? Our schools must grow empathetic community members who have compassion for the struggles of others, and who are motivated to help all members in their communities thrive and live healthy lives with dignity. How can we truly develop this compassion if we do not spend time interacting with people of diverse backgrounds because our communities and schools are so segregated? Finally, we must produce future workforce members who will use their knowledge, skills, and economic privilege to accomplish the first two purposes, with the clarity that in this time of global connectedness, cooperation is key to creating a sustainable and peaceful path forward for all people.

Applying a social justice purpose to schools requires disrupting the mechanisms that have created the current state of affairs. We must start by considering if schools should serve as sorting mechanisms that reproduce and strengthen the historical injustices that already exist, or if we can transform them into mechanisms for creating opportunity and equity [6]. We see the sorting that creates the current unequal opportunity landscape manifest in different ways throughout the public schooling experience. School attendance boundaries are drawn in a manner that tends to concentrate minoritized students and students growing up in poverty in certain schools [7]. For example, we learned in our interviews in Minneapolis that structural problems must be addressed with structural solutions driven by purpose and mission. To enact the social justice purpose the district has clearly articulated, Minneapolis Public Schools began implementing a Comprehensive District Design plan that included re-examining current policies through an equity lens [8]. Using the results of its school boundary study, the district has redrawn school boundary lines to reduce the racial and ethnic segregation in its schools. It has also streamlined confusing school choice policies and procedures, eliminating those that disadvantage students of color by segregating them in certain schools. The district is currently examining its procedure for assigning teachers to schools, after extensive study and feedback from educators, students, and parents in the community, to make sure all students have equal access to the most experienced teachers. While these changes have been challenging and contributed to leadership turnover, a teacher strike, and enrollment fluctuations at different points during and after the pandemic, the district has not deviated course from its strategic vision, leveraging clarity of purpose to navigate its way to a more just education system through an ongoing process of annual diversity and equity impact assessment [9].

Purpose-Driven Assessment

If the future of education is to serve a social justice purpose, assessment practices will play an important role in several ways. Throughout schooling, testing data are used to determine decisions of educational opportunity within schools, reinforcing the sorting of students discussed in the previous section. Assessment data are used to determine if students have met the criteria for grade completion, and to distribute access to limited academic opportunities, such as gifted and talented programs. Poorly designed identification approaches for these programs consistently result in inequitable access for students of color and those growing up in poverty [10]. Aggregated testing data are used to rate teacher performance and school quality, with ratings potentially playing an influential role in teacher compensation and school funding decisions. While standardized tests and state accountability policies were implemented with the goal of raising student achievement and supporting greater educational equity across student groups [11], a growing body of research suggests a host of negative consequences for instructional practices. From teachers narrowing the curriculum to teach to the test at the expense of building critical thinking skills [12], to investing energy and resources on students who are more likely to pass the test [13], assessment strategies have been implemented in ways that threaten actual opportunities for students to learn. If the social justice purpose of education is to be reflected in the learning experiences of a diverse student body, we must move public school education to a more growth-focused orientation.

With the educational disruptions of the COVID-19 pandemic came several opportunities to think more innovatively about educational assessment. In some cases, the inability to administer standardized tests during the pandemic creates natural opportunities for their abandonment. For example, once colleges and universities waived college entrance exams such as the SAT and the ACT during the pandemic to accommodate applicants who were not able to access the tests during lockdowns, higher education institutions were able to experiment with more holistic admissions processes. With long-standing concerns about the equity issues associated with college entrance exams as a backdrop, approximately 80% of four-year institutions dropped standardized test score requirements for admissions in fall 2023, choosing to either adopt test-optional or test-blind admissions criteria [14]. This replacement of one of the most high-stakes tests that college-bound students take during their K-12 years by a more holistic admissions process has increased the pressure on states to develop more innovative approaches toward assessment for accountability purposes as well.

With state testing requirements waived in the spring of 2020 during virtual schooling, many K-12 education systems found themselves in a unique position to experiment with new assessment approaches. State education agencies have leveraged large infusions of emergency relief funds into their coffers to develop and pilot novel approaches to state accountability systems that reduce the reliance on standardized testing, and that reduce the time schools spend on testing so it can be reallocated to instruction [15]. Several innovative assessment practices have emerged from these efforts that align with the CIRCLE Model and can support the social justice purpose of school. For example, Kentucky focused its accountability and assessment reforms on the development of a public engagement process that used radical inclusion and liberatory design. To gather and incorporate the lived experiences of community stakeholders, the Kentucky Coalition for Advancing Education has established local learning laboratories across the state that are testing locally inspired assessment innovations to inform state system development [16].

In New Hampshire, the Performance Assessment of Competency Education is reducing the standardized testing burden by allowing local development of performance assessments that will use double-blind calibration scoring to support standardization [17]. A network of at least eight states has been collaborating in the development of Stackable, Instructionally-Embedded, Portable Science (SIPS) assessment tasks, which will be modular performance assessments that can be flexibly administered through the year as classes complete instruction on related topics [18]. SIPS would transform the tendency of *teaching to the test* into *testing as you teach*. By integrating assessment intentionally into teaching, students and families will also be able to receive timely, structured feedback throughout the year, without sacrificing large amounts of learning time in the spring to days of standardized testing. While these strategies are prioritizing more local control in accountability assessment procedures to meet the needs of their context, some states are more intentionally bringing the local community into their assessments.

The state of Washington has included a High School and Beyond Plan as a graduation requirement in its schools. Students start building this portfolio toward the end of middle school, adding information related to their career and educational interests and goals, academic and social-emotional competencies, and an activity log of learning experiences, work experiences, and community service from inside and outside of school [19]. The plan supports accountability and greater educational equity through state-mandated requirements for communication, including evidence that students have received information on a range of financial aid opportunities for post-secondary education. By documenting individual educational experiences and goals extensively, students work with educators to align their high school experience with their evolving needs and future aspirations.

Individualized assessment strategies have also played a role in the New Mexico Public Education Department's partnership with non-profit Future Focused Education in its New Mexico Graduate Equity Initiative [20]. While state testing requirements remain in place during this development work, the goal of the project is to replace traditional standardized testing with more innovative approaches. This initiative uses community-based capstones—student-led projects that incorporate the culture and wisdom of the local community to demonstrate the skills and characteristics captured in the high school graduate profiles in place of standardized testing [21]. These profiles were developed with community and industry input, and often include cultural competencies and social-emotional skills that impact employability, in addition to traditional academics. This powerful approach engages in active, self-directed, and community-based learning experiences to produce a body of work or to solve a problem, with the final results being publicly exhibited or presented to school, family, and community stakeholders [22]. Because this assessment approach is deeply integrated with local communities, it is being enacted as part of a broader systemic education movement toward a community schools model that includes three pillars: student support, community engagement, and learning by doing.

Whatever innovative assessment practices we choose, their use must always be guided by purpose [23]. If we collect testing data, we must use it with clear intention—formatively, to inform instructional choices, and diagnostically, to provide more individualized learning supports [24]. Instead of punishing students for what they do not know with lower grades and fewer options, we must consider where we need to adapt our practices to motivate and support students in the learning process. We must start by accepting that our job as educators is to meet students, families, and communities wherever they happen to be, and use every tool at our disposal to support their growth and learning. As we consider these many innovative approaches to assessment that can support a social justice purpose for education, the CIRCLE Model guides us to further integrate our statements of purpose within the local context and the needs of students within them. How can we more intentionally bring the community into the school and the school into the community? What challenges are inherent in this type of partnership? What opportunities exist that can create more responsive and just educational opportunities for students?

SITUATING SCHOOLS IN ECOLOGICAL SYSTEMS

State educational agencies and school districts have to think about opportunities in their context for mutually beneficial innovation that can support schools in terms of purpose and funding and support the needs of the community in novel ways. We learned from our interviews in the Bronx that partnership with the hospital nearby provided essential mental health services for educators during the traumatic events of the early pandemic. Massive death tolls and isolation highlighted the mental health crisis in American schools, and have resulted in acceleration of mental health services in school settings [25]. While an increasing number of schools have been leveraging relationships with health care to set up community health clinics to support vaccination or subsidized dental care for children, and these have been increased since the start of the pandemic, the school-community partnerships that emerged out of necessity during a time of crisis have also created increased openness to more innovative connections between schools and their communities. For example, setting up community centers and senior centers in schools [26] can provide opportunities for mutual financial benefit, but can also support multigenerational learning opportunities that leverage community cultural wealth and local funds of knowledge [27].

One very successful example of this type of school-community partnership can be seen in Swampscott, Massachusetts, where the need to build a new high school and a new senior center serendipitously arose at the same time, and community leaders decided to place both on the same plot of land. While both organizations have separate entrances, their proximity has afforded numerous authentic opportunities for engagement. The school is able to share facilities such as lecture halls, library, computer lab, and auditorium when not in use, and high school students are able to spend time with seniors and learn life skills like cooking or knitting. When members of the senior center need help navigating technology, high school students can volunteer their time to help them. When teachers in the school are looking for guest speakers, the pool of seniors with deep local knowledge and interesting lived experiences of history are available to be called on. At a time when extended families are often dispersed across the country in search of career opportunities, and an aging population is often without extended family support, the partnership in Swampscott offers mutually beneficial intergenerational engagement that can promote community learning and well-being across the lifespan [28].

As schools contend with declining enrollments since the pandemic, they also face losses in funding resulting from reduced student counts [29]. Creative partnerships that open up unused school facilities for community events, child care providers, or other social services might provide more integrated learning opportunities for students and more funds for much-needed school infrastructure and resources as pandemic-related emergency funding expires.

Full Service Community Schools

A more comprehensive approach to community school interdependence that is particularly well-aligned with the CIRCLE Model is the Full Service Community Schools (FSCSs) approach, which has been highlighted in the work of Joy Dryfoos over the course of almost three decades [30]. First developed in the 1980s and 1990s through innovative legislation across multiple states that integrated youth service programs into public schools, these FSCSs continue to be funded through the U.S. Department of Education as community service hubs that work in partnership with a range of agencies and organizations [31]. As defined by the U.S. Department of Education's Office of Innovation and Improvement:

> A full-service community school means a public elementary or secondary school that works with its local educational agency and community-based organizations, nonprofit organizations, and other public or private entities to provide a coordinated and integrated set of comprehensive academic, social, and health services that respond to the needs of its students, students' family members, and community members. In addition, a full-service community school promotes family engagement by bringing together many partners in order to offer a range of supports and opportunities for students, students' family members, and community members. [32]

While each FSCS looks different based on the needs and resources of the community in which it is located, several key features are common to schools that take this approach. First, the overarching rationale for FSCSs is that school-community partnerships create high-quality learning experiences for students that result in improved academic performance, even in under-served and under-resourced neighborhoods. While housed in school buildings, FSCSs tend to provide services for extended hours throughout the year, often including extensive afterschool and summer programming, medical and mental health services, parent education programs, and services related to food, shelter, and case management from a range of social service providers. They also involve high levels of parental and community engagement and shared leadership structures that bring together school principals and service coordinators in decision-making. While these components bring the community into the school, students from these schools are also often engaged in service learning and community service opportunities that bring them into the community and create mutual benefit [33].

Community schools have existed for decades, in some form or another, and according to the Coalition for Community School, approximately 5000 community schools exist in the United States [34]. Although the data on the exact number of FSCSs is more limited and includes a smaller number, the increase in federal funding toward this strategy since the pandemic began in 2020 suggests that there is growing interest in increasing school-community partnership in this way. In December of 2022, the White House announced the passage of a bipartisan funding bill that increased investment in the Full Service Community Schools Program to $150 million, doubled from the $75 million the previous year [35]. The following month, the U.S. Department of Education announced $63 million in funding being awarded to 42 new grantees in 8 states and territories to establish FSCSs [36]. The successful stories of school-community interdependence that have emerged from the pandemic, and a growing research base that shows powerful positive impacts on student learning and overall well-being in community schools [37], support further innovation in the FSCS space to maximize the benefits of this approach. For example, the workforce of every field depends on teachers to support early learning. How can corporate and industry partnerships within an FSCS framework help address teacher shortages? How might schools use FSCS models to strengthen post-secondary pipelines that leverage education to lift families and communities out of poverty? How can the efficiencies of time and space that an FSCS affords be translated into more individualized learning opportunities for students?

Finding Innovative Funding Solutions

Ultimately, all innovation must be funded to take root and become systemic, and school-based innovations are no different. Inequities in education funding that result from housing segregation will always be a challenge under our current school funding system that relies so heavily on local property taxes. Research suggests that community school models are a promising approach to funding equity through more efficiency in education spending, as demonstrated in the example from Swampscott in this chapter [37]. Increasing the role of federal funding, and to some extent state funding, toward schools could open doors to address the structural and resource issues of educational equity. Public school finance policies in the U.S. tend to produce limited options, but federal funds remain essential, especially in times of crisis. An examination of data since the Great Recession of 2008 suggests that we must remain vigilant as emergency federal funding from the pandemic dries up. Many states disinvested from public education after the recession, and while their spending continued to increase slowly over the subsequent years, by the time the COVID-19 pandemic began, education expenditures in many states, particularly in the South, had not returned to pre-recession levels [38].

One model of education finance reform that has garnered much international acclaim and can be instructive when considering innovative funding approaches comes from the Brazilian municipality of Sobral [39], and has been expanded through the entire state of Ceará, where Sobral is located, due to the initiative's success. Over the course of a decade, Ceará, one of the poorest states in Brazil, engaged in several practices that helped communities practically eliminate a school dropout crisis, dramatically improve lagging literacy outcomes, and developed a well-trained teacher workforce. Some of Ceará's finance reforms included changing how funds are distributed and attaching funding levels to meeting state academic outcome targets that are set annually. While this creates some competition between districts, it is augmented with a funding process that rewards municipalities with incentive funds based on growth rather than average scores; research suggests much of this funding is awarded to municipalities that have been underperforming and drives continuous improvement by traditionally under-resourced schools. Unlike the traditional education funding streams, these incentive funds can be used by municipalities in more flexible ways to address issues in the community, creating better conditions for education [40].

While this mechanism has helped redistribute resources in the state in ways that create greater education equity, they were introduced with several policies and resources that have supported their success. First, the state provides access to extensive technical assistance, monthly professional development for teachers, and scripted curricula, lesson plans, and materials in its target area of literacy to ensure that all teachers can implement a baseline level of literacy instruction with ease. Perhaps the most innovative incentive that clearly aligns with the interdependence ethos we value in the CIRCLE Model is that high-performing schools are incentivized to mentor low-performing schools, with incentive funds tied to improved outcomes demonstrated by low-performing schools [41]. This investment in shared goals and outcomes offers a policy mechanism that clearly values and rewards equity-oriented behaviors in schools, and brings to bear the financial resources of the State in an alignment of educational purpose and school context.

As we look forward to the future of public education, we would be remiss to ignore what was likely the biggest lesson we can take away from the pandemic years: the future of education is not grounded in an economic, social, or civic purpose, rather in its ability to comprehensively address the dual epidemics of inequality (economic and racial) that America has been struggling with through a social justice purpose. Public schools in every context must be responsive to this reality in the ways needed by their community. As Principal Purkeypile reminded us in Lubbock, not doing so is not really an option:

> *In my humble opinion, public schools have never been more necessary than they are right now. The "safe port" for the exchange of ideas may be more important now than it ever has. We will work to lead the next generation back to the idea of "civil discourse" and if we do not; it will not be due to a lack of effort. At least not from this little public high school on the high plains of West Texas.*

As the field integrates new ideas on education structures and personnel that have emerged from this turbulent time into the mainstream of pedagogical thought and classroom praxis, we must keep our eyes on the needs of the next generation of Americans that are currently in our schools. We believe the answers lie in developing comprehensive curriculum and instructional practices that combine both critical skills needed for the twenty-first-century economy and the critical consciousness needed for the twenty-first-century citizen.

Reflect and Discuss

We invite you to consider what you have read in this chapter and apply it to your own community context. Use the following questions as a starting point for your personal reflection and for discussion with stakeholders in your community.

1. How can we better design institutions and school districts to support educational equity?
2. What role can you play in supporting educational equity in your local schools?
3. In what ways might educators improve assessment to be more purposeful and responsive to the needs of student learning and development?
4. How do schools fit within the larger context of community and ecological systems in your area? How can you advocate for deeper connections?
5. What is the role of community schools in modern society? What positive impacts could a community school bring about in your area?

References

1. Covey, S. R. (2020). *The 7 habits of highly effective people*. Simon & Schuster.
2. Spring, J. (2017). *American education*. Routledge.
3. Nowicki, J. M. (2022, June 16). *K-12 Education: student population has significantly diversified, but many schools remain divided along racial, ethnic, and economic lines*. US Government Accountability Office. Retrieved April 14, 2023, from https://www.gao.gov/assets/gao-22-104737.pdf
4. Danieli, Y. (1998). *International handbook of multigenerational legacies of trauma*. Springer Science & Business Media.
5. Drutman, L. (2021, March 4). How much longer can this era of political gridlock last? *FiveThirtyEight*. https://fivethirtyeight.com/features/how-much-longer-can-this-era-of-political-gridlock-last/
6. Lubienski, C., Perry, L. B., Kim, J., & Canbolat, Y. (2022). Market models and segregation: Examining mechanisms of student sorting. *Comparative Education, 58*(1), 16–36.
7. Owens, A. (2020). Unequal opportunity: School and neighborhood segregation in the USA. *Race and Social Problems, 12,* 29–41.

8. Minneapolis Public Schools (2021, November 9). *Comprehensive District Design (CDD): Implementation progress updates.* Minneapolis Public Schools. https://accountability.mpls.k12.mn.us/comprehensive_district_design_cdd
9. Minneapolis Public Schools. (2022, August 19). *Equity and diversity impact assessment.* MPS EDIA. Retrieved April 13, 2023, from https://sites.google.com/mpls.k12.mn.us/mpsedia/home
10. Peters, S. J. (2022). The challenges of achieving equity within public school gifted and talented programs. *Gifted Child Quarterly, 66*(2), 82–94.
11. US Department of Education. (2019). *Standards, assessments, and accountability.* US Department of Education. Retrieved April 13, 2023, from https://www2.ed.gov/admins/lead/account/saa.html
12. Berliner, D. (2011). Rational responses to high stakes testing: The case of curriculum narrowing and the harm that follows. *Cambridge Journal of Education, 41*, 287–302.
13. Horn, I. S. (2018). Accountability as a design for teacher learning: Sensemaking about mathematics and equity in the NCLB era. *Urban Education, 53*, 382–408. https://doi.org/10.1177/0042085916646625
14. Nietzel, M. T. (2022, November 15). More Than 80% of four-year colleges won't require standardized tests for fall 2023 admissions. *Forbes.* https://www.forbes.com/sites/michaeltnietzel/2022/11/15/more-than-80-of-four-year-colleges-wont-require-standardized%2D%2Dtests-for-fall-2023-admissions/?sh=16b7c3557fb9
15. Pace, L. (2020, April 22). *State guidance for building resilient and equitable education systems.* Knowledge Works. Retrieved April 13, 2023, from https://knowledgeworks.org/wp-content/uploads/2020/04/restoring-hope-in-crisis-Covid19.pdf
16. Dodd, K. (2022). *Kentucky coalition for advancing education.* Kentucky Department of Education. Retrieved April 13, 2023, from https://education.ky.gov/CommOfEd/Pages/Kentucky-Coalition-for-Advancing-Education.aspx
17. White, M. (2023). *Performance assessment of competency education.* State of New Hampshire. Retrieved April 13, 2023, from https://www.education.nh.gov/who-we-are/division-of-learner-support/bureau-of-instructional-support/performance-assessment-for-competency-education
18. SIPS (2021). *Stackable, instructionally-embedded, portable science (SIPS) assessments project.* SIPS Partners. Retrieved April 15, 2023, from https://sipsassessments.org/sips-measurement-models-and-psychometric-methods/
19. Washington State Board of Education. (2021). *High school and beyond plan.* Washington State Board of Education. Retrieved April 13, 2023, from https://www.sbe.wa.gov/our-work/high-school-and-beyond-plan
20. Innovations in Assessment. (2020). *The New Mexico graduation equity initiative. The innovations in assessment and new measure grant program.* Retrieved

April 15, 2023, from https://www.education-first.com/wp-content/uploads/2022/08/NewMexico-case-study-08.22.pdf
21. Hand, T. (2023, January 27). *Innovation zones offer fertile ground for high school transformation*. Future Focused Education. Retrieved April 15, 2023, from https://futurefocusededucation.org/2023/01/27/innovation-zones-offer-fertile-ground-for-high-school-transformation/
22. Good, D. (2021, Mar 10). *Senior capstones are replacing bubble tests at some high schools*. Future Focused Education. Retrieved, April 13, 2023, from https://futurefocusededucation.org/2021/03/10/senior-capstones-are-replacing-bubble-tests-at-some-high-schools-how-this-will-change-our-education-system/
23. McTighe, J., & Thomas, R. S. (2003). Backward design for forward action. *Educational Leadership, 60*(5), 52–55.
24. Deonovic, B., Chopade, P., Yudelson, M., de la Torre, J., & von Davier, A. A. (2019). Application of cognitive diagnostic models to learning and assessment systems. In M. von Davier & Y. S. Lee (Eds.), *Handbook of diagnostic classification models: Models and model extensions, applications, software packages* (pp. 437–460).
25. Cummings, J. R., Wilk, A. S., & Connors, E. H. (2022). Addressing the child mental health state of emergency in schools—Opportunities for state policy makers. *JAMA Pediatrics, 176*(6), 541–542.
26. Peetz, C. (2023, March 13). A town put a senior center in its high school, offering a model for an aging nation. *Education Week*. https://www.edweek.org/leadership/a-town-put-a-senior-center-in-its-high-school-offering-a-model-for-an-aging-nation/2023/03
27. Llopart, M., & Esteban-Guitart, M. (2018). Funds of knowledge in 21st century societies: Inclusive educational practices for under-represented students. *Journal of Curriculum Studies, 50*(2), 145–161.
28. Stephan, A. (2021). Intergenerational learning in the family as an informal learning process: A review of the literature. *Journal of Intergenerational relationships, 19*(4), 441–458.
29. Syverson, E., & Duncombe, C. (2022). *Student counts in k-12 funding models*. Education Commission of the States.
30. Dryfoos, J. (2005). Full-service community schools: A strategy—Not a program. *New Directions for Youth Development, 107*, 7–14.
31. Min, M., Anderson, J. A., & Chen, M. (2017). What do we know about full-service community schools? Integrative research review with NVivo. *School Community Journal, 27*(1), 29–54.
32. U.S. Department of Education. (2014, June 5). *Frequently asked questions about FSCSs*. U.S. Department of Education. Retrieved April 14, 2023, from http://www2.ed.gov/programs/communityschools/faq.html

33. Dryfoos, J., & Maguire, S. (2019). *Inside full-service community schools*. Simon and Schuster.
34. Lubell, E. (2011). *Building community schools: A guide for action*. Children's Aid Society.
35. The White House. (2023, January 18). *Fact sheet: Biden-Harris administration announces efforts to support community schools*. The White House. Retrieved April 14, 2023, from https://www.whitehouse.gov/briefing-room/statements-releases/2023/01/18/fact-sheet-biden-harris-administration-announces-efforts-to-support-community-schools/
36. U.S. Department of Education. (2023, January 18). *U.S. Department of Education announces $63 million to expand community schools and increase social, emotional, mental health, and academic support for students, educators, and families*. U.S. Department of Education. Retrieved April 15, 2023, from https://www.ed.gov/news/press-releases/us-department-education-announces-63-million-expand-community-schools-and-increase-social-emotional-mental-health-and-academic-support-students-educators-and-families
37. Maier, A., Daniel, J., Oakes, J., & Lam, L. (2017). *Community schools as an effective school improvement strategy: A review of the evidence*. Learning Policy Institute.
38. Allegretto, S., García, E., & Weiss, E. (2022). *Public education funding in the US needs an overhaul: How a larger federal role would boost equity and shield children from disinvestment during downturns*. Economic Policy Institute.
39. The Economist. (2021, December 18). What a Brazilian state can teach the world about education. *The Economist*. https://www.economist.com/the-americas/2021/12/18/what-a-brazilian-state-can-teach-the-world-about-education
40. Loureiro, A., Cruz, L., Lautharte, I., & Evans, D. K. (2020, June). *The State of Ceará in Brazil is a role model for reducing learning poverty*. World Bank. Retrieved April 14, 2023, from https://documents1.worldbank.org/curated/en/281071593675958517/pdf/The-State-of-Ceara-in-Brazil-is-a-Role-Model-for-Reducing-Learning-Poverty.pdf
41. Sondergaard, L. (2020, September 30). *In Ceará, Brazil, mayors have to improve education outcomes to receive more funds*. World Bank. Retrieved April 14, 2023, from https://blogs.worldbank.org/latinamerica/ceara-brazil-mayors-have-improve-education-outcomes-receive-more-funds

CHAPTER 9

Reimagine How Schools Work: Structures and Personnel

> *The work makes your identity, who you are as a teacher and educator. If you feel good about that, then it builds that resiliency to keep going during hard times.*
> —Holly Kleppe, Principal, Ella Baker Global Studies & Humanities School

Once we have used the CIRCLE Model to situate schools in their surrounding purpose and context, it is time to reimagine what occurs within the innovative schools of the future. In this chapter we focus on opportunities in school structures and personnel that can be leveraged for a brighter educational future. First, we examine how schools can think more flexibly about learning formats and time to make room for more responsive learning solutions. The pandemic years revealed the importance of high-speed internet access, and its inaccessibility in many parts of the country. As districts aggressively rolled back online learning options in the summer of 2021 [1], a flexible future where students could learn using the tools and approaches that best met their needs was in danger of being abandoned, and it appeared that the large investments in broadband connectivity needed for equitable access to quality education may not come. As the nation's population grows increasingly diverse, equitable access to high-quality learning experiences may require structural changes in

© The Author(s), under exclusive license to Springer Nature Switzerland AG 2023
F. M. Jamil, J. E. Siddiqi, *Public Education in Turbulent Times*, https://doi.org/10.1007/978-3-031-43237-8_9

schools, and a more pluralistic approach to the types of learning experiences students can benefit from may need to be adopted [2]. Instructional time may have to be reconfigured to adapt to the needs of a new generation of tech-savvy students who have survived global trauma and developed a voice. We propose moving the conversation about school choice beyond choice *between* schools and focusing more on choices *within* schools.

To create a responsive exchange between school structures and personnel, we will explore options for reconceptualizing the educator pipeline. As schools across the nation manage historic learning losses resulting from pandemic education disruptions [3], and teacher preparation programs battle declining enrollments [4], we must wonder as a society how we will continue to serve the educational needs of future generations of learners. In the short term, we must consider how we communicate the value of teachers in society and reduce barriers to entry into the teaching profession. In the long term, how might we support the localized, multi-generational aspects of the teacher pipeline that strengthen communities [5], while simultaneously developing systems that bring in fresh ideas and tap into talent pools from farther away? As the needs of students and society change, different types of teachers and workforce efficiencies may be needed. Instead of dividing school personnel into teachers *and* leaders, we suggest ways in which the reimagined school can view teachers *as* leaders, increasingly empowered to impact the learning of more students as they demonstrate success.

Planning for Pluralistic Structures

When we consider the range of student needs that public schools must address, it is important to keep in mind the CIRCLE Model's proposition that dichotomies represent oversimplification in educational thought. The pandemic revealed dichotomies at every turn that seldom considered the reality that teachers in public schools spend every day of their careers trying to differentiate their practice to meet the vastly different needs of the students in their classrooms. Was online or in-person instruction the right approach in the fall of 2020? Did wearing masks in school help students or harm them? Did learning online cause learning loss and harm mental health among students, or was it a helpful intervention that kept students and their communities safe? There are likely stakeholders in education that would take a strong position in response to any of these questions, but the data suggest that in every one of these situations each option helped some students and hurt others depending on individual and school factors. A study by Cowger and colleagues published in the *New England Journal of Medicine* showed that universal masking mitigated the rates of virus transmission in schools, which they suggested was important because teachers being homesick could be especially disruptive for student learning [6]. On the other hand, Ramdani and colleagues conducted a review of studies on the topic and found that universal masking disrupted the reading of facial expressions and non-verbal social cues in ways that were particularly distressing for people with certain socioemotional psychiatric issues [7]. Masking in schools helped some people and hurt others, and for the people it hurt, perhaps online options might have created a more responsive learning environment during the time when masks were required for virus prevention.

Reports from around the country have also questioned the length of time schools stayed online during the pandemic, with test score data showing that, on average, students around the country experienced learning losses, and adolescents especially experienced mental health challenges after extended periods of isolation [8]. At the same time, there is a growing awareness that for some students, freedom from peer pressure and bullying, or the ability to experience uninterrupted learning even though chronic health conditions might have put them at greater risk of negative outcomes if they contracted the coronavirus, made virtual learning largely beneficial. The safety of learning from home allowed them to thrive academically in ways they never had, resulting in states like Texas rolling back school district funding for online learning once federal funding expired, and then reinstituting online and hybrid options only months later due to high demand from families [9]. Yet again, when the debate was contextualized, and proper consideration given to the needs of different students, policymakers realized that providing flexible options for students to choose online, hybrid, and in-person learning would allow more students to be successful over the long run. If we were to reframe the question from *whether* we should invest in virtual learning to *how* we can make virtual learning options worthy of investment, we open up space to create more responsive, equitable options for all students. We can learn from the areas where virtual learning failed students, and instead of abandoning the endeavor, we can improve it!

Keep in mind that the outcomes of changes undertaken rapidly during a crisis do not represent what is possible when those same changes are undertaken as part of a process of gradual, considered innovation. A review of research on online learning by Tate and Warschauer from 2022 frames the educational equity issues the field must contend with in relation to virtual education along the lines of physical, human, and social resources [10]. This framing is instructive as we consider a path forward, especially because it differentiates between emergency online learning and planned online learning. The physical resources that create challenges to effective online learning—computers, internet connectivity, access to appropriate software—often stem from funding disparities across schools and families. Human resources needed for successful online learning include the self-regulated learning skills that students must have to effectively manage their online engagement experience. These skills can vary a great deal across individuals based on their level of maturity and the sources of their motivation. Finally, social resources can include the online instruction skills of teachers, and parental and peer support. Addressing inequities in all three of these areas is an essential first step in a reimagined education future where students have flexible options to choose from across learning formats.

While many schools have been able to leverage emergency educational funding during the pandemic to acquire appropriate technologies and broadband connections for students and teachers, physical resources such as individual devices must be replaced regularly to remain useful. As emergency funds are rolled back, school-community-industry partnerships can be incredibly helpful for meeting these physical resource needs. As mentioned in the previous chapter when we discussed full-service community schools, school-community partnerships are especially beneficial in ensuring that students have their essential human needs met. One challenge we have yet to contend with is how, in modern society, broadband internet connectivity is becoming as important to leading a life where you reach your full potential as access to electricity and clean water. In other words, to achieve educational equity, broadband connectivity must be a public utility, and communities should move to universal access to support thriving for all their members [11].

Many large technology companies, such as Apple and Microsoft, have negotiated special pricing for education entities and educators, but another way that schools can manage technology replacement costs and improve their capacity for online instruction is by partnering with educational technology companies for teacher professional development needs as part of their purchase contracts. All too often, school districts make large investments in purchasing new physical resources, without the corresponding investment in adequate human and social resources to ensure new technologies are put to the most effective use. As education technologies become seamlessly integrated into public school learning, we must take advantage of the robust training tools and workshops created by educational technology developers—often available for free online—and pair these with professional learning communities where teachers can collaboratively support each other in refining their use of new technologies in the context of their school and student population. A growing research literature on *microlearning*, professional development experiences for teachers that can be accessed in small chunks as needed, highlights the effectiveness of this approach for increasing the teacher's effective incorporation of new educational technologies in their practice, especially when paired with a social learning component [12]. Financial efficiencies from conceptualizing educational technology plans and teacher professional development in this interrelated way can be reinvested toward technology replacement costs, while simultaneously increasing the social resources brought to student learning by skilled teachers that are comfortable using online learning tools.

Viewed through the lens of the CIRCLE Model, virtual and hybrid learning options are in themselves democratizing approaches in ways that can reduce academic inequalities over time when situated in contexts that have a lower capacity for unique course offerings. For example, smaller rural schools often have difficulties supporting a range of advanced courses and foreign language electives for their students because not enough students in the school would take a course for it to make financial sense to hire a teacher for it. But if a group of schools pooled their resources and coordinated their scheduling, a synchronous online version of the course offering could create new opportunities for students in all their schools. In many ways, this idea is just an institutional-level extension of the pandemic pods that so many parents opted for to return their children to in-person learning during lockdown—joining a group of families in a quarantine bubble and pooling their resources together to hire a teacher for their children [13]. By providing more online learning opportunities, and in turn, more affordances for practicing self-regulated learning in online settings, schools would also address some of the human resource challenges of virtual learning. Students cannot grow their capacity of self-regulated learning online if they do not have the option for practice. Gaining that practice during one class, while maintaining a largely in-person learning schedule, could be an approach to building that skill without potentially jeopardizing a whole year of learning.

Taking the Time to Thrive

Structural innovation in schools must consider how schools prioritize and use time—for learning, for planning, and for healing—in addition to the learning formats they offer students to support their learning needs. As we consider purpose-driven learning experiences designed with respect for and in response to the community, we are moving the finish line of public school education from providing our students the basic skill for surviving the challenges of the world to a robust set of tools for thriving in it. In the wealthiest nation on the planet, this seems like a reasonable adjustment to make. As with all aspects of education we have discussed using the CIRCLE Model in this book, we believe that in a diverse society the approach to thriving must be responsive to individual needs by creating a range of opportunities for learners to choose from. In addition, any structural changes that schools undertake must come with a corresponding assessment of personnel training and needs to achieve a successful outcome. Coming out of the greatest disruption to American education in generations, innovation and change in education must start with repairing the harm done to the learning and development of the current generation of students during the pandemic.

Time to Recover Learning

Since returning to in-person learning after pandemic lockdowns, schools have had to approach time in flexible ways to accommodate fluctuating coronavirus infection rates in the community, and this has, perhaps, created more openness for unconventional approaches. Around the country, school districts have made space in school schedules to offer additional academic support to students, and added time to their school calendars to provide essential professional development that teachers need for the changing demands of teaching in the post-pandemic era. One particularly important change has been the increased effort schools have put into providing teachers with common planning time to collaborate with colleagues. A growing body of research suggests that creating space for teachers to build collective knowledge and learn from each other's experiences helps professionalize teaching and breaks down the structural isolation that is commonplace in school settings [14]. This shift in thinking is incredibly beneficial as schools try to attract new talent to a shrinking field, but it has also been helpful in bringing teacher teams together to understand how to support learning recovery for students that fell behind academically during the pandemic.

A more comprehensive approach that builds a standard block of *flex time* into the master schedule of the school is becoming increasingly popular since the pandemic because it creates a designated time for individualized learning supports to be enacted [15]. For example, in Anderson School District 1 in South Carolina, plans for pandemic learning losses included the introduction of a 40-minute flex time block to the high school schedule between morning core classes on four days of the week. During this time, students can meet with teachers for extra support, make up tests, or complete homework collaboratively with peers. The latter provides opportunities for peer learning, but also creates structured time to make up for lost peer interaction time and the social-emotional learning that was hampered during pandemic virtual instruction. On Wednesdays, there is no flex block, and by shortening each class by a few minutes, students are released an hour early, clearing the way for school data and problem-solving teams to hold meetings to discuss individual student needs and adjustment to learning times. This time is also used by teachers in professional learning communities that are addressing various challenges in their school. In addition, this early release time allows students time to engage in learning and work experiences outside of school, including internships and community service. While flex blocks in schedules have different names and are structured differently across districts and schools, there is no doubt, this mechanism has shown promising results for supporting students individually in the interest of recovering lost learning [16].

Time to Master Learning

Another way in which the pandemic has created opportunity for educators to rethink school structures is in regard to how we conceptualize the time needed for learning a concept. Mastery learning, or competency-based learning, is an approach to learning and assessment that was first introduced in the late 1960s. It posited that by providing necessary individual learning support and additional time, teachers could adjust the rate of learning required of students and eventually bring most students to a mastery of concepts, effectively closing gaps in learning outcomes [17]. Mastery learning approaches have variations in how they are conceptualized and implemented, but the overarching concept is that because students learn things at a different pace, often reflecting the baseline from where they start learning a concept, they should not be assessed and moved forward to the next topic in lock step [18]. Unlike traditional approaches, where classes move through curricular topics based on a predetermined schedule of instruction and assessment, whether or not individual students fully understand the concepts, mastery learning favors a more individualized approach. Students are allowed to receive feedback, practice, and resubmit assignments and assessments until they have demonstrated mastery of the concept. When considered through the CIRCLE Model's conceptualization of educational purposes, we have to ask some guiding questions. Do we value *what* students learn in school or *when* they learn it? If one student masters a grade level standard in the fall and another student masters it in the spring, is it fair for their grades to consider one student as passing and the other as failing on that content or skill solely based on the timing of the assessment? Is the goal of assessments to measure what students know as it changes dynamically over the year, or to document what they do not know at a given time?

Proponents of the approach cite several factors in its favor. First, where traditional approaches often leave gaps in student understanding that can increase the challenge of learning later topics as students progress through the curriculum, mastery learning ensures that when students reach the next learning objectives, they will have the requisite understanding to build on. Second, the approach is more clearly grounded in the science of learning and human development, with a plethora of evidence that human beings require different amounts of time to acquire different skills, and that the time it takes to master a skill says little about the level of competence with which they will eventually function. Finally, more recent research has suggested that mastery learning approaches might be fruitful in raising motivation and encouraging persistence toward learning goals.

A survey by *Education Week* in 2023 asked a nationally representative sample of students aged 13–19, and secondary teachers, what would motivate students to work harder in school. Among the students, the most selected option of the 24 possible, with about 35% of students endorsing it, was the opportunity to redo assignments if they receive a low grade [19]. Among teachers, this option ranked 11th out of 24, with the more often endorsed ideas including providing students with more hands-on experiences, or showing students the application of the concepts being taught to support student motivation [20]. While all of these approaches are beneficial, students were clearly indicating the need for different affordances in learning than their teachers thought they needed.

The mastery learning approach has been used by individual schools and organizations around the world with a range of student populations, but it has not had widespread adoption because of the increased challenge for teachers to manage students at different points in the curriculum simultaneously. Several advances in the field have made this approach a more viable option for further innovation and adoption than ever before. First, the field has a deeper understanding of the science of learning and human development as they occur in technology-mediated and real-world contextual systems that suggest mastery approaches can promote deeper learning [21]. Second, the existence of mastery-based online tools for individualized learning, such as Khan Academy, can efficiently provide students with independent skills practice to reduce the content creation and lesson planning burden on teachers when students need more time and support [22]. Finally, growing evidence that mastery learning approaches can close the widened learning outcome disparities, caused by the disproportionately negative impact of pandemic learning losses on the most vulnerable students, has created an increased interest in the approach among leaders of large school districts across the country. In October 2021, a group of six school district superintendents from California, Texas, Florida, Pennsylvania, Nevada, and Maryland, founding members of the Superintendents Alliance at the National Center on Education and the Economy, penned an influential op-ed highlighting the distinction between learning and time as criteria for graduation. This publication brought the long-brewing debate of education purpose to center stages, putting the onus on the field to invest time and resources on approaches that resulted in lasting student learning [23].

Time to Heal for Learning

As we learned during our interviews with educators in different parts of the country and from our own lived experiences, between the trauma of death and sickness, the struggles with economic uncertainty, and the pain of racial violence, recovery from lost learning is not the only place where educators must invest their time in order for students to thrive. The trauma experienced by students through this disruptive series of events was pervasive and complex—touching their sense of physical and emotional safety, altering developmental trajectories of cognition, emotion, and behavior, and challenging their identity development and sense of belonging in school and wider society [24]. And these experiences of trauma were not limited to students. All members of school communities, from students, families, teachers, staff, and administrators experienced the traumatic effects of the pandemic in a variety of ways. Beyond individual experiences of illness and death, the COVID-19 pandemic was an event that resulted in a layer of collective trauma, disrupting and changing societal norms and connections locally and globally [25]. Adopting practices that support healing from these layers of trauma, and dedicating the time to fully engage in these practices, will be an essential part of structuring education for the future.

Based on the proposition of *working from the outside-in* that we articulated in Chap. 7, we contend that academic recovery and healing from the trauma of the pandemic go hand in hand. For students to thrive academically, they must be learning in environments where every individual is dedicated to creating a healing space and has the skills and resources to do so. We must create schools that are not just trauma-informed, rather trauma-engaged and healing-centered spaces that take a whole system approach to building safe and just schools [26]. Much like the systems approach toward educational equity that we observed in interviews in Minneapolis, these healing-centered schools of the future will articulate trauma-informed policies that make it incumbent on all members of the school community to consider the root cause of academic and behavioral challenges, including the role trauma might have played, and respond in ways that make space for healing. For example, schools might replace zero-tolerance discipline policies such as suspension, an exclusionary practice that tends to exacerbate harm and trauma, with restorative circles and mediation-based conflict resolution that prioritizes healing damaged relationships over punishment [27]. Systems approaches also provide training to all community members on understanding, recognizing, and appropriately addressing trauma within the purview of their role. They empower adults in the school community to support student healing by incorporating resources like mindfulness, meditation, and calming spaces into their classroom norms [28].

Chicago Public Schools provides an excellent example of a district that has undertaken intensive, systemic change to address community trauma through its Healing Centered Framework [29]. The framework is grounded in an understanding that healing from collective trauma requires collective effort, and includes a role for school leaders, staff, students and families, and community partners. With five main components, the multi-year initiative aims to:

- increase education and awareness of trauma among all stakeholders
- provide skills training related to coping with stress and cultivating well-being
- promote a culture of equity and belonging
- provide the resources to prevent future trauma and create healing
- build capacity for crisis support

By centering healing in this sweeping strategic initiative, the school district has decided that it will take the time to heal, moving forward with empathy and humanity [30]. To support this process and keep it responsive to the needs of the community, the district has also committed to tracking progress. Instead of just focusing assessment on academic aspects of education, it will also be collecting more humanizing data from all stakeholders—social, emotional, and psychological indicators of well-being—to ensure that mental health challenges are being recognized and addressed, and the district investments continue to be targeted intentionally for systemic healing to occur [26].

Establishing Resilient Educator Pipelines

For the structural changes outlined above to occur and be successful, the CIRCLE Model recognizes that complementary innovations in the recruitment and retention of education personnel need to be a part of future-oriented solutions. The size and training of the teacher workforce in many districts could make some of these practices impossible to implement. While workforce challenges take different forms in different contexts, a few issues facing the current teacher pipeline include the declining number of individuals entering the field, the low levels of diversity in the workforce, and licensing restrictions that are a barrier to entry and movement in the profession.

The widespread teacher shortage that was already concerning education leaders before the COVID-19 pandemic has been exacerbated by the low pay, burnout, and political battles over curriculum and teaching practices, with over one million teachers leaving their jobs between 2020 and the end of 2022 [31]. Education systems, including school districts, higher education institutions, and state and federal governments, have created pathways and partnerships to reduce the cost of teacher education, removing a large barrier to entry for some in an era of rising costs in higher education. For example, the Teacher Pipeline Project, a partnership between American University and D.C. Public Schools, recruits high school students to the field so that they can take advantage of dual enrollment credits and take teacher education courses while in high school. Some students even earn a Child Development Associate degree by the time they graduate. At that point, students are provided with full scholarships to complete their teacher education, ongoing coaching and mentoring, guaranteed teaching jobs once they complete their degrees, and a seamless transition experience with a supportive professional community through their first year in the field. Freed from financial burden and debt, these new teachers are able to focus on their development as professionals and fill much-needed teaching positions after graduation [32]. Similar pipeline pathways, some of them targeting paraprofessionals already working in the school, are taking a *Grow Your Own* approach to invest in the local community to increase capacity.

The One Million Teacher of Color campaign is aimed at creating a resilient and more diverse teacher workforce by adding one million teachers of color and thirty-thousand leaders of color to the education workforce over the next decade. While 52% of students in the United States identify as people of color, nearly 80% of teachers are white, and 78% of principals are white. Over 40% of public schools don't have a single teacher of color. For the teacher workforce to mirror student demographics in America, we know we need to add one million new teachers of color to our nation's schools. In February of 2021, The Hunt Institute and TNTP, together with EdTrust, MCEL, New Leaders, and Teach Plus, formed a coalition dedicated to eliminating the educator diversity gap by 2030. Together they have leveraged local and state partners to address challenges at the federal, state, and community levels. While this work is in its infancy, it will take creative thinking and bold innovations to fortify the teacher pipeline.

State-funded initiatives to reduce the cost of teacher education and fill critical positions have also played an important role in strengthening the teacher pipeline. For example, the North Carolina Teaching Fellows, which aims to recruit high achieving high school students into the teaching profession, has provided scholarships and forgivable loans to reduce or eliminate the cost of traditional teacher preparation in partner programs across the state. An early iteration of the program provided scholarships to future teachers in exchange for a four-year commitment to teach in North Carolina public schools. Graduates from this program had higher retention rates than the field, with about 75% of them remaining in teaching after five years. This was attributed to strong preparation, professional networking, and ongoing mentorship that accompanied the financial support [33]. In 2015, the state's legislature ended the popular program as enrollment in teacher education underwent a sharp decline, redirecting the funds toward the nonprofit organization Teach for America [34, 35]. In 2017, North Carolina reinstated a revised Teaching Fellows program, now only targeting new teachers in STEM and Special Education, and replacing the scholarships with forgivable student loans, each year of which can be repaid by teaching for a single year in a low-performing public school in the state, or two years in any public school in North Carolina. While data are clouded by impacts of the COVID-19 pandemic, the results of this new iteration suggest that while it is building the teacher workforce, more students are choosing to pay back the loan after graduation than are teaching in low-performing schools for the faster pay-off, suggesting the financial incentive may not be enough to address that challenge [36].

As we think forward to the future of public education in America, there is no doubt that attracting the next generation of teachers to a profession that has been embattled and underpaid for decades is a looming challenge. But how will we educate doctors for our hospitals, engineers and scientists for our industries, and lawmakers to run our government, if we cannot provide them with a high-quality K-12 education for a lack of teachers in our schools? While school-university partnerships and state financial aid programs are making a difference, trajectory-changing solutions to our leaky teacher pipeline require more integral intervention. We saw during the pandemic that large investments of emergency funding by the federal government can have dramatic impacts. With 55% of current teachers considering leaving the profession earlier than they had previously planned, Americans must consider sweeping solutions to the teacher shortage [37].

We can look across the globe for solutions, starting with nations that have strong education systems and produce competitive students. Finland and Singapore have consistently ranked in the top ten across Reading, Mathematics, and Science scores on the Programme for International Student Assessment (PISA) test, administered to 15-year-olds in over 90 countries by the Organization for Economic Cooperation and Development (OECD) [38]. In Finland and Singapore, the government completely covers the cost of teacher education, even paying stipends or salaries to students in teacher preparation programs while they learn, much like the model used by many doctoral programs to support Ph.D. students in the United States. Because teachers are considered an important investment in the country's future, teaching is a highly regarded profession in both countries, with competitive entrance into teacher education, and salaries that are on par with other professions with similar levels of education [39].

When we consider the massive investments made by the U.S. government into our defense budget, maintaining the largest and most powerful military in the world, we must ask, how safe is the country when it has a weakened and understaffed education system? At a time when information is power, wars can be fought using information technologies as well as conventional weapons. Investing in a well-educated citizenry that can think critically about the information it consumes and develop a deep understanding of the issues that govern its vote is as important for maintaining a strong democracy as developing cutting-edge military technology [40]. Could a robust federal investment in America's public school teachers and their preparation not raise the prestige and desirability for teaching? How can we build on these ideas to not only recruit excellent teacher candidates into our teacher preparation programs, but also encourage them to stay in the profession once they are there?

Rewarding Excellence to Retain Teachers

Because of the somewhat unique structure of the education system in the United States, with responsibility largely falling to states and local governments constitutionally, federal government involvement comes with high political hurdles that must be navigated. This is why programs like the National Teacher Corps (NTC), created as part of the Higher Education Act of 1965, did not fare as well as other parts of the landmark legislation, which also created federal financial aid and loans. The NTC was established to develop a cadre of highly trained teachers with skills especially targeted toward underserved urban and rural schools [41]. NTC programs were developed in a partnership between higher education institutions and school districts. The structure was designed so districts could request assistance, and teams with one expert teacher mentoring four interns would be dispatched to work in the school, their salaries paid by the federal government. Like their contemporaries in the Peace Corps, NTC interns were often young graduates of prestigious colleges, engaged in social activism and national service [42]. Corps members had reduced teaching loads because they were expected to do community service in the district, complete summer training, and continue to take university courses to obtain master's degrees. The program was revised over several iterations, each further removing the national service focus of the corps and giving more control back to local education systems, until it was finally disbanded in 1981. Although short-lived, the program established that educators working with children in poverty may need special skills and strategies to teach effectively, and laid the foundation for future alternate certification programs run by nonprofit organizations, like Teach for America [43]. The NTC program also set a precedent for a federally funded teacher corps, and several calls for its reintroduction in some form have been made over the decades since it was disbanded [44].

We contend that the current moment in time may be well-suited for the introduction of a national service program like the National Teacher Corps that is targeted toward teacher retention more than teacher recruitment. We draw on a proposal for *America's Teacher Corps (ATC)*, made by the Brookings Institute in 2010, which envisioned that a national pool of highly effective teachers, as demonstrated by a district or state evaluation system, could be awarded membership in ATC [45]. Conceptualized as a prestigious designation, ATC membership would come with national recognition of teaching excellence, a salary supplement contingent on teaching in a Title I school, and a portable credential that would be accepted across all 50 states. This approach presents a strategy for increasing professional prestige and salaries for teachers, while also developing a mechanism to encourage retention, and the ability to attract highly skilled teachers to the places where they are the most needed. As teacher shortages grow, there has also been significant interest in a more easily portable teaching credential, with an increasing number of states joining an Interstate Teacher Mobility Compact to grow their hiring candidate pools [46].

The complexity of teacher shortages, driven by both recruitment and retention challenges, requires a flexible set of solutions that simultaneously addresses challenges at different points in the teacher pipeline to build a resilient teacher workforce for the future. While mobility and recognition for a highly skilled corps of teachers is an important mechanism, there is no escaping the fact that public school teachers in America are underpaid: teachers earn approximately 23% less than their peers in other professions who have similar levels of education [47]. Raising teacher salaries across the board is imperative. The American Teacher Act (H.R. 9566) was introduced in the U.S. House of Representatives on December 14, 2022, with the aim of raising minimum teacher salaries to $60,000 annually through grants to states. The bill includes language referring to the "enhanced awareness of the value of the teaching profession," hinting at the growing magnitude of the teacher workforce crisis the country has entered [48]. A more direct way that the federal government could, in effect, boost teacher salaries would be through permanent tax credits to teachers. For example, the Center for American Progress, a non-partisan policy institute, has proposed a $10,000 federal Teacher Tax Credit for educators in high poverty schools [49]. We imagine this mechanism could be used in a tiered way, perhaps creating a standard tax credit for all teachers, and additional ones focusing on teachers in high-need schools or high-need content areas.

As a final component to these interventions to strengthen the teacher pipeline, we propose rethinking what "retention" means in the current climate. While teachers remaining in the classroom in a full-time capacity is ideal, there are several ways that borrowing models from other organizations can be instructive in managing the needs of teaching, especially when less-than-ordinary conditions occur. For example, in the early part of 2022, New Mexico had to deploy members of its National Guard to fill vacancies in classrooms brought about by a COVID-19 surge and a shortage of substitutes [50]. Imagine if the individuals that were being called up to fill classroom vacancies were members of a National Teacher Reserve? As we envision a resilient teacher pipeline for the future, perhaps there is an opportunity to consider a form of "partially retaining" teachers in the pipeline through a reserve program, where, like their military counterparts, teachers who have left the field would commit to maintaining training through regular workshops and summer institutes and stay prepared for deployment to a teaching assignment in a time of critical need. With proper legislation to protect the rights of teacher reservists with their employers, this approach could allow the field to retain the experience and wisdom of an educator for longer and create options for teachers who are on the verge of burnout to explore other career opportunities. Perhaps reservists could pass on skills and mentor teachers still in the field as part of regular training commitments, and employers might find brief deployments to result in job stress relief and re-engagement upon the return home, a benefit that research studies have suggested members of the Army

Reserves can experience, with deployment sometimes serving as a sabbatical [51].

Another way to expand our thinking on retention could also include teacher job-sharing. Job-sharing is an arrangement where two individuals sign a contract sharing the responsibilities, pay, and benefits of a single job between them. While uncommon in the United States, this type of arrangement occurs more regularly in educational settings in England and Australia [52]. Job-sharing can be a helpful way to achieve work-life balance and is often undertaken if employees need to work part-time to meet family care obligations or manage a health condition along with employment. It can also help at least partially retain a teacher in the workforce, while making room for personal responsibilities or new professional opportunities like returning to school for an advanced degree. Job-sharing arrangements tend to most often occur in the United States as a result of individual arrangements, and there are not enough structured policies to support more regular use of these arrangements to prevent burnout or support career advancement [53]. One way job-sharing arrangements might keep teaching financially viable for some teachers is by freeing up time for them to engage in more lucrative contract work using their professional skills in the corporate world. After all, the highly translatable skills of curriculum development, instructional design, and training have been in great demand since the COVID-19 lockdowns forced all jobs online. The proliferation of remote work created an important space for individuals who could effectively navigate online learning spaces, and after the dramatic transition to pandemic virtual learning, teachers definitely meet that description [54]. Ultimately, the greater retention value of a job-sharing arrangement may not be in the additional income, but in the opportunity to transfer the skills from both positions back and forth and grow professionally from the diverse professional experiences across different settings.

Public education has faced and overcome many challenges since the start of the COVID-19 pandemic in 2020. Navigating pandemic lockdowns, economic instability, social unrest, and now the long-term recovery of our students and educators from the societal disruptions of this challenging time has led to incredible adaptations in schools. Bolstered by new educational technologies, and a growing focus on mastery and thriving, schools can more effectively meet the needs of a more diverse pool of students. Educators who bring their own diverse educational and developmental experiences, and are prepared to approach teaching in flexible, responsive ways, will be the key to restructuring schools successfully for the future. As we look forward to the future of education in the post-pandemic era, it is important to consider how the structural and personnel decisions in schools, if made in conjunction with each other, can afford opportunities for innovation and inclusion.

> **Reflect and Discuss**
> We invite you to consider what you have read in this chapter and apply it to your own community context. Use the following questions as a starting point for your personal reflection and for discussion with education stakeholders in your community.
>
> 1. How can institutions of learning be more amenable to changing structures and evolving societal needs? What role can you play to support these improvements?
> 2. In what ways can leaders better support the professional development and mental health of new educators? What impact would that have on the children in your community?
> 3. How could the local schools in your context ensure educators are well-supported in mastering the skills of teaching and leading? What opportunities exist?
> 4. In what ways have you created space for healing and growth for yourself and those in your community after the recent years of trauma and challenges?
> 5. How can we better retain and recruit excellent teachers? In what ways might you support the recruitment and retention mechanisms in your area?"

REFERENCES

1. Belsha, K. (2021, May 26). Cheers and questions as some states and big school districts remove virtual learning option for fall. *Chalkbeat*. https://www.chalkbeat.org/2021/5/26/22455236/no-remote-learning-virtual-option-fall
2. Bamberger, C. (2022, June 23). NYC rolling out 2 virtual learning programs with aim to turn them into fully remote schools by 2023. *New York Post*. https://nypost.com/2022/06/23/new-nyc-hybrid-high-school-program-could-be-fully-remote-by-2023/

3. Kuhfeld, M., Soland, J., & Lewis, K. (2022). Test score patterns across three COVID-19-impacted school years. *Educational Researcher, 51*(7), 500–506.
4. Wilson, S. M., & Kelley, S. L. (2022). *Landscape of teacher preparation programs and teacher candidates.* National Academy of Education Committee on Evaluating and Improving Teacher Preparation Programs.
5. Hayes, C. (2014). What I know about teaching, I learned from my father: A critical race autoethnographic/counternarrative exploration of multigenerational transformative teaching. *Journal of African American Males in Education (JAAME), 5*(2), 247–265.
6. Cowger, T. L., Murray, E. J., Clarke, J., Bassett, M. T., Ojikutu, B. O., Sánchez, S. M., Linos, N., & Hall, K. T. (2022). Lifting universal masking in schools—Covid-19 incidence among students and staff. *New England Journal of Medicine, 387*(21), 1935–1946.
7. Ramdani, C., Ogier, M., & Coutrot, A. (2022). Communicating and reading emotion with masked faces in the covid era: A short review of the literature. *Psychiatry Research, 114755.*
8. Toness, B. V., & Gecker, J. (2022, October 21). Online schools put US kids behind. Some adults have regrets. *AP News.* https://apnews.com/article/online-school-covid-learning-loss-7c162ec1b4ce4d5219d5210aaac8f1ae
9. Henvey, A. (2022, January 13). Frisco's ISD's online learning platform will turn a district dream into a reality. *Star Local Media.* https://starlocalmedia.com/friscoenterprise/frisco-isds-online-learning-platform-will-turn-a-district-dream-into-reality/article_96925cc8-73f5-11ec-8506-278ae80a7e30.html
10. Tate, T., & Warschauer, M. (2022). Equity in online learning. *Educational Psychologist, 57*(3), 192–206.
11. McDaniels, T. (2022). Improving broadband in Appalachia: How municipal broadband networks can bring high-speed internet to millions. *Public Contract Law Journal, 52*(1), 133–155.
12. Zhang, J., & West, R. E. (2020). Designing microlearning instruction for professional development through a competency based approach. *TechTrends, 64*(2), 310–318.
13. Horn, M. B. (2021). The rapid rise of pandemic pods: Will the parent response to Covid-19 lead to lasting change? *Education Next, 21*(1), 93–95.
14. Carl, N. M., Jones-Layman, A., & Quinn, R. (2022). Taking back teaching: The professionalization work of teacher activist organizations. *Journal of Teacher Education, 73*(3), 314–327.
15. Bastoni, A., Pickering, B., & Bisson, N. (2021). *Making room for change: Finding ways to leverage time to benefit all students.* Rowman & Littlefield.
16. Durrance, S. (2023). *Implementing MTSS in secondary schools: Challenges and strategies.* SERVE Center at UNC Greensboro.
17. Bloom, B. S. (1974). Time and learning. *American Psychologist, 29*(9), 682.

18. Guskey, T. R. (2022). *Implementing mastery learning*. Corwin Press.
19. Prothero, A. (2023, February 23). What would motivate teens to work harder in school? the chance to redo assignments. *Education Week*. https://www.edweek.org/leadership/what-would-motivate-teens-to-work-harder-in-school-the-chance-to-redo-assignments/2023/02
20. Heubeck, E. (2023, March 10). Should students get a 'do over'? The debate on grading and re-doing assignments deepens. *Education Week*. https://www.edweek.org/teaching-learning/should-students-get-a-do-over-the-debate-on-grading-and-re-doing-assignments-deepens/2023/03
21. Darling-Hammond, L., Flook, L., Cook-Harvey, C., Barron, B., & Osher, D. (2020). Implications for educational practice of the science of learning and development. *Applied Developmental Science, 24*(2), 97–140.
22. Khan, S. (2023, November 18). Sal Khan says reinventing education will close the learning gap. *The Economist*. https://www.economist.com/the-world-ahead/2022/11/18/sal-khan-says-reinventing-education-will-close-the-learning-gap
23. Beaseley, M., Carvalho, A., Hite, W., Jara, J., Goldson, M., & Almendarez, J. (2021, October 12). Graduation must depend on learning, not time. *Education Week*.https://www.edweek.org/leadership/opinion-graduation-must-depend-on-learning-not-time/2021/10
24. Márquez Aponte, E. (2020). Trauma-informed strategies to support complexly traumatized adolescents in schools in the time of the COVID-19 pandemic. *Theory in Action, 13*(3), 124–139.
25. Crosby, L. M. S. W., Shantel, D., Penny, B., & Thomas, M. A. T. (2020). Teaching through collective trauma in the era of COVID-19: Trauma-informed practices for middle level learners. *Middle Grades Review, 6*(2), 5.
26. Portilla, X. A. (2022). *Healing school systems. Solutions for educational equity through social and emotional well-being*. MDRC.
27. Barsky, A. E. (2008). A capacity-building approach to conflict resolution. In *Handbook of conflict analysis and resolution* (pp. 241–251). Routledge.
28. Erricker, C., & Erricker, J. (Eds.). (2001). *Meditation in schools: Calmer classrooms*. A&C Black.
29. Chicago Public Schools. (2023). *The healing centered framework*. Retrieved April 13, 2023, from https://www.cps.edu/strategic-initiatives/healing-centered/framework/
30. Tran, H., Hardie, S., & Cunningham, K. M. (2020). Leading with empathy and humanity: Why talent-centred education leadership is especially critical amidst the pandemic crisis. *International Studies in Educational Administration (Commonwealth Council for Educational Administration & Management (CCEAM)), 48*(1), 39–45.

31. Morrison, N., (2022, December 30). The biggest challenge for schools in 2023 is keeping hold of teachers. *Forbes.* https://www.forbes.com/sites/nickmorrison/2022/12/30/the-biggest-challenge-for-schools-in-2023-is-keeping-hold-of-teachers/?sh=5d5ac75725f7; https://www.forbes.com/sites/nickmorrison/2022/12/30/the-biggest-challenge-for-schools-in-2023-is-keeping-hold-of-teachers/?sh=5d5ac75725f7
32. Holcomb-McCoy, C. (2023). Creating teacher education programs to solve the teacher shortage. *Childhood Education, 99*(2), 72–78.
33. Henry, G. T., Bastian, K. C., & Smith, A. A. (2012). Scholarships to recruit the "best and brightest" into teaching: Who is recruited, where do they teach, how effective are they, and how long do they stay? *Educational Researcher, 41*(3), 83–92.
34. Wagner, L. (2015, May 13). The final class of the North Carolina teaching fellows. *NC Newsline.* https://ncpolicywatch.com/2015/05/13/the-final-class-of-the-north-carolina-teaching-fellows/
35. Lovison, V. S. (2022). *The effects of high-performing, high-turnover teachers on long-run student achievement: Evidence from Teach For America.* (EdWorkingPaper: 22–675). Annenberg Institute at Brown University. Retrieved April 13, 2023, from https://doi.org/10.26300/9mhe-1w08
36. Way, D. E. (2023, February 13). *Is the N.C. teaching fellows program worth the money?* The James G. Martin Center for Academic Renewal. Retrieved April 13, 2023, from https://www.jamesgmartin.center/2023/02/is-the-n-c-teaching-fellows-program-worth-the-money/https://www.jamesgmartin.center/2023/02/is-the-n-c-teaching-fellows-program-worth-the-money/
37. Walker, T. (2022, February 1). *Survey: Alarming number of educators may soon leave the profession.* NEA News. Retrieved April 13, 2023, from https://www.nea.org/advocating-for-change/new-from-nea/survey-alarming-number-educators-may-soon-leave-profession
38. OECD. (2023). *Programme for international student assessment.* Retrieved April 13, 2023, from https://www.oecd.org/pisa/
39. Darling-Hammond, L., Burns, D., Campbell, C., Goodwin, A. L., Hammerness, K., Low, E. L., McIntyre, A., Sato, M., Zeichner, K. (2017). Empowered educators: How high- performing systems shape teaching quality around the world. Jossey-Bass.
40. Glaeser, E. L., Ponzetto, G. A., & Shleifer, A. (2007). Why does democracy need education? *Journal of Economic Growth, 12,* 77–99.
41. Rogers, B. (2009). "Better" people, better teaching: The vision of the national teacher corps, 1965–1968. *History of Education Quarterly, 49*(3), 347–372.
42. Rogers, B. L. (2008). Teaching and social reform in the 1960s: Lessons from national teacher corps oral histories. *The Oral History Review., 35*(1), 39–67.
43. Eckert, S. A. (2011). The National Teacher Corps: A study of shifting goals and changing assumptions. *Urban Education, 46*(5), 932–952.

44. DLC New Dem Daily. (1999, July 12). *Idea of the week: A national teachers corps.* Beaconfire Consulting. Retrieved April 13, 2023, from https://web.archive.org/web/20050905041016/http://www.dlc.org/ndol_ci.cfm?kaid=131&subid=207&contentid=58
45. Glazerman, S., Goldhaber, D., Loeb, S., Staiger, D. O., & Whitehurst, G. J. (2010). *America's teacher corps.* Brown Center on Education Policy at Brookings.
46. National Center for Interstate Compacts. (2023). *Interstate teacher mobility compact.* The Council of State Governments. Retrieved April 13, 2023, from https://teachercompact.org/
47. Allegretto, S. (2022, August 16). *The teacher pay penalty has hit a new high: Trends in teacher wages and compensation through 2021.* Economic Policy Institute. Retrieved April 13, 2023, from https://www.epi.org/publication/teacher-pay-penalty-2022/
48. Wilson, F. S. (2022, December 14). *H.R.9566—American teacher act.* Education & Labor Committees, U. S. House of Representatives. Retrieved April 14, 2023, from https://www.congress.gov/bill/117th-congress/house-bill/9566
49. Benner, M., Roth, E., & Johnson, S. (2018, July 13). *How to give teachers a $10,000 raise.* Center for American Progress. Retrieved April 14, 2023, from https://www.americanprogress.org/article/give-teachers-10000-raise/
50. Green, E., & Malcom, A. (2022, February 20). Why some teachers in New Mexico wear camo. *The New York Times.* https://www.nytimes.com/2022/02/20/us/politics/substitute-teachers-national-guard-new-mexico.html
51. Etzion, D., Eden, D., & Lapidot, Y. (1998). Relief from job stressors and burnout: Reserve service as a respite. *Journal of Applied Psychology, 83*(4), 577.
52. Williamson, S., Cooper, R., & Baird, M. (2015). Job-sharing among teachers: Positive, negative (and unintended) consequences. *The Economic and Labour Relations Review, 26*(3), 448–464.
53. Watton, E., Stables, S., & Kempster, S. (2019). How job sharing can lead to more women achieving senior leadership roles in higher education: A UK study. *Social Sciences, 8*(7), 209.
54. Nworie, J. (2022). The increasing quest for instructional designers and technologists in higher education and corporate settings. *Contemporary Educational Technology, 14*(1).

CHAPTER 10

Conclusion: Innovation and Inclusion

> *Every challenge creates new opportunities. As educators, we have to capitalize on that. We cannot go back to what we had. We have to move forward and reimagine education.*
> —Marcos Hernandez, Principal, Ellen Ochoa Learning Center

As we conclude this journey, drawing lessons from the lived experiences of brave educators during the COVID-19 pandemic, it is important to reflect on how much has happened since those early days of lockdowns. For a short while, schooling around the world either stopped completely or was relegated to interactions between people in tiny boxes on a computer screen. While the formal processes of education suddenly moved from classrooms to virtual spaces in people's homes, the amount of learning that took place for society in the weeks that followed was unprecedented. It is easy to overlook the tremendous amounts of adaptation and innovation that occurred among all education stakeholders during this tumultuous period, if we become too distracted with the constant news stories highlighting the learning losses experienced by students during the pandemic [1]. We cannot serve the needs of our students without building on the important lessons of this trying time.

No doubt, as we outlined in the first section of this book, the year 2020 was full of trauma and danger—physical, economic, and social. Yet, it was also a year of incredible heroism and solidarity, as communities united to meet the dangers together. We examined the narratives of four schools in four different communities in the second section of this book, putting faces to the challenges and incredible resilience that emerged from this unique year in modern history. In the third section of this book, we leveraged the lessons and learnings that emerged from the pandemic to introduce the CIRCLE Model, with the understanding that after times of great disruption, we can never truly go back to the way things were. We must reimagine a way forward for public education that meets the needs of a population that has been fundamentally transformed; schools must be places of innovation and inclusion [2].

How will we move forward as a society, and what role will public education play in creating and sustaining the changes we take from the pandemic disruption? These are issues that every individual with a stake in public education must wrestle with and make a contribution to answering. It is time for policymakers, educators, parents, industry leaders, and even students to evaluate their local schools or school systems and ask two questions. First, are we using all the resources at our disposal to create the best educational opportunities for the next generation of American public school students? Second, are we doing everything we can to serve the needs of all students in our public schools? We invite you to reflect on these questions and pose them to those in your circle of influence, as we all bear responsibility for what comes next.

Leadership and Learning in Communities

It is hard to believe that at the time of writing, two years have passed since we started this project in the spring of 2021. At that time, many schools were still engaged in virtual learning across the United States, and the country was still contending with large numbers of coronavirus infections and deaths each day. In fact, the country was recovering from a winter COVID surge that caused over 200,000 cases of the virus each day [3]. While a vaccine was available to many American adults after an unprecedented rate of vaccine development, uptake of the vaccine was lower than many hoped for [4]. Debates over mask mandates were a regular feature on the news. At the time, it was hard to imagine that things could get much worse, but in many ways, they did.

The world had not yet faced the increasingly contagious virus that emerged with the delta and omicron variants, at one time causing around one million people to test positive for the virus each day in the United States [5]. Since that time, the world has reopened, emergency declarations made by governments have elapsed, and students are back in schools. People are traveling again, many at higher rates than they were before the pandemic [6]. Life seems to have returned to normal by many metrics. It would be easy to forget that at the end of the pandemic, the virus has claimed the lives of over one million Americans, and orphaned over 200,000 American children [7]. As we look ahead to the future of public education in America, we cannot overlook the fact that our schools are not just responsible for helping children recover from the academic challenges brought about by the pandemic—for some of our students, the scars from this traumatic period in history will continue to be a part of their lives [8]. We owe it to them to ensure that the lessons from this period in our educational history are used to envision an education system that will serve them better than the one we have.

The strong leadership shown by educators and community members through the darkest days of the pandemic will continue to be important in addressing the needs of a generation of children who have lived through incredible tragedy. We can attest from our interviews for this project, leadership at every level of the education system was instrumental in navigating a path through the challenges. At the district level, superintendents developed and communicated a vision of collective responsibility and built relationships with local government agencies, nonprofit organizations, and industry partners to increase capacity and shore up resources for their district's pandemic response. They expanded their roles in response to the situation, and they reimagined the role of their schools to meet the needs of the moment. We cannot simply turn the page on the inventiveness that district leaders showed when many of their actions improved lives and addressed long-standing needs once they were empowered and resourced to act.

At the school level, principals worked tirelessly to create cultures of care during remote learning, committed to meet the needs of the entire community: students, parents, and essential workers, alike. In many cases, the pandemic forced building leaders to prioritize the human needs in their schools in new ways, from investing deeply in more inclusive and consistent communication practices to quell student and parent anxieties, to embracing fair expectations and authentic recognition of efforts for teachers in light of the overwhelming challenges facing schools [9]. Their dedication of time and infusion of daily practices that tightened community connections, from regular virtual check-ins with families to increased social and emotional support for teachers as they struggled through the daily challenges of this period, highlighted the important caretaking potential of their positions [10].

At the classroom level, teachers navigated new technologies, reprioritized learning objectives, and served as vital lifelines into student homes, while themselves struggling through trauma, uncertainty, and illness in their personal lives. In many cases, having students learning from home provided new opportunities for teachers to connect with families, and for families to contribute their own cultural perspectives and funds of knowledge more easily to classroom learning, creating deep connections in times of physical isolation. When schools started moving toward a more relationship-centered approach during virtual learning, teachers collaborated with colleagues and families, grounding their practice in compassion for students, families, and each other [11]. Empowered educators at all levels of the system led with empathy, creativity, and professionalism to support their communities in their darkest hour. We must remember their commitment and self-sacrifice as we envision education for the future.

Unfortunately, through this period of strong leadership and community-building, public education has also become a battleground for the political divisions that have plagued the country over recent years. There has been a sharp increase in politicization and conflict related to curriculum and pedagogy as the country has emerged from the pandemic years. From banning school library books that represent identities and perspectives diverging from local norms to presenting singular perspectives in the teaching of history, bad actors have been sowing fear and mistrust in public education [12]. This aggressive stance is believed to be a backlash toward the social unrest that surfaced in the summer of 2020 after the murder of George Floyd, who was one in a far too long list of individuals killed as a result of racial profiling by police: Stephon Clark, Rashon Washington, Anton Black, Manuel Ellis, Breonna Taylor, Andre Hill, Daunte Wright [13]. We have to question, with an eye to the future, how America's students can receive a globally competitive education without inclusive books in their libraries or curriculum in their classrooms that accurately represents the complexity of their nation's past. No doubt, the history of America, as the history of every other nation, includes points of deep patriotic pride, and periods of regrettable darkness, all of which make up a rich tapestry of unique lived experiences.

Our friend Doug Straley, Superintendent of Louisa County Schools in Virginia, made an observation about the current political climate, and shared wisdom in a conversation we had with him while conceptualizing this book. He highlighted the importance of educational discourse, which may not always result in agreement, but must remain a part of our decision-making processes. We offer it here as an important part of how we build the bridges between schools and communities, navigating diversity with purpose.

> *A key in dealing with the environment of increased politicization is being open, honest, and upfront with your community. A quote we say here often is, "Where there's a void in communication, negativity will fill it," and that's the truth. We do everything we can to be as thorough as possible in our reasoning behind the decisions we make, and we also try to have an honest conversation with individuals or groups who may disagree with something we're doing. The goal isn't to get everyone to agree with every aspect of your plan, but to help them develop an understanding and respect for the process*

In an increasingly diverse and interconnected reality, children need to be educated to understand and respect the different experiences of the human beings who walk the earth beside them, and the adults in their lives must model how to communicate across those differences. Otherwise, we destine young people to repeat the mistakes of the past, instead of building on the experiences of those that came before them.

Americans broadly trusted public school educators to lead in dark times by keeping our children not only learning, but safe and connected to the outside world. We trusted them to innovate, and they rose to that challenge. Now, we must build on that empowerment and autonomy, borne of professional expertise and experience, and allow them the academic freedom to do their jobs well [14]. In a world where being a discerning consumer of information, one who can separate fact from opinion and evaluate viewpoints on their merit, is an essential life skill, we cannot hamper the development of the next generation of Americans by limiting their access to ideas. Public education cannot serve the needs of an increasingly diverse student population if it erases the lived experiences and cultural perspectives of half those students from its curriculum. Our schools cannot recruit much-needed teachers to the profession if we cannot guarantee they will be treated as professionals and empowered to succeed. Americans must move public education from being a target for conflict to a space for collective action to secure their future.

Collective Responses Beyond the Crisis

Much has been written since the start of the COVID-19 pandemic about leadership in times of crisis. This comes as no surprise, considering the scope of the global crisis, and the many opportunities that it afforded for learning. Scholarship on crisis leadership suggests that in our orientation toward caring for others, our leadership success can be attributed to our openness to collective wisdom in times where the stakes are high and the options are limited [15]. Perhaps it is easier to approach challenges with humility when we are aware that no one knows the way out of the crisis, and we must rely on each other, value the relationships we have with each other, and work toward the common goal of survival [16]. The resilience and courage with which school communities faced times of crisis, and the ways in which these collective responses built on local assets and shared values of compassion and connectedness, cannot be left behind as the current crisis fades into distant memory.

We observed a common thread that ran through our interviews for this book: schools navigated the pandemic by leveraging the good work they had put in motion before the crisis began. Preparation for what comes next matters, and the best time to prepare for the next challenge is while the lessons of the last crisis are fresh in our minds [17]. Maintaining an approach that values perspectives from multiple education stakeholders and focuses on common ground for the greater good can help us keep establishing flexible approaches to education that can be adapted to individual needs, instead of getting stuck in the endless mire of political discord.

As the crisis of the pandemic years fades, we must remind ourselves that our collaborative approaches and humility do not have to fade with it. Our schools and our communities can maintain the interdependence through which they survived and build on it to thrive in the years ahead. To do so, we must identify our shared values and communicate a collective vision for the public schools in our communities. We may not agree on many things, but we can take heart in our care for the students our schools educate, and the future they will build for themselves and those around them. Our responsibility as stakeholders in public education is to ensure that the needs, voices, and interests of these young people are centered in our educational policies and practices, and that they are being served in an equitable manner. As much as we may want to make the assessment of what is best for them ourselves, we saw throughout the pandemic the incredible self-awareness and ownership with which many students approached their learning and well-being. It is time to trust them to tell us what they need and include them in reimagining education for the future [18].

During the pandemic, we saw young people assert themselves and advocate for their peers, showing themselves to be an important voice in their own futures. They served as advisors to school leaders, proposing solutions to the social disconnection of remote learning. They asked for flexibility in class attendance during the height of the 2020 recession, so they could support their families by starting jobs while continuing school. We even saw them take to the streets in protest to advocate for racial justice and schools free from gun violence. It is important that we give the youth of our communities a voice in the conversations about what education looks like for their future, and we ask them how we can best meet their needs in schools. Not only does this provision for youth voices allow us to directly engage the young minds at the center of every education debate, but this approach is also backed by research. Schools that are responsive to youth voices tend to have more engaged students, with higher grades and lower absenteeism [19]. Let's empower the young people in our schools to be our partners in creating educational experiences that reflect their needs, hopes, and dreams for the future.

FUTURE SCHOOLS: PLACES OF INCLUSION, SAFETY, AND PURPOSE

When we ask American youth what they want out of school, the results are unsurprising, because their responses reflect the basic needs of all human beings for safety, connection, and purpose. They want to safely learn meaningful things in places where they feel they belong [20]. Yet the Adolescent Behavior and Experiences Survey administered to a nationally representative sample of American high school students in 2021 suggests that this desire for inclusion, safety, and purpose is not being realized: one-third of respondents are experiencing poor mental health, with persistent feelings of sadness and hopelessness [21]. In many ways, societal and school disruptions since 2020 have contributed to the mental health challenges of American teens, but these findings also reflect longer-standing challenges that have come to the forefront. American youth are stressed about the future—the state of the nation, gun violence, climate change, economic instability—teens were stressed about these before the pandemic started [22], and the trauma and isolation of the pandemic have only exacerbated the mental health challenges young people have faced [23]. We would be remiss if we did not learn the biggest lesson of all from the pandemic: public schools must be safe and inclusive places for learning and innovation to occur, and right now, too many children do not feel safe in school.

The sudden rise in crime across the nation since 2020 is broadly seen to result from the confluence of the same three challenges that were the focus of this book. First, the COVID-19 lockdowns resulted in trauma for millions and started a cascade of mental health issues stemming from isolation and fear. Lockdowns also resulted in high unemployment rates and economic instability during the early part of the pandemic, which, coupled with the financial pressures of rising inflation, can lead to increases in crime rates [24]. Finally, the murder of George Floyd and the protests that followed resulted in lower trust for the police among members of the American public, leading to a dramatic increase in gun sales across the country. Whether purchased to defend themselves in *the absence of* the police, or to protect themselves *from* police officers, American gun sales soared during the pandemic [25].

Regardless of the individual reasons that prompted people to purchase more guns during the pandemic, what is not disputed by scholars is that places with higher rates of gun ownership and more lax gun laws experience higher rates of violent crime [26]. For schools in particular, the greatest danger related to guns and violence is that of school shooters. The nation was reminded of this on May 24, 2022, when 18-year-old Salvador Ramos entered Robb Elementary School in Uvalde, Texas, and murdered 19 children and 2 teachers using legally purchased firearms [27]. Since the Columbine Massacre of 1999, school shootings and armed intruder drills are a normal part of school life for students in America. After the trauma of the global pandemic, we must do better for our kids.

The responsibility of adult stakeholders in education to be responsive to the calls of young people requires that we create ongoing opportunities for them to share their needs. What opportunities do you have to engage the youth of your community about their educational needs? Perhaps this engagement takes place as a discussion in your classroom, or maybe it is a conversation with the children in your home. Perhaps your inquiry takes the form of a survey of the students in the school that you lead, or maybe you hold a town hall for youth you represent in local government. Regardless of our role, we all have opportunities to elevate the voice of young people in society and engage them in co-creation of their education. They have proven to be resilient and enterprising in the most challenging of times, and they deserve a voice in the future of what and how they will learn.

To further the power of our collective response in the post-pandemic era of education, we must each consider our local context and all it has to offer in partnership, both in cultural capital and engagement capacity. Let us move forward to the next stage of American public school education, developing community schools that serve the diverse needs of our country's youth by bringing the community into the school and the school into the community. What connections between the school and the community can be enhanced in your context to support this process? How can you support the diverse cultural traditions of various community members to help inform academic learning in your local schools? Can you bring community stories to life in a classroom, transmitting intergenerational wisdom, but also creating an identity-affirming space where students learn compassion and respect for their peers? Perhaps you are an educator who can reach out to the families of your students, or a community member with a tradition or story to share. How can you help bring learning out into your community, connecting the curriculum to service activities that address real problems in the community through collective action? Perhaps you work for a local organization and can envision such a learning opportunity, or you are a concerned citizen that would like to volunteer your time to bring school and community together in such an endeavor.

Ultimately, we must all contend with the role we want to play in the future of an innovative and inclusive society, and whether we are educators, community members, technology providers, or philanthropists, we all have a stake in the health of our public schools. Even if you do not have children attending those schools, your economic future depends on critical thinkers with robust academic skills to come through public schools and contribute to the workforce. If you are a community member, you depend on ethical, media-literate individuals to lend their voices and their votes to supporting a thriving democracy in the years to come. Finally, if you are a parent, you likely want your children to grow up in a safe, healthy world where they can live a life of opportunity and dignity regardless of who wields political power. We must all ask ourselves, what part can we play to support public schools in our context? How can we play a part in our community, regardless of our role, to contribute to public schools that are not only encouraged to innovate for future economic prosperity, but center inclusion and equity to ensure a free, democratic future for all?

THE RUBBER BAND: A FINAL THOUGHT

We have covered a lot of ground in this book. Between the philosophical questions, lived experiences, and plans for the future, it can be challenging to find an appropriate end. When we started this project, we might have been tempted to provide some ultimate solution at the end of this book, the final correct answer that would solve all the problems that public education faces in the post-pandemic era. Of course, that would be folly. If anything, this process has reinforced the complexity of public education in turbulent times and reminded us at each stage of the importance of contextualizing leadership and learning in the needs of children and their communities. After three years of heroic efforts, educators, students, and parents are exhausted. Everyone has been stretched far beyond the limits of what is comfortable and appropriate. During this period of stretching, we innovated in unexpected ways, and we gave more than we thought we possibly could to support those in our communities. As the pandemic comes to an end, like an overstretched rubber band that has been released, we risk snapping back to our resting shape—a return to *normal*. It is a reasonable desire, given all we have endured as a society and as an educational system. As we find ourselves returning to a more comfortable position, it is vitally important that we not forget how far we were able to stretch when the need arose. It showed us our true capacity, and the true potential of public education in the future. We are now challenged to use what we have learned more intentionally, stretching to meet the diverse needs of the students in our schools. Let us work together with purpose to address the long-standing needs in our schools and reimagine education for the future.

Reflect and Discuss

We invite you to consider what you have read in this chapter and apply it to your own community context. Use the following questions as a starting point for your personal reflection and for discussion with education stakeholders in your community.

1. What novel approaches or learning opportunities do you believe have the potential to increase educational outcomes and success in public schools?
2. What possibilities do you have in your current role to advocate for positive changes that will create greater innovation and inclusion in your local schools?
3. How does the power of collective response promote buy-in and communal support as we envision the next steps in American public education?
4. How does this book affect the ways in which you will engage in your local schools now and in the future?
5. What will you do next to improve the educational opportunities in your community?

References

1. Zhao, Y. (2022). Build back better: Avoid the learning loss trap. *Prospects, 51*(4), 557–561.
2. Ladson-Billings, G. (2021). I'm here for the hard re-set: Post pandemic pedagogy to preserve our culture. *Equity & Excellence in Education, 54*(1), 68–78.
3. Katella, K. (2023, February 3). Omicron, delta, alpha, and more: what to know about the coronavirus variants. *Yale Medicine.* https://www.yalemedicine.org/news/covid-19-variants-of-concern-omicron
4. AJMC. (2021, June 3). A timeline of COVID-19 vaccine developments in 2021. *AJMC.* https://www.ajmc.com/view/a-timeline-of-covid-19-vaccine-developments-in-2021
5. Huang, J., Jacoby, S., Lee, J. C., Murphy, J. M., Smart, C., & Sun, A. (2023, April 10). Track Covid-19 in the U.S. *The New York Times.* https://www.nytimes.com/interactive/2023/us/covid-cases.html

6. Kellman, L. (2022, July 1). After two pandemic years, a summer travel bounce—And chaos. *AP News*. https://apnews.com/article/inflation-covid-technology-health-travel-a84678f1d1512ae9e84b77a632d12b9f
7. Imperial College of London. (2020). *COVID-19 orphanhood*. Imperial College of London. Retrieved April 14, 2023, from https://imperialcollegelondon.github.io/orphanhood_calculator/#/country/United%20States%20of%20America
8. Requarth, T. (2022, April 6). America's pandemic orphans are slipping through the cracks. *The Atlantic*. https://www.theatlantic.com/health/archive/2022/04/covid-orphan-kids-lost-parent/629436/
9. Kraft, M. A., Simon, N. S., & Lyon, M. A. (2021). Sustaining a sense of success: The protective role of teacher working conditions during the COVID-19 pandemic. *Journal of Research on Educational Effectiveness, 14*(4), 727–769.
10. Hayes, S. D., Flowers, J., & Williams, S. M. (2021). "Constant communication": Rural principals' leadership practices during a global pandemic. *Frontiers in Education, 5*(618067).
11. Darling-Hammond, L., Schachner, A., & Edgerton, A. K. (2020). *Restarting and reinventing school: Learning in the time of COVID and beyond*. Learning Policy Institute.
12. Nadeau, S. (2022, September 19). *Book banning and curriculum restrictions driven by political polarization are widely unpopular*. The Center for American Progress. Retrieved April 15, 2023, from, https://www.americanprogress.org/article/book-banning-curriculum-restrictions-and-the-politicization-of-u-s-schools/
13. Crenshaw, K. (2021). The panic over critical race theory is an attempt to whitewash us history: Banning discussion of race makes it impossible to discuss the past accurately. In C. Kimberlé (Ed.), *Foundations of critical race theory in education* (pp. 362–364). Routledge.
14. Kim, R. (2021). Under the law: 'Anti-critical race theory' laws and the assault on pedagogy. *Phi Delta Kappan, 103*(1), 64–65.
15. McLeod, S., & Dulsky, S. (2021). Resilience, reorientation, and reinvention: School leadership during the early months of the COVID-19 pandemic. *Frontiers in Education, 6*, 637075. https://doi.org/10.3389/feduc.2021.637075
16. Mutch, C. (2015). The impact of the Canterbury earthquakes on schools and school leaders: Educational leaders become crisis managers. *Journal of Educational Leadership, Policy and Practice, 30*(2), 39–55.
17. Stern, E. (2013). Preparing: The sixth task of crisis leadership. *Journal of Leadership Studies, 7*(3), 51–56.
18. Duane, A., & Mims, L. C. (2022). "Listen when I come to the table": Reimagining education with and for black elementary-aged youth and their mothers. *Frontiers in Education, 7*, 970443.

19. Kahne, J., Bowyer, B., Marshall, J., & Hodgin, E. (2022). Is responsiveness to student voice related to academic outcomes? Strengthening the rationale for student voice in school reform. *American Journal of Education, 128*(3), 389–415.
20. The Learning Network. (2019, December 19). What students are saying about how to improve American education. *The New York Times.* https://www.nytimes.com/2019/12/19/learning/what-students-are-saying-about-how-to-improve-american-education.html
21. Jones, S. E., Ethier, K. A., Hertz, M., DeGue, S., Le, V. D., Thornton, J., & Geda, S. (2022). Mental health, suicidality, and connectedness among high school students during the COVID-19 pandemic—Adolescent behaviors and experiences survey, United States, January–June 2021. *MMWR Supplements, 71*(3), 16.
22. American Psychological Association, & American Psychological Association. (2018). Stress in America: Generation Z. *Stress in America Survey, 11.*
23. Zolopa, C., Burack, J. A., O'Connor, R. M., Corran, C., Lai, J., Bomfim, E., & Wendt, D. C. (2022). Changes in youth mental health, psychological well-being, and substance use during the COVID-19 pandemic: A rapid review. *Adolescent Research Review, 7*(2), 161–177.
24. Ajimotokin, S., Haskins, A., & Wade, Z. (2015, April 14). *The effects of unemployment on crime rates in the US.* Georgia Institute of Technology. Retrieved April 15, 2023, from https://smartech.gatech.edu/bitstream/handle/1853/53294/theeffectsofunemploymentoncimerates.pdf?sequence=1&isAllowed=y
25. Alcorn, C. (2021, April 1). Gun background checks soar to record in March following mass shootings and gun-control bills. *CNN Business.* https://www.cnn.com/2021/04/01/business/gun-sales-march/index.html
26. Tucker, E., & Krishnakumar, P. (2022, March 27). States with weaker gun laws have higher rates of firearm related homicides and suicides, study finds. *CNN.* https://www.cnn.com/2022/01/20/us/everytown-weak-gun-laws-high-gun-deaths-study/index.html
27. Romo, V. (2022, May 25). Texas community struggles with second-deadliest school shooting in U.S. history. *NPR.* https://www.npr.org/2022/05/24/1101037902/texas-elementary-school-shooting-uvalde

Index[1]

A
Abdullah, Yusuf, 126–130, 134, 136–139
Access, vii, 6, 8, 12, 15, 28–31, 34, 54, 60, 61, 78, 79, 86, 90, 98, 109, 110, 122–124, 128, 131, 132, 148, 152, 153, 156, 157, 166, 167, 174, 179, 182, 205
Accountability, vii, 120, 126, 131–133, 137–138, 167, 168
  assessment for, 167
Adolescent Behavior and Experiences Survey, 207
Alvarez, Rafael, 42–44, 46, 48–56, 58–60, 62–65
  developmental thinking and, 64
  response to COVID-19 pandemic, 43
American Dream, 8, 9, 15, 164

American Teacher Act, 194
America's Teacher Corps (ATC), 193
Aspirational capital, 106, 107

B
Beutner, Austin, 99–102, 105, 106, 109, 113
  response to COVID-19 pandemic, 99
Book banning, 204
Booker v. Special School District No. 1, Minneapolis, Minnesota, 123
Brazil, 173
  education funding in, 173
Bridges, 15–16, 100, 205
Broadband connectivity, 109, 179, 182

---

[1] Note: Page numbers followed by 'n' refer to notes.

Bronx Community School District 7 (CSD 7)
   democratic communication practices in, 58–60
   implementation of CIRCLE model in, 148, 151, 157
   Regional Enrichment (REC) Centers in, 55
   school closures in, 44, 48
Bronx, NY
   COVID-19 pandemic in, 28, 29, 50
   poverty in, 42, 49
   See also Concourse Village Public School
Brown v. Board of Education decision, 123
Brown, Brené, 3
Bullying, 22, 181

C

Capital, forms of, 101, 106, 107, 112
Ceará (Brazil), 173
Chauvin, Derek, 26, 128
Chicago Public Schools, viii, 188
Choice, 8, 10, 41, 61, 64, 69–91, 111, 120, 122, 124, 148, 166, 169, 180
   communication of, 85
Coalition for Community School, 172
Cobb County, Georgia, 12, 13
Collective response, 206–207, 209, 211
Columbine Massacre, 22, 208
Comanche tribe, 75
Communication styles, 58
   communication of danger, 82, 85
Community cultural wealth, 96, 98, 103, 105–112, 114, 115, 170
Community organizations, 33, 46, 50, 56
   See also School-community partnerships

Community schools, *see* Full Service Community Schools (FSCSs); School-community partnerships
Competency-based learning, 185
Comprehensive District Design (CDD)
   implementation of, 134, 166
   social justice education and, 166
Comprehensive, Innovative, Resilient, and Contextualized Lens on Education (CIRCLE) model
   complexity and, 158
   educational assessment and, 168, 169
   educational funding and, 174
   evolving educator roles and, 154
   Full Service Community Schools (FSCSs) and, 171–172
   guiding principles of, 155–159
   pluralistic structures and, 180–184
   school context section of, 151
   school innovation and, 152–153, 156
   teacher recruitment/retention and, 152, 189
   virtual learning and, 156, 157
Compromise, 73
Concourse Village Public School (CVES) (Bronx, NY), 28, 42, 44–46, 57, 60–62, 64
   decision making in, 44, 46, 55, 60–62
Cosell, Howard, 49
Covey, Stephen, 41, 164
COVID-19 pandemic
   danger and, 23, 72, 73
   district readiness and, 34
   economic effects of, 128
   economic inequality and, 29, 103, 127–128
   educational assessment and, 167
   educators' response to, 157, 201

effect of on school funding, 24–25, 110, 172–173
effects of in California, 30, 96
effects of in Minneapolis, 26, 119
effects of in New York City, 28, 41
effects of in Texas, 29, 69
increased crime rates and, 208
job loss and, 9, 96
mask mandates and, 202
misinformation and, 70, 81
politicization of pandemic, 70, 189
post-pandemic crisis leadership and, 202–204, 206
psychological impact of lockdowns, 56
risk tolerance and, 70
school closures and, 4, 20
teacher shortages and, 189
trauma and, 5, 8, 21, 28, 41, 43, 47, 50, 188, 208
2021 surge, 202
Cowger, T. L., 181
Crime rates, increases in, 77, 208
Crisis leadership, 206
Critical Race Theory (CRT), 6, 7, 27
laws prohibiting teaching of, 6–7, 204
Cruz, Cynthia, 45, 46, 54, 57, 59, 61–63
democratic communication practices and, 59
Cudahy, CA
cultural capital and, 107
effect of COVID-19 pandemic on, 103
Cultural wealth, 33, 96, 98, 103, 105–112, 114, 115, 170

D
Dakota Sioux, 121
Danger
communication of, 85, 86
evolving experience of, 74–80
DeBlasio, Bill, 47
Decision-making, 16, 35, 52, 58, 60–62, 70, 74, 80, 85, 111, 137, 138, 172, 205
Democratic communication practices, 58–60
Depersonalizing, 71, 81, 82
Depoliticizing, 71, 85, 89, 148
Desegregation, 123
Developmental thinking, 16, 59, 64, 158
Discipline policies, 188
Distance learning, 5, 12, 15, 20, 21, 25, 31, 46, 47, 52, 53, 64, 77, 79, 85, 86, 88, 89, 109, 127, 128, 135, 137, 148, 156, 157, 179, 181–183, 195, 202, 204
intergenerational learning and, 135
See also School closures
District context, 42–47, 65, 71–74, 91, 96, 120–127
District readiness, 34
District structure, 43–47, 72–74, 98, 124–127

E
Ecological systems, 170–172, 175
Economic inequality
COVID-19 effects on, 29, 103, 127–128
cultural capital and, 106–110, 112
in Los Angeles, 97
in Minneapolis, 120
racial discrimination and, 120
Education funding
in Brazil, 173
community schools and, 172
housing segregation and, 172
innovative sources, 172–174

Educator student match, 114
Einstein, Albert, 16
Elementary and Secondary School Emergency Relief (ESSER) Fund, 25
Ellen Ochoa Learning Center (EOLC) (Los Angeles, CA), 30, 96, 100–103, 105, 108, 110, 115
    effect of COVID-19 pandemic on, 30, 96, 100
Ellison, Kim, 139
Environmental racism, 103, 104
Equity training, 133
Evolving educator roles, 154
Exide Battery Plant, 103

F
Familial capital, 107–111
Fender Guitars, 151
Finland, 191, 192
Flex time, 185
Floyd, George, 5, 20, 26, 27, 30, 61, 89, 119, 122, 125, 128–130, 133–136, 204, 208
    protests following murder of, 26, 129, 130, 208
Frankl, Victor, 41
Frazier, Darnella, 5
Fujita, Ted, 76
Full Service Community Schools (FSCSs), viii, 43, 132, 169, 171–173, 182, 209
Future Focused Education, 169

G
Graff, Ed, 125, 128–131, 133, 134, 136, 138, 139, 148
    Comprehensive District Design and, 131, 134

Grow Your Own (GYO) programs, 114, 190
Guidance counselors, 57
Gun ownership, 208

H
Happy Land Social Club fire, 50
Healing Centered Framework, 188
Henry, Patrick, 126
Hernandez, Marcos, 100, 101, 104, 105, 108, 109, 111, 114
High School and Beyond Plan (WA State), 168
Human resources, 125, 182, 183
Hunt Institute, 14, 15, 190
Hunt, Jim, 14
Hybrid learning, 183
    See also Distance learning

I
Individual Freedom Act (Stop Wrongs Against our Kids and Employees "Stop WOKE" Act), 7
Innovation in schools, 152–153, 156, 184
    "outside-in" principle of, 156
Interdependence, 105, 148, 156–158, 164, 171, 172, 174, 206
Intergenerational learning, 135

J
Jamil, Faiza, vii, ix, 10–13
Job-sharing, 195

K
Kentucky Coalition for Advancing Education, 168
Key, Patrick, 12

Keys, Alicia, 105
Khan Academy, 187
Kleppe, Holly, 179

L
Ladson-Billings, Gloria, 148
Leadership philosophies, 32, 34, 72, 99
Linguistic capital, 106
Llano Estacado, 71, 75, 75n1
Los Angeles, CA, city and county of, 95, 96, 110, 111, 113, 151, 155
  effect of COVID-19 pandemic on, 29, 96
Los Angeles Unified School District (LAUSD), 30, 34, 98, 99, 102, 105–107, 111–115, 148
  effect of COVID-19 pandemic on, 29, 99
  environmental racism and, 103–104, 107–108
  implementation of CIRCLE model in, 148, 151
  See also Ellen Ochoa Learning Center
Lozano, Elida, 101, 108, 110–112, 114
Lubbock Independent School District
  communication styles within, 34, 82, 85
  effect of COVID-19 pandemic, 29
  implementation of CIRCLE model in, 148, 151, 155–156, 174
  school closures and, 29, 77–79, 86–87
  See also Monterey High School
Lubbock Tornado of 1970, 76
Lubbock, TX, city of
  crime in, 76
  native American history of, 71
  poverty, 71, 77, 86, 156

M
Marjory Stoneman Douglas High School, 88
Mask mandates, 82, 202
Maslow's hierarchy of needs, 157
Mastery learning, 185–187
McDonnell, Bob, 14
Microlearning, 183
Minneapolis Branch of NAACP et al. v. State of Minnesota et al., 124
Minneapolis Federation of Teachers (MTF), 139
Minneapolis, MN
  economic inequality, 119, 127, 136
  racial injustice, 30, 120, 140
Minneapolis Public Schools (MPS)
  accountability and, 120, 131, 137, 138
  Comprehensive District Design, 131–133, 166
  desegregation of, 123
  implementation of CIRCLE model in, 152, 155
  leadership structure of, 124–125, 137–138
  response to racial injustice, 30
  social justice education and, 134, 152, 166
Misinformation, 70, 81, 150
Monterey High School (Lubbock, TX), 29, 70, 73, 77, 78, 82, 84, 85, 88, 90, 91
Muhammad, Nafeesah, 127, 129, 135–137
Multigenerational learning, 170

N
National Teacher Corps (NTC), 192, 193
Navigational capital, 107–109

New Mexico Public Education Department, 169
New York City
  COVID-19 pandemic, 28, 41, 47
  school closures, 20
  See also Bronx, NY
North Carolina Teaching Fellows, 190

O

Office of Family and Community Empowerment, 56
One million teachers of color campaign, 189, 190
Online learning, *see* Distance learning
Opioid epidemic, 49

P

Park Avenue Elementary (PAE), 104, 107
Patrick Henry High School (PHHS), 30, 120, 126–128, 130, 131, 134–139
Physical resources, 182, 183
Pluralistic structures, 180–184
Policy
  educational equity, 167
  for social justice, 134, 152
Political polarization, 6–8, 12, 69, 85, 206–210
Poverty, 30, 42, 49, 71, 77, 86, 97, 104, 122–124, 148, 156, 166, 167, 172, 193, 194
Psychological safety, 52, 55–58, 64, 65
Public school systems
  CIRCLE model in (*see* Comprehensive, Innovative, Resilient, and Contextualized Lens on Education (CIRCLE) model)
  complexity and, 158
  danger and, 139
  discipline policies in, 188
  district readiness and, 34
  economic inequality and, 29, 48–49, 54, 77, 97–98, 103–105, 127–128
  economic purpose of, 7
  effect of COVID-19 pandemic on, 188
  evolving educator roles in, 31, 154–155
  innovation in schools, 152–153, 156, 184
  interdependence and, 171
  mental health crisis in, 21–22, 24–25, 48, 51–52, 55–56, 85–88, 180–181, 189, 207–208
  political polarization and, 6–8, 12, 69, 85, 206–210
  political purpose of, 6–7, 149–151, 164–166
  purpose-driven assessment and, 166–169
  resources available to schools, 151
  school closures in, 48
  school-community partnerships and, 32–33, 53–55, 62–63, 99–102, 108, 151, 158, 169–172
  school/student empowerment, 205
  segregation within, 123, 165
  social justice education and, 165, 167, 174
  social purpose of, 9
  structural flexibility in, 153
  teacher shortages and, 189, 191
  trauma and, 111, 188
  See also Bronx Community School District 7; Concourse Village Public School; Los Angeles Unified School District; Lubbock Independent School

INDEX

District; Minneapolis Public Schools; Monterey High School
Purkeypile, John, 71, 73–85, 87–90, 174
  response to COVID-19 pandemic by, 73, 88
Purpose-driven assessment, 166–169

R
Racial covenants, 122
Racism
  classroom discussions, 27
  economic inequality, 5, 136
  environmental racism, 103, 104
  murder of George Floyd, 5, 20, 27, 30, 119, 125, 129, 130, 133–136, 204, 208
  racial reckoning, 5, 26–28, 30, 34, 138, 163
  systemic racism, 5, 26, 131, 147
  teaching of CRT, 6, 27
Ragsdale, Chris, 12
Ramdani, C., 181
Ramos, Salvador, 208
Reading Wars, 158
Recession of 2020, 112
Regional Enrichment Centers (REC Centers), 54
Relationships, 33, 45–47, 53, 56–59, 62, 63, 73, 81, 82, 100, 102, 112, 133, 134, 156, 170, 188, 203, 206
Representation, 15, 59, 60
Resilience, 9, 13, 16, 19, 28, 30, 41–65, 89, 103, 105, 107, 111, 202, 206
Resilient teacher pipelines, 194
Resistance capital, 107, 130
Riordan, Sean, 165
Risk tolerance, 70, 83
Robb Elementary School, 208

Robinson, Ken, 3
Rollo, Kathy, 72–75, 78, 79, 81, 85–88
  response to COVID-19 pandemic by, 47

S
School closures
  in New York City, 20
  reopening and, 11–12, 23, 51, 78–80, 89, 114
  in Texas, 78–79
School-community partnerships, viii, 33, 43, 132, 169–173, 175, 182, 209
School empowerment, 60
School shootings, 22, 70, 88, 208
  protests following, 88
Segregation in public schools, 123, 165
  test-score gaps and, 165
September 11 terrorist attacks, 50
Siddiqi, Javaid, vii, ix, 13–15
Singapore, 191, 192
Social capital, 107, 108, 111, 112
Social justice education, 165–167, 169
Social resources, 182, 183
Socrates, 3
Sorden, Alexa, 44, 45, 53, 54, 56–61, 63–65
  democratic communication practices, 58–60
Spring, Joel, 6, 164
Stackable, Instructionally-Embedded, Portable Science (SIPS) assessment tasks, 168
Standardized tests, 167
Straley, Doug, 205
Structural flexibility, 153
Structural racism, 28, 136, 165
Student empowerment, 131

Suicide attempts, 21
Superintendents Alliance at the National Center on Education and the Economy, 187
Susko, Jennifer, 12

T
Tate, T., 182
Teacher Pipeline Project, 190
Teacher reserve programs, 194
Teacher salaries, 194
Teacher shortages
  international solutions to, 191, 193
  teacher recruitment, 25, 193
  teacher retention, 46, 137, 193
Teacher strikes, 166
Teacher Tax Credits, 194
Teacher-student racial matches, 114
Teach for America, 191, 193
Technological inequity, 31
Thriving, 4, 24, 48, 50, 74–77, 81, 82, 96, 106, 112, 115, 120, 122, 150, 152, 156–157, 182, 184, 195, 209
Time management, 153, 184–185
Trauma
  academic recovery, 188
  adaptation, 52
  teachers and, 13, 28, 34
Tutu, Desmond, 4

U
Unemployment, 24, 29, 49, 103, 122, 208

V
Virtual learning, *see* Distance learning
Vulnerability, 3–9, 148

W
Warschauer, M., 182
White flight, 49
Williams, Sarah, 73, 74, 79, 83–88, 90
Workforce, 4, 8, 9, 26, 32, 78, 113, 120, 127, 152, 154, 155, 164, 166, 172, 173, 180, 189–191, 193–195, 209
Wormholes, 16

Y
Yosso, Tara, 106
Yousefzai, Malala, 4

GPSR Compliance

The European Union's (EU) General Product Safety Regulation (GPSR) is a set of rules that requires consumer products to be safe and our obligations to ensure this.

If you have any concerns about our products, you can contact us on

ProductSafety@springernature.com

In case Publisher is established outside the EU, the EU authorized representative is:

Springer Nature Customer Service Center GmbH
Europaplatz 3
69115 Heidelberg, Germany

www.ingramcontent.com/pod-product-compliance
Lightning Source LLC
LaVergne TN
LVHW020344260326
834688LV00045B/1519